Single-Family Builder Compensation Study

Salary, Bonus & Benefits for 39 Jobs

2017 Edition

Economics and Housing Policy Group

NAHB®
National Association
of Home Builders

Single-Family Builder Compensation Study, 2017 Edition

Robert Dietz, Ph.D.   NAHB Chief Economist and Senior Vice President.
Paul Emrath, Ph.D.   Vice President, Survey and Housing Policy Research
Rose Quint   Assistant Vice President, Survey Research
Ashok Chaluvadi   Senior Research Associate

BuilderBooks, a Service of the National Association of Home Builders
Elizabeth M.R. Hartke   Acquisitions & Managing Editor

Gerald M. Howard   NAHB Chief Executive Officer
Lakisha A. Woods, CAE   NAHB Senior Vice President & Chief Marketing Officer

Disclaimer

Published in the United States of America

20 21 20 19 18   1 2 3 4 5

ISBN-13: 978-0-86718-766-3
eISBN-13: 978-0-86718-767-0

For further information, please contact:
National Association of Home Builders
1201 15th Street, NW
Washington, DC 20005-2800
800-223-2665
BuilderBooks.com

Table of Contents

I. EXECUTIVE SUMMARY

- The *Single-Family Builder Compensation Study,* 2017 Edition shows data on compensation and benefits for 39 common positions at single-family home building companies. The data are broken down by region and size of the builder (starts, dollar volume, and employees).

- Nearly all single-family builders (95 percent) responding to the survey have a full-time President/CEO. Forty-four percent have a full-time Superintendent, 25 percent a full-time Bookkeeper (20 percent have it part-time), 36 percent a full-time VP of Construction, 30 percent a full-time Project Manager, and 26 percent a full-time CFO/Head of Finance. The remaining 33 positions listed exist as full-time jobs at less than 20 percent of the responding firms.

- Respondents were asked to report the annual salary and bonus/commission (if any) of each position existing at their firm. To produce the average total compensation for each full-time position, its average annual salary and average bonus/commission (computed among all respondents reporting a salary for the position on a full-time basis) were combined.

- The top five highest average total compensation levels are:

  - **Head/Director of Land Acquisition:** $173,466 (full-time position exists at 8 percent of responding firms).
  - **President/CEO:** $157,401 (full-time position exists at 95 percent of responding firms).
  - **CFO/Head of Finance:** $148,583 (full-time position exists at 26 percent of responding firms).
  - **Head/Director of Sales & Marketing:** $135,890 (full-time position exists at 19 percent of responding firms).
  - **VP of Construction:** $131,918 (full-time position exists at 36 percent of responding firms).

- The lowest five average total compensation levels are:

  - **Receptionist:** $34,805 (full-time position exists at 8 percent of responding firms).
  - **Administrative Assistant:** $40,751 (full-time position exists at 9 percent of responding firms).
  - **Bookkeeper:** $45,357 (full-time position exists at 25 percent of responding firms).
  - **Executive Assistant:** $48,687 (full-time position exists at 11 percent of firms).
  - **Selections Coordinator:** $53,678 (full-time position exists at 10 percent of firms).

- Respondents were also asked about which of a list of 13 fringe benefits (health insurance, dental insurance, vision program, prescription program, life insurance, short term disability, long term disability, flex spending, 401k plan, paid vacation leave, paid sick leave, tuition reimbursement, and training) they offered to each of the positions existing at the firm.

- The most commonly offered benefits are paid vacation leave and health insurance: all of the positions are offered paid vacation leave by at least 79 percent of the builders where they exist, while health insurance is offered by at least 70 percent.

- The least likely benefits builders offer their employees are tuition reimbursement and flex spending. None of the positions is offered tuition reimbursements by half or more of the builders where they exist. The same holds true for flex spending, with one exception: 50 percent of builders who have a Director of IT offer that person flex spending.

II. INTRODUCTION

One of the most consequential business decisions a company has to make is how much to pay its employees. Single-family home building companies are no exception, and they often turn to the National Association of Home Builders (NAHB) for industry standards. In July 2017, the Economics & Housing Policy Group at the NAHB conducted a nationwide survey of single-family builders covering the most common 39 positions at these companies. The survey's objective was to produce industry benchmarks on employees' salaries, bonuses/commissions, and benfits.

A sample of 5,221 single-family builder members received the survey electronically. The sample was stratified to accurately represent builders across the four Census regions of the country as well as across builder size categories (in terms of number of single-family units started). In all, 311 builders took the survey, for a response rate of six percent. Of that number, 308 reported single-family home building to be their principal operation. This report is based on their responses. Appendix A shows combined findings for all single-family builders in the survey, but also detailed breakdowns by Census region, 2017 expected dollar volume, 2017 expected single-family starts, and number of employees on payroll. A distribution of responses across these categories is shown in Exhibit 1, as well as the distribution of actual single-family units started in the four Census Regions of the country in 2016.

Exhibit 1. Distribution of Responses

Category	% of Respondents	% of Single-family Starts in 2016
Region		
Northeast	8%	8%
Midwest	19	15
South	52	54
West	21	23
2017 Expected Dollar Volume		
Less than $1 million	10%	
$1 million–$4,999,999	40	
$5 million–$9,999,999	20	
$10 million–$14,999,999	10	
$15 million or more	20	

	% of Respondents
2017 Expected Single-Family Starts	
Zero	1%
1–10	52
11–99	37
100 or more	11
Number of Employees	
Zero	1%
1–2	17
3–4	21
5–9	29
10 or more	33

III. BUILDER PROFILE

PRINCIPAL OPERATION

More than half (56 percent) of survey respondents report their principal operation to be single-family custom building. Another 27 percent are primarily single-family spec/tract builders, and 16 percent are single-family general contractors (Exhibit 2). Only one percent report 'other' principal activity. The analysis in this report is based solely on the 99 percent of respondents who are primarily single-family home builders.

Exhibit 2. Principal Operation
(Percent of Respondents)

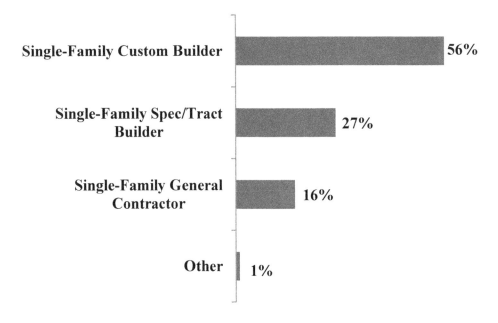

4

NUMBER OF SINGLE-FAMILY UNITS STARTED

On average, survey respondents expect to increase production of single-family units from 31 in 2016 to 38 in 2017, while the median is expected to rise from 8−10 units. In 2016, 55 percent of respondents started 1−10 units, just slightly higher than the 52 percent who expect that level of output for 2017. Instead, 21 percent expect to start 11−25 units in 2017 (up from 17 percent in 2016), 16 percent expect to start 26−99 units (up from 15 percent in 2016), and 10 percent expect to start 100−499 single-family units in 2017 (up from the seven percent in 2016) (Exhibit 3).

Exhibit 3. Number of Single-Family Starts
(Percent of Respondents)

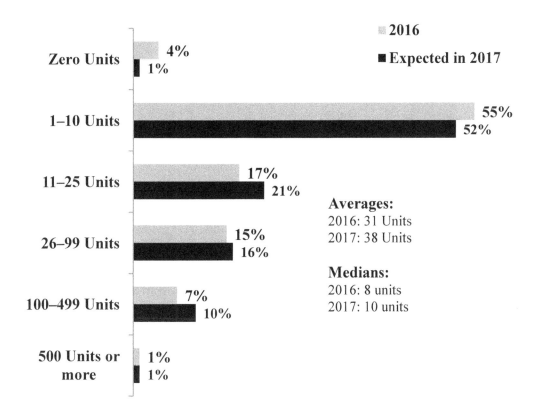

5

EXPECTED DOLLAR VOLUME OF BUSINESS IN 2017

Only 10 percent of builders responding to the survey expect their companies' total dollar volume in 2017 to be below $1 million. The plurality—40 percent—expect it to be somewhere between $1 million and $4.9 million. A non-trivial 20 percent expect it to top $15 million (Exhibit 4). Overall, the median dollar volume expected for 2017 is about $5 million.

Exhibit 4. Expected Total Dollar Volume of Business in 2017
(Percent of Respondents)

Category	Percent
Less than $500,000	2%
$500,000–$999,999	8%
$1 million–$4,999,999	40%
$5 million–$9,999,999	20%
$10 million–$14,999,999	10%
$15 million or over	20%

Median: $5 million

YEARS COMPANY HAS BEEN IN BUSINESS

About half of the respondents report their companies have been in business more than 20 years, while a small minority—5 percent—report less than five years in business. On average, single-family builders in the survey have been in business for 24 years (Exhibit 5).

Exhibit 5. How Long Company Has Been in Business
(Percent of Respondents)

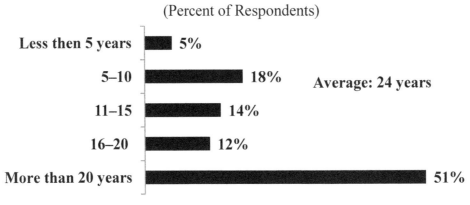

Category	Percent
Less then 5 years	5%
5–10	18%
11–15	14%
16–20	12%
More than 20 years	51%

Average: 24 years

NUMBER OF EMPLOYEES

One-third of survey respondents report there were 10 or more employees on their companies' payroll as of June 30, 2017 (Exhibit 6). Seventeen percent report 1–2 employees, 21 percent 3–4, 29 percent 5–9, and only one percent report no employees at all. The median number of employees was six and the average 14 employees.

Exhibit 6. Number of Employees as of June 30, 2017 (Including Owner/ President/CEO)
(Percent of Respondents)

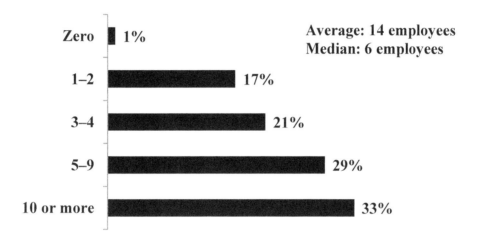

TOTAL PAYROLL

The average payroll among those builders who reported it is $577,689[1]. Of that group, more than half—54 percent—had an annual payroll somewhere between $100,000 and $499,999 as of the last day of June, 2017. For another 11 percent, total payroll was below $100,000, for 16 percent it ranged from $500,000 to less than $1 million, and for the remaining 19 percent, it was $1 million or more (Exhibit 7).

---

[1] Nearly half of respondents—46 percent—chose not to answer the payroll question.

Exhibit 7. Total Annual Payroll as of June 30, 2017 (Including Owner/ President/CEO)
(Percent of Respondents to this Question)

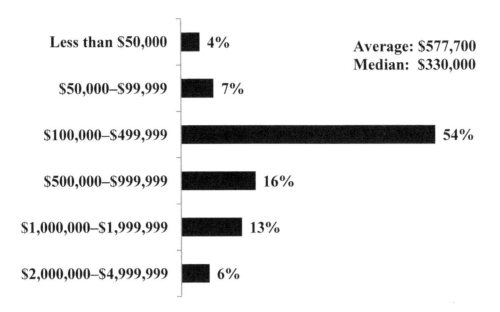

Less than $50,000 — 4%

$50,000–$99,999 — 7%

$100,000–$499,999 — 54%

$500,000–$999,999 — 16%

$1,000,000–$1,999,999 — 13%

$2,000,000–$4,999,999 — 6%

Average: $577,700
Median: $330,000

The remainder of this report is divided into two sections that present the survey findings from two different perspectives:

- Compensations and Benefits Across 39 Positions—this section provides a broad view of the prevalence of 39 positions at single-family building companies as well as a comparison of average total compensation and benefits across those positions. For the purpose of this study, the average total compensation is the sum of the average salary and the average bonus/commission (among all reporting a salary). For brevity, the term 'bonus' is used throughout this report to refer to either a bonus and/or a commission.

- Compensation and Benefits by Position—this section provides a more detailed view of each position's average compensation and benefits. It also shows how compensation can vary across firms of different size.

IV. COMPENSATION AND BENEFITS ACROSS 39 POSITIONS

PREVALENCE OF 39 POSITIONS

According to the survey, the top three most common positions at single-family home building companies are **President/CEO** (95 percent of respondents have it full-time, three percent part-time), **Superintendent** (44 percent have it full-time, one percent part-time), and **Bookkeeper** (25 percent full-time, 20 percent part-time) (Exhibit 8).

Exhibit 8. Three Most Common Jobs at Single-Family Building Companies
(Percent of Respondents Who Have the Position)

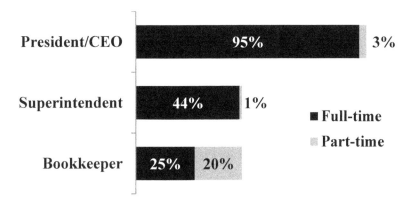

Less than 40 percent of respondents report any of the remaining 30+ positions exist in their companies, whether in a full-time or part-time capacity. **VP of Construction, Project Manager**, and **CFO/Head of Finance** exist as full-time positions at 36 percent, 30 percent, and 26 percent, respectively, of respondents' companies. Between 15 and 19 percent have a full-time **Head/Director of Sales & Marketing, Controller, Office Manager, Head/Director of Purchasing, Salesperson, Home Services/ Warranty Manager, Production Manager**, and **Estimator**. Between 10 and 14 percent report the following full-time positions exist at their companies: **Head/Director of Production, Executive Assistant, Staff Accountant, Selections Coordinator,** and **Architect**. Every position below Architect in Exhibit 9 exists as a full-time job at fewer than 10 percent of all single-family building companies in the survey. Fewer than half a percent of builders report the existence of a full-time Head/Director of Development and Training or a full-time Recruiter.

Exhibit 9. Other Jobs at Single-Family Building Companies
(Percent of Respondents Who Have the Position)

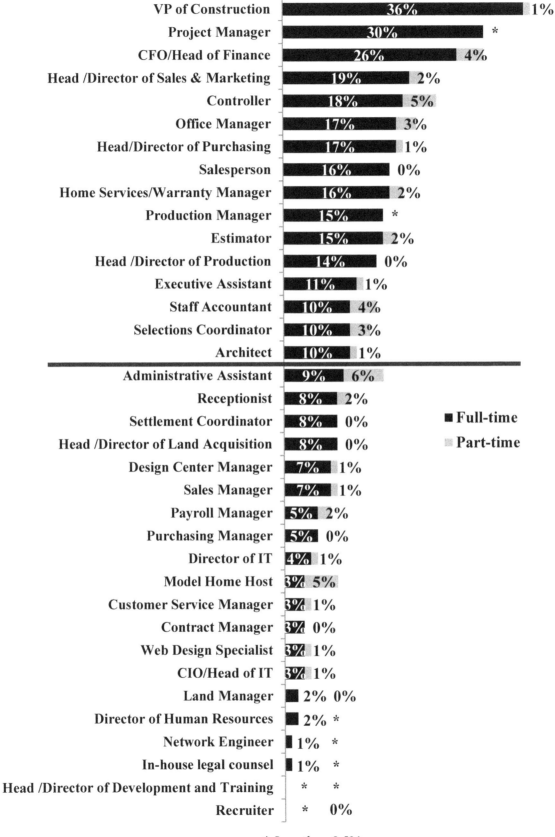

Position	Full-time	Part-time
VP of Construction	36%	1%
Project Manager	30%	*
CFO/Head of Finance	26%	4%
Head /Director of Sales & Marketing	19%	2%
Controller	18%	5%
Office Manager	17%	3%
Head/Director of Purchasing	17%	1%
Salesperson	16%	0%
Home Services/Warranty Manager	16%	2%
Production Manager	15%	*
Estimator	15%	2%
Head /Director of Production	14%	0%
Executive Assistant	11%	1%
Staff Accountant	10%	4%
Selections Coordinator	10%	3%
Architect	10%	1%
Administrative Assistant	9%	6%
Receptionist	8%	2%
Settlement Coordinator	8%	0%
Head /Director of Land Acquisition	8%	0%
Design Center Manager	7%	1%
Sales Manager	7%	1%
Payroll Manager	5%	2%
Purchasing Manager	5%	0%
Director of IT	4%	1%
Model Home Host	3%	5%
Customer Service Manager	3%	1%
Contract Manager	3%	0%
Web Design Specialist	3%	1%
CIO/Head of IT	3%	1%
Land Manager	2%	0%
Director of Human Resources	2%	*
Network Engineer	1%	*
In-house legal counsel	1%	*
Head /Director of Development and Training	*	*
Recruiter	*	0%

Legend: Full-time, Part-time

* Less than 0.5%

TOTAL COMPENSATION BY JOB GROUP

Survey participants were asked to report the annual salary and bonus (if any) of each of the positions existing at their companies. Only full-time positions were considered in this analysis. To produce the average total compensation for a position, the average annual salary and the average bonus were combined. The average bonus was calculated taking into account "zero bonuses" (those who received a salary but not a bonus). When comparing average compensation levels, keep in mind that not all of the positions exist (at all or as a full-time job) at any one respondent's company. Thus, the average total compensation for a particular position is only the average among those who actually have the full-time position at their company.

Also, the salary and bonus for positions that did not have 10 or more responses were tested for their homogeneity, and only included if their standard error was less than 20 percent of the mean[2]. The salary and bonus were not reported for the Head/Director of Development & Training, Director of Human Resources, Recruiter, In-House Legal Counsel, and Network Engineer. Although the salaries of the Web Design Specialist, Land Manager, Contract Manager, Model Home Host, and Customer Service Manager passed the standard error test, their bonus did not and is not reported.

Appendix B lists all positions and their prevalence as full-time jobs at responding companies (column A) as well as the average total compensation for each position (column D). In addition, a second bonus calculation is presented (column E) where only those who actually reported a bonus were averaged out (no "zero bonuses" were included). This bonus calculation is missing from four additional positions because it did not pass the standard error test: CIO/Head of IT, Payroll Manager, Director of IT, and Administrative Assistant.

---

[2] In general, results were suppressed for questions/breakdowns with less than 10 responses.

Executive Jobs

Respondents report that Presidents/CEOs at single-family home building companies have an average annual salary of $113,222 and an average bonus (across all those who got a salary) of $44,179. This gives the President/CEO an average total compensation of $157,401. The CFO/Head of Finance has an average total compensation of $148,583 ($107,758 salary and $40,825 bonus), followed by the VP of Construction with a total compensation of $131,918 ($94,293 salary and $37,625 bonus), and the CIO/Head of IT with a total compensation of $98,850 ($79,600 salary and $19,250 bonus) (Exhibit 10).

Exhibit 10. Total Compensation for Executive Jobs

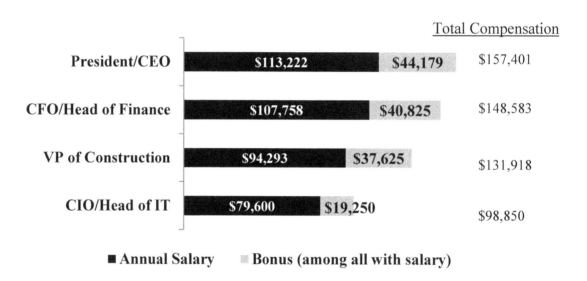

■ Annual Salary ▪ Bonus (among all with salary)

Operations Jobs

The Head/Director of Land Acquisition has an average annual salary of $124,114, and a bonus, averaged among all those with a salary, of $49,352, for a total compensation of $173,466. The Head/Director of Sales & Marketing has an average total compensation of $135,890 ($88,027 salary and $47,863 bonus), the Head/Director of Purchasing receives $100,898 ($80,884 salary and $20,014 bonus), and the Head/Director of Production receives $100,833 ($74,496 salary and $26,337 bonus) (Exhibit 11).

Exhibit 11. Total Compensation for Operations Jobs

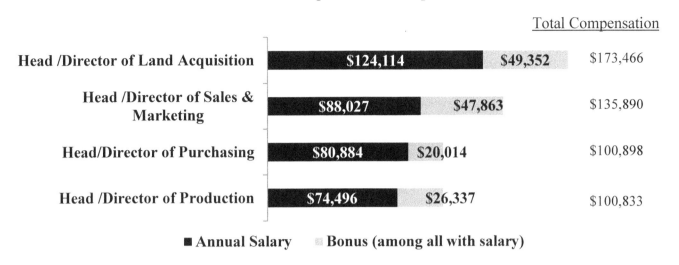

Finance Jobs

The Controller has an average annual salary of $72,002, and a bonus, averaged among all those with a salary, of $11,697, for a total compensation of $83,699. The Payroll Manager has an average total compensation of $58,678 ($54,571 salary and $4,107 bonus), the Staff Accountant has an average total compensation of $58,514 ($53,290 salary, and $5,224 bonus), and the Bookkeeper has an average total compensation of $45,357 ($42,478 salary and $2,879 bonus) (Exhibit 12).

Exhibit 12. Total Compensation for Finance Jobs

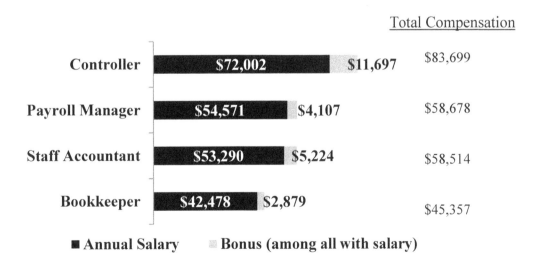

Human Resources

None of the positions in Human Resources received enough responses to report a salary or bonus.

IT Jobs

The Director of IT has an average annual salary of $70,491, and a bonus, averaged among all those with a salary, of $5,773, for a total compensation of $76,264 (Exhibit 13). The Web Design Specialist has an average salary of $56,222. Its bonus cannot be reported due to low response count.

Exhibit 13. Total Compensation for IT Jobs

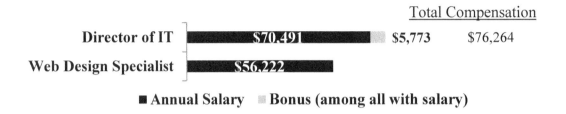

Administrative Jobs

The Settlement Coordinator has an average annual salary of $51,486, and a bonus, averaged among those with a salary, of $7,459, for a total compensation of $58,945. The Office Manager has an average total compensation of $55,717 ($50,287 salary and $5,430 bonus), the Executive Assistant has an average total compensation of $48,687 ($44,732 salary, and $3,955 bonus), the Administrative Assistant has an average total compensation of $40,751 ($38,473 salary, and $2,278 bonus), and the Receptionist has an average total compensation of $34,805 ($32,464 salary and $2,341 bonus) (Exhibit 14).

Exhibit 14. Total Compensation for Administrative Jobs

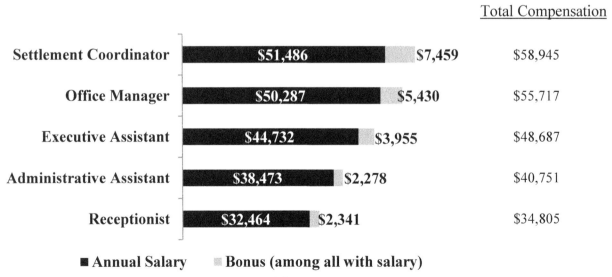

Production Jobs

The Architect has an average annual salary of $80,858, and a bonus, averaged among all those with a salary, of $10,461, for a total compensation of $91,319. The Purchasing Manager has an average total compensation of $81,906 ($69,875 salary and $12,031 bonus), the Production Manager has an average total compensation of $80,657 ($69,520 salary, and $11,137 bonus), the Project Manager has an average total compensation of $78,917 ($67,247 salary and $11,670 bonus), the Superintendent has an average total compensation of $67,706 ($59,888 salary, and $7,818 bonus), while the Estimator receives $55,306 in salary and $5,466 in bonus, for total compensation of $60,772, and the Home Services/Warranty Manager receives $53,373 in salary and $6,938 in bonus, for total compensation of $60,311. The Land Manager and the Contract Manager receive average annual salaries of $87,500 and $62,222, respectively. However, not enough builders specified their bonuses to report industry averages (Exhibit 15).

Exhibit 15. Total Compensation for Production Jobs

Sales & Marketing Jobs

The Sales Manager has an average annual salary of $65,142, and a bonus, averaged among all those with a salary, of $48,444, for a total compensation of $113,586. The Salesperson has an average total compensation of $98,415 ($34,050 salary and $64,365 bonus—the only position whose bonus exceeds its salary), the Design Center Manager has an average total compensation of $65,553 ($57,701 salary and $7,852 bonus), while the Selection Coordinator has an average total compensation of $53,678 ($47,285 salary and $6,393 bonus). The Customer Service Manager and the Model Home Host receive average annual salaries of $53,913 and $33,938, respectively. Not enough builders specified their bonuses to report industry averages (Exhibit 16).

Exhibit 16. Total Compensation for Sales & Marketing Jobs

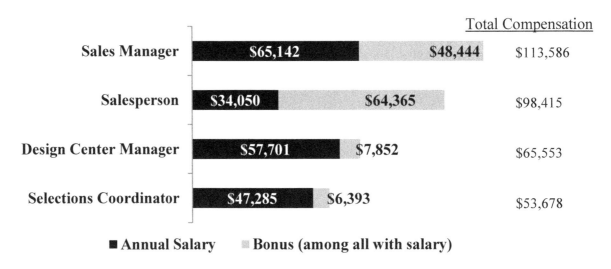

	Total Compensation
Sales Manager $65,142 $48,444	$113,586
Salesperson $34,050 $64,365	$98,415
Design Center Manager $57,701 $7,852	$65,553
Selections Coordinator $47,285 $6,393	$53,678

■ **Annual Salary** ▪ **Bonus (among all with salary)**

BENEFITS

In addition to providing information on the current salary and bonus level of the full-time positions existing at their companies, survey participants also reported which of 13 fringe benefits are offered to those positions. When comparing the frequency of any particular benefit across jobs, it is important to remember that not all positions exist (at all or as a full-time job) at any one respondent's firm. Thus, the average share of employees in any particular position who get health insurance, for instance, is only the average among those who actually have the position full-time at their company.

Fewer than 10 builders provided any information on benefits for the following 11 positions, and therefore these results are not reported: CIO/Head of IT, Head/Director of Development & Training, Director of Human Resources, Recruiter, In-house Legal Counsel, Network Engineer, Web Design Specialist, Land Manager, Contract Manager, Model Home Host, and Customer Service Manager. This section shows a comparison of the prevalence of each of the 13 fringe benefits across the remaining 28 positions.

Health Insurance

All 28 positions are offered health insurance by 70 percent or more of the respondents who report their existence at their firms. In fact, at least 90 percent of builders who have the first 10 positions in Exhibit 17 offer them health insurance, from Selections Coordinator down to CFO/Head of Finance. Another 10 positions are offered health insurance by 80−89 percent of respondents—from Home Services/Warranty Manager down to Estimator. Between 70 and 76 percent of respondents provide health insurance to the remaining eight positions—from Payroll Manager to Office Manager.

Exhibit 17. Health Insurance
(Percent of Respondents with Position)

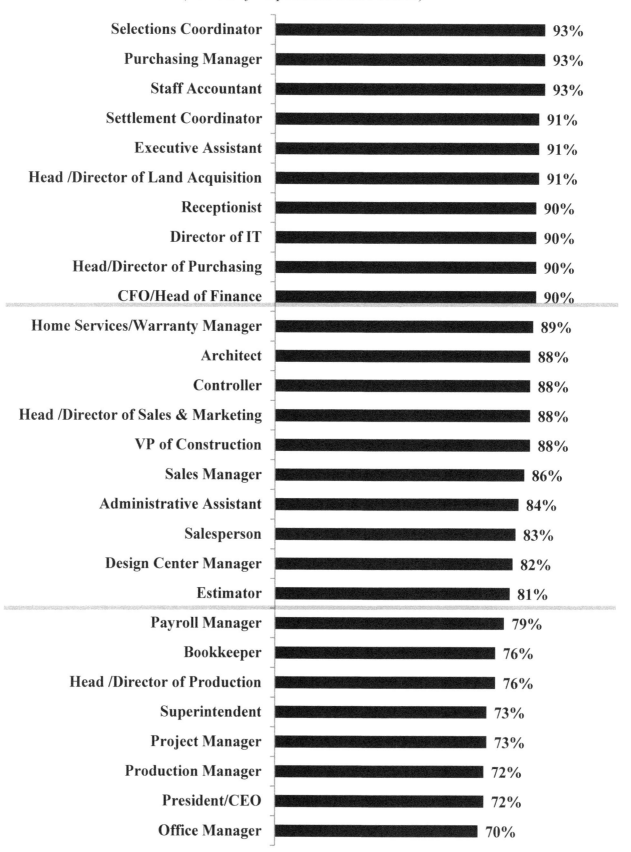

Position	Percent
Selections Coordinator	93%
Purchasing Manager	93%
Staff Accountant	93%
Settlement Coordinator	91%
Executive Assistant	91%
Head /Director of Land Acquisition	91%
Receptionist	90%
Director of IT	90%
Head/Director of Purchasing	90%
CFO/Head of Finance	90%
Home Services/Warranty Manager	89%
Architect	88%
Controller	88%
Head /Director of Sales & Marketing	88%
VP of Construction	88%
Sales Manager	86%
Administrative Assistant	84%
Salesperson	83%
Design Center Manager	82%
Estimator	81%
Payroll Manager	79%
Bookkeeper	76%
Head /Director of Production	76%
Superintendent	73%
Project Manager	73%
Production Manager	72%
President/CEO	72%
Office Manager	70%

Dental Insurance

Compared to health insurance, dental insurance is less commonly offered as a benefit. In fact, in only four cases do more than 70 percent of builders where positions exist offer it: Head/Director of Land Acquisition (82 percent), Director of IT (80 percent), Receptionist (75 percent), and Purchasing Manager (73 percent). Fifteen positions are offered dental insurance by somewhere between 50 and 67 percent of the builders who report them: from Selections Coordinator (67 percent) down to Payroll Manager (50 percent) in Exhibit 18. The remaining nine positions are offered dental insurance by less than half of respondents. The three least likely positions to get this benefit are President/CEO (33 percent), Office Manager (36 percent), and Project Manager (39 percent).

Exhibit 18. Dental Insurance
(Percent of Respondents with Position)

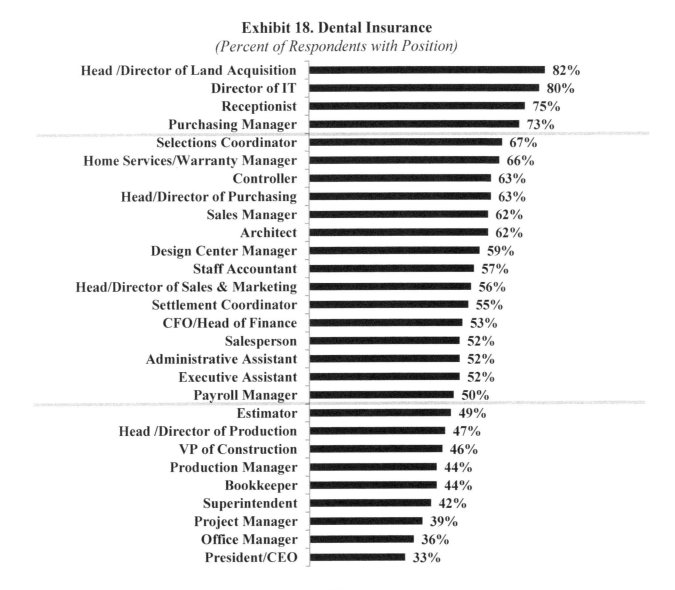

Position	Percent
Head /Director of Land Acquisition	82%
Director of IT	80%
Receptionist	75%
Purchasing Manager	73%
Selections Coordinator	67%
Home Services/Warranty Manager	66%
Controller	63%
Head/Director of Purchasing	63%
Sales Manager	62%
Architect	62%
Design Center Manager	59%
Staff Accountant	57%
Head/Director of Sales & Marketing	56%
Settlement Coordinator	55%
CFO/Head of Finance	53%
Salesperson	52%
Administrative Assistant	52%
Executive Assistant	52%
Payroll Manager	50%
Estimator	49%
Head /Director of Production	47%
VP of Construction	46%
Production Manager	44%
Bookkeeper	44%
Superintendent	42%
Project Manager	39%
Office Manager	36%
President/CEO	33%

Vision Program

Only five positions are offered a vision program by half or more of the respondents that report having them in their firm: Receptionist (60 percent), Director of IT (60 percent), Purchasing Manager (53 percent), and Staff Accountant and Head/Director of Land Acquisition (both 50 percent). In the majority of cases, 17 positions to be precise, a vision benefit is only offered by 30–49 percent of builders: from Head/Director of Purchasing (49 percent) down to Office Manager (30 percent) in Exhibit 19. Less than 30 percent of builders who have the remaining seven positions on staff offer them a vision program, from Head/Director of Production and VP of Construction (both 29 percent) down to President/CEO (20 percent).

Exhibit 19. Vision Program
(Percent of Respondents with Position)

Position	Percent
Receptionist	60%
Director of IT	60%
Purchasing Manager	53%
Staff Accountant	50%
Head /Director of Land Acquisition	50%
Head/Director of Purchasing	49%
Sales Manager	48%
Executive Assistant	45%
Controller	43%
Head /Director of Sales & Marketing	42%
Selections Coordinator	41%
Home Services/Warranty Manager	41%
Estimator	40%
Administrative Assistant	40%
CFO/Head of Finance	40%
Salesperson	38%
Payroll Manager	36%
Architect	35%
Production Manager	33%
Design Center Manager	32%
Settlement Coordinator	32%
Office Manager	30%
Head /Director of Production	29%
VP of Construction	29%
Project Manager	27%
Bookkeeper	26%
Superintendent	25%
President/CEO	20%

Prescription Program

Only three positions are offered a prescription program by half or more of the respondents that report having them in their firm: Head/Director of Land Acquisition (59 percent), Executive Assistant (52 percent), and Design Center Manager (50 percent). Much like the vision benefit, the majority of positions—22 of them—are offered a prescription program by more than 30 percent but fewer than half of builders who have the positions on staff, starting with Head/Director of Purchasing (49 percent) down to Head/Director of Production (32 percent) in Exhibit 20. The three least likely positions to be offered this benefit are Project and Payroll Managers (each 29 percent) and President/CEO (27 percent).

Exhibit 20. Prescription Program
(Percent of Respondents with Position)

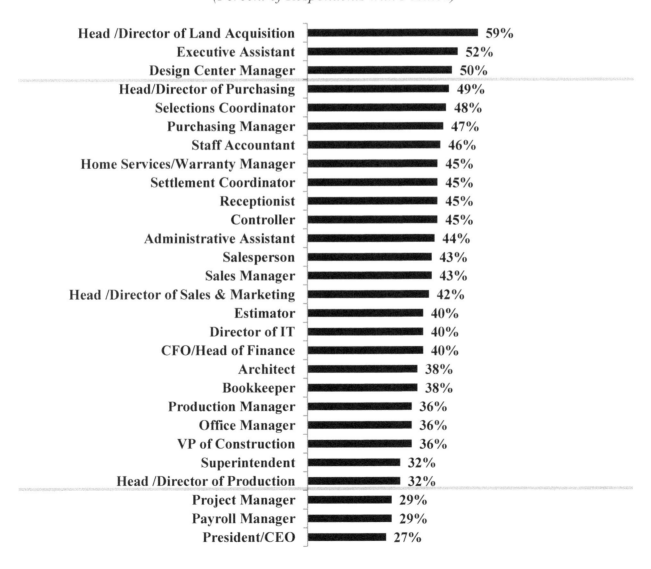

Position	Percent
Head /Director of Land Acquisition	59%
Executive Assistant	52%
Design Center Manager	50%
Head/Director of Purchasing	49%
Selections Coordinator	48%
Purchasing Manager	47%
Staff Accountant	46%
Home Services/Warranty Manager	45%
Settlement Coordinator	45%
Receptionist	45%
Controller	45%
Administrative Assistant	44%
Salesperson	43%
Sales Manager	43%
Head /Director of Sales & Marketing	42%
Estimator	40%
Director of IT	40%
CFO/Head of Finance	40%
Architect	38%
Bookkeeper	38%
Production Manager	36%
Office Manager	36%
VP of Construction	36%
Superintendent	32%
Head /Director of Production	32%
Project Manager	29%
Payroll Manager	29%
President/CEO	27%

Life Insurance

Of the 28 positions for which enough data are available to produce results on the prevalence of benefits, 15 are offered life insurance by more than half of the respondents where those positions exist. Leading the way is the Director of IT (70 percent), followed by Payroll Manger (64 percent) and Selections Coordinator (63 percent). Another dozen positions are offered life insurance by 50–59 percent of builders: from Design Center Manager (59 percent) to Head/Director of Purchasing (51 percent) in Exhibit 21. The remaining 13 positions are offered life insurance by less than half but more than a quarter of respondents who have them on staff, starting with Estimator (49 percent) down to Project Manager (27 percent).

Exhibit 21. Life Insurance
(Percent of Respondents with Position)

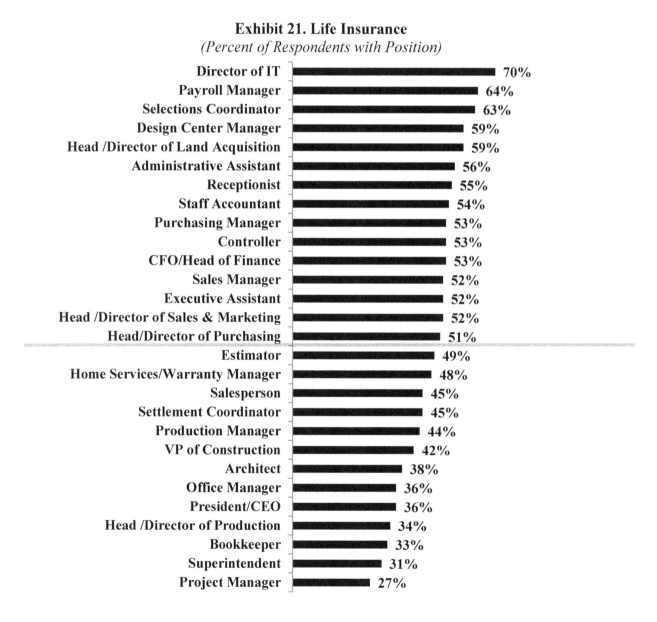

Position	Percent
Director of IT	70%
Payroll Manager	64%
Selections Coordinator	63%
Design Center Manager	59%
Head /Director of Land Acquisition	59%
Administrative Assistant	56%
Receptionist	55%
Staff Accountant	54%
Purchasing Manager	53%
Controller	53%
CFO/Head of Finance	53%
Sales Manager	52%
Executive Assistant	52%
Head /Director of Sales & Marketing	52%
Head/Director of Purchasing	51%
Estimator	49%
Home Services/Warranty Manager	48%
Salesperson	45%
Settlement Coordinator	45%
Production Manager	44%
VP of Construction	42%
Architect	38%
Office Manager	36%
President/CEO	36%
Head /Director of Production	34%
Bookkeeper	33%
Superintendent	31%
Project Manager	27%

Short Term Disability

Only two positions are offered short term disability by half or more of the respondents that report them in their firm: Sales Manager (52 percent) and Design Center Manager (50 percent). Another 17 positions are offered this benefit at 30–49 percent of the companies where they exist: from Selections Coordinator (48 percent) down to CFO/Head of Finance (31 percent) in Exhibit 22. An additional seven positions get short-term disability from 20–29 percent of builders who report them, from Staff Accountant (29 percent) to Bookkeeper (21 percent). Only 18 percent and 16 percent, respectively, of builders offer short-term disability benefits to their Office Managers and President/CEO.

Exhibit 22. Short Term Disability
(Percent of Respondents with Position)

Position	Percent
Sales Manager	52%
Design Center Manager	50%
Selections Coordinator	48%
Purchasing Manager	47%
Payroll Manager	43%
Receptionist	40%
Director of IT	40%
Settlement Coordinator	36%
Estimator	35%
Head /Director of Sales & Marketing	34%
Production Manager	33%
Executive Assistant	33%
Head/Director of Purchasing	33%
Home Services/Warranty Manager	32%
Administrative Assistant	32%
Head /Director of Land Acquisition	32%
Salesperson	31%
Controller	31%
CFO/Head of Finance	31%
Staff Accountant	29%
Architect	27%
VP of Construction	27%
Head /Director of Production	24%
Project Manager	23%
Superintendent	22%
Bookkeeper	21%
Office Manager	18%
President/CEO	16%

Long Term Disability

Only three positions are offered long term disability by half or more of the respondents that report having them at their companies: Director of IT (60 percent), Selections Coordinator (52 percent), and Head/Director of Land Acquisition (50 percent). Another 12 positions are offered long term disability by less than half, but by at least 30 percent of builders: from Purchasing Manager (47 percent) down to Head/Director of Sales & Marketing (30 percent) in Exhibit 23. The remaining 13 positions are offered long-term disability by less than 30 percent of firms where they exist, from Salesperson (29 percent) down to President/CEO (17 percent).

Exhibit 23. Long Term Disability
(Percent of Respondents with Position)

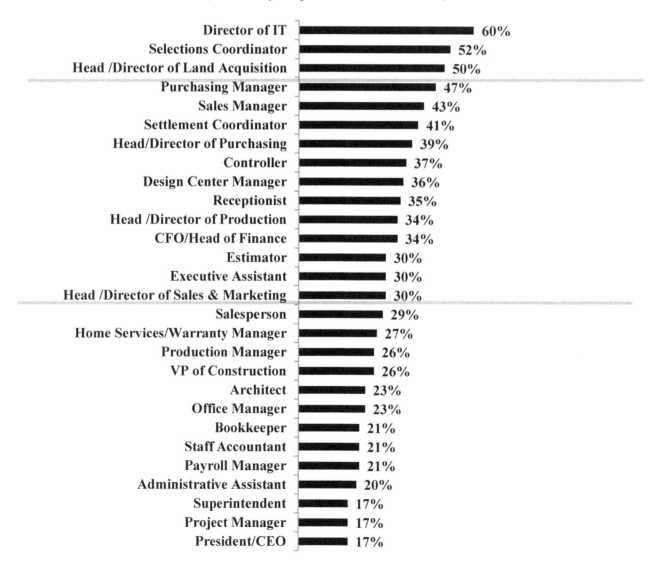

Director of IT — 60%
Selections Coordinator — 52%
Head /Director of Land Acquisition — 50%
Purchasing Manager — 47%
Sales Manager — 43%
Settlement Coordinator — 41%
Head/Director of Purchasing — 39%
Controller — 37%
Design Center Manager — 36%
Receptionist — 35%
Head /Director of Production — 34%
CFO/Head of Finance — 34%
Estimator — 30%
Executive Assistant — 30%
Head /Director of Sales & Marketing — 30%
Salesperson — 29%
Home Services/Warranty Manager — 27%
Production Manager — 26%
VP of Construction — 26%
Architect — 23%
Office Manager — 23%
Bookkeeper — 21%
Staff Accountant — 21%
Payroll Manager — 21%
Administrative Assistant — 20%
Superintendent — 17%
Project Manager — 17%
President/CEO — 17%

Flex Spending

Flex spending is not a common benefit at single-family home building companies. In fact, only one position is offered this benefit by at least half of the builders who have it on staff: Director of IT (50 percent). Less than half, but at least 30 percent of builders offer flex spending to another 13 positions: from Purchasing Manager (47 percent) down to Home Services/Warranty Manager (30 percent) in Exhibit 24. The remaining 14 positions (half of the 28 for which reliable benefit data were collected) are offered flex spending by less than 30 percent of builders who have them on staff, starting with Salesperson and CFO/Head of Finance (both 29 percent) down to Office Manager (11 percent).

Exhibit 24. Flex Spending
(Percent of Respondents with Position)

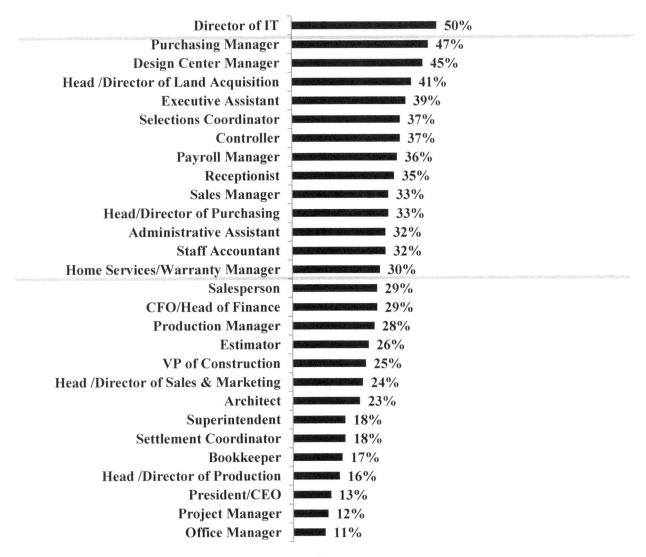

Position	Percent
Director of IT	50%
Purchasing Manager	47%
Design Center Manager	45%
Head /Director of Land Acquisition	41%
Executive Assistant	39%
Selections Coordinator	37%
Controller	37%
Payroll Manager	36%
Receptionist	35%
Sales Manager	33%
Head/Director of Purchasing	33%
Administrative Assistant	32%
Staff Accountant	32%
Home Services/Warranty Manager	30%
Salesperson	29%
CFO/Head of Finance	29%
Production Manager	28%
Estimator	26%
VP of Construction	25%
Head /Director of Sales & Marketing	24%
Architect	23%
Superintendent	18%
Settlement Coordinator	18%
Bookkeeper	17%
Head /Director of Production	16%
President/CEO	13%
Project Manager	12%
Office Manager	11%

401k

Every one of the 28 positions in this analysis is offered access to a 401k plan by more than half of the builders who have them on staff. In fact, 90 percent of builders with a Director of IT offer this benefit to that position. Between 80 and 89 percent also offer it to another 10 positions: from Sales Manager (86 percent) down to Controller (80 percent) in Exhibit 25. Another 15 positions get the benefit of a 401k plan from 60–79 percent of builders where they exist, while 53 percent provide it to the President/CEO and 57 percent to the Payroll Manager.

Exhibit 25. 401k
(Percent of Respondents with Position)

Position	Percent
Director of IT	90%
Sales Manager	86%
Selections Coordinator	85%
Administrative Assistant	84%
Head /Director of Sales & Marketing	82%
Head /Director of Land Acquisition	82%
Architect	81%
Home Services/Warranty Manager	80%
Purchasing Manager	80%
Receptionist	80%
Controller	80%
Estimator	79%
Design Center Manager	77%
Head/Director of Purchasing	73%
Salesperson	71%
Staff Accountant	71%
Executive Assistant	70%
Project Manager	69%
Settlement Coordinator	68%
Head /Director of Production	66%
CFO/Head of Finance	66%
Production Manager	64%
Office Manager	64%
Superintendent	63%
VP of Construction	63%
Bookkeeper	62%
Payroll Manager	57%
President/CEO	53%

Paid Vacation Leave

Paid vacation leave is the most universal fringe benefit at single-family home building companies. Every position is offered paid vacation by more than 75 percent of respondents where they exist. In fact, the Purchasing Manager, Production Manager, Receptionist, and Director of IT are offered paid vacation leave by 100 percent of the builders who have these positions. Ninety percent or more offer it to another 14 positions: from Home Services/Warranty Manager (98 percent) down to VP of Construction (90 percent) in Exhibit 26. The remaining 10 positions are offered paid leave by at least 79 percent of respondents.

Exhibit 26. Paid Vacation Leave
(Percent of Respondents with Position)

Position	Percent
Purchasing Manager	100%
Production Manager	100%
Receptionist	100%
Director of IT	100%
Home Services/Warranty Manager	98%
Office Manager	98%
Controller	98%
Head /Director of Production	97%
Administrative Assistant	96%
Head/Director of Purchasing	96%
Sales Manager	95%
Head /Director of Land Acquisition	95%
Superintendent	94%
Executive Assistant	94%
Project Manager	92%
Bookkeeper	92%
Head /Director of Sales & Marketing	90%
VP of Construction	90%
Selections Coordinator	89%
Estimator	88%
CFO/Head of Finance	87%
Design Center Manager	86%
Salesperson	86%
Settlement Coordinator	86%
Staff Accountant	86%
Architect	85%
President/CEO	83%
Payroll Manager	79%

Paid Sick Leave

Every position is offered paid sick leave by more than half of the respondents where they exist. Ninety percent of builders who have a Director of IT offer that person this benefit, and 80–89 percent offer it to another six positions: from Purchasing Manager (87 percent) down to Head/Director of Purchasing (80 percent) in Exhibit 27. The majority of positions (16 of the 28) are offered paid sick leave by 70–79 percent of respondents where they exist, starting with Staff Accountant (79 percent) down to Receptionist (70 percent). Architects are the least likely to receive paid sick leave, but even in this case, 58 percent of builders offer it to them.

Exhibit 27. Paid Sick Leave
(Percent of Respondents with Position)

Position	Percent
Director of IT	90%
Purchasing Manager	87%
Controller	86%
Home Services/Warranty Manager	84%
Office Manager	84%
Sales Manager	81%
Head/Director of Purchasing	80%
Staff Accountant	79%
Production Manager	77%
Settlement Coordinator	77%
Head /Director of Land Acquisition	77%
Salesperson	76%
Administrative Assistant	76%
Executive Assistant	76%
Selections Coordinator	74%
Design Center Manager	73%
Superintendent	73%
VP of Construction	73%
Head /Director of Sales & Marketing	72%
Head /Director of Production	71%
Estimator	70%
Project Manager	70%
Receptionist	70%
CFO/Head of Finance	69%
Bookkeeper	67%
Payroll Manager	64%
President/CEO	62%
Architect	58%

Tuition Reimbursement

Only five positions are offered tuition reimbursement by 30 percent or more of the respondents who report having them in their firm: Purchasing Manager (40 percent), Sales Manager (38 percent), Selections Coordinator (33 percent), and Receptionist and Director of IT (both 30 percent). Seven other positions are offered tuition reimbursement by 20–29 percent of respondents: from Design Center Manager (27 percent) down to Controller (20 percent) in Exhibit 28. The remaining 16 positions are much more unlikely to receive this benefit, as fewer than 20 percent of respondents said they offer it to them. The President/CEO (13 percent) and the Payroll Manager (14 percent) are the two unlikeliest positions to be offered tuition reimbursement.

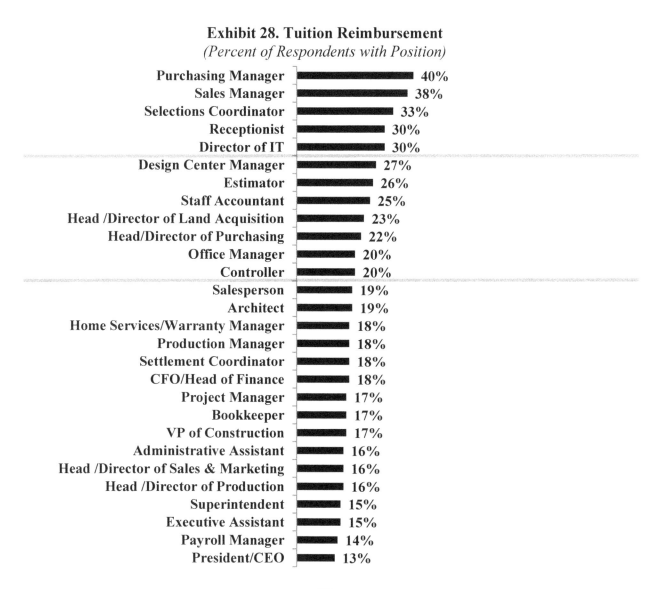

Exhibit 28. Tuition Reimbursement
(Percent of Respondents with Position)

Position	Percent
Purchasing Manager	40%
Sales Manager	38%
Selections Coordinator	33%
Receptionist	30%
Director of IT	30%
Design Center Manager	27%
Estimator	26%
Staff Accountant	25%
Head /Director of Land Acquisition	23%
Head/Director of Purchasing	22%
Office Manager	20%
Controller	20%
Salesperson	19%
Architect	19%
Home Services/Warranty Manager	18%
Production Manager	18%
Settlement Coordinator	18%
CFO/Head of Finance	18%
Project Manager	17%
Bookkeeper	17%
VP of Construction	17%
Administrative Assistant	16%
Head /Director of Sales & Marketing	16%
Head /Director of Production	16%
Superintendent	15%
Executive Assistant	15%
Payroll Manager	14%
President/CEO	13%

Training

The only two positions offered training by more than half of the respondents reporting their existence are Administrative Assistant (56 percent) and Estimator (51 percent). The vast majority of positions, the next 22 in Exhibit 29, are offered training by 30–48 percent of respondents: from Selections Coordinator (48 percent) down to Home Services/Warranty Manager (30 percent). The four positions least likely to be offered training as a benefit are Head/Director of Production and Salesperson (both 26 percent), Head/Director of Sales & Marketing (28 percent), and Head/Director of Purchasing (29 percent).

Exhibit 29. Training
(Percent of Respondents with Position)

Position	Percent
Administrative Assistant	56%
Estimator	51%
Selections Coordinator	48%
Sales Manager	48%
Production Manager	46%
Design Center Manager	45%
Staff Accountant	43%
Head /Director of Land Acquisition	41%
Purchasing Manager	40%
Director of IT	40%
Superintendent	37%
Settlement Coordinator	36%
Office Manager	36%
Executive Assistant	36%
Payroll Manager	36%
Architect	35%
Project Manager	35%
Receptionist	35%
Bookkeeper	35%
CFO/Head of Finance	35%
VP of Construction	34%
Controller	33%
President/CEO	31%
Home Services/Warranty Manager	30%
Head/Director of Purchasing	29%
Head /Director of Sales & Marketing	28%
Salesperson	26%
Head /Director of Production	26%

Other

Outside of the 13 benefits listed, between four and 20 percent of builders reported offering additional benefits to some of their employees (Exhibit 30). Some of the "other" benefits mentioned are a cell phone, a company vehicle, profit sharing, ownership shares, and paid bereavement leave.

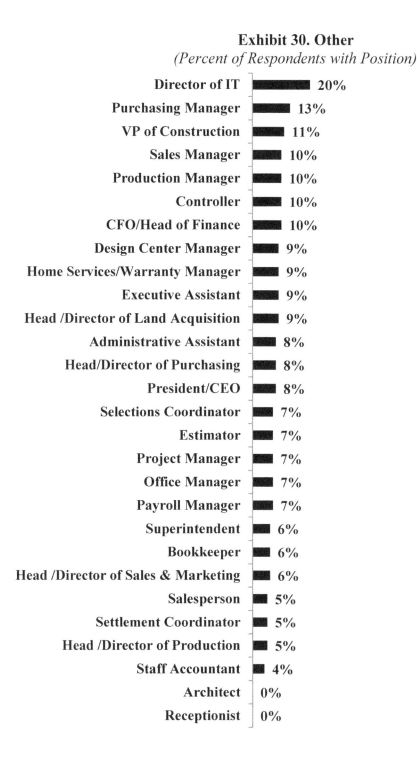

Exhibit 30. Other
(Percent of Respondents with Position)

Position	Percent
Director of IT	20%
Purchasing Manager	13%
VP of Construction	11%
Sales Manager	10%
Production Manager	10%
Controller	10%
CFO/Head of Finance	10%
Design Center Manager	9%
Home Services/Warranty Manager	9%
Executive Assistant	9%
Head /Director of Land Acquisition	9%
Administrative Assistant	8%
Head/Director of Purchasing	8%
President/CEO	8%
Selections Coordinator	7%
Estimator	7%
Project Manager	7%
Office Manager	7%
Payroll Manager	7%
Superintendent	6%
Bookkeeper	6%
Head /Director of Sales & Marketing	6%
Salesperson	5%
Settlement Coordinator	5%
Head /Director of Production	5%
Staff Accountant	4%
Architect	0%
Receptionist	0%

V. <u>COMPENSATION AND BENEFITS BY POSITION</u>

This section provides a more detailed view of each position's average compensation and benefits grouped by job category (Appendix C), while also highlighting how compensation for the same position can vary according to the size of the company (measured by the expected number of single-family starts in 2017) (Appendix D).

EXECUTIVE JOBS

President/CEO

Nearly all single-family builders responding to the survey have someone serving as President/CEO: 95 percent report the job exists as a full-time position and another three percent as part-time (Exhibit 31). Eighty-nine percent report the person in this job "always" has experience in the construction trades, while four percent said "sometimes", and seven percent "never or almost never" (Exhibit 32).

Exhibit 31. Does this Position (President/CEO) Exist?

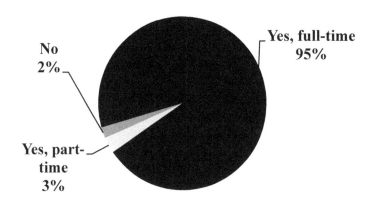

Exhibit 32. Is it Filled by Person with Construction Trades Experience?

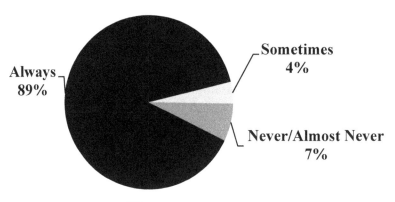

For those firms that have the position full-time, 11 percent report that their President/CEO has an annual salary of less than $50,000, 42 percent between $50,000 and $99,999, and 47 percent report it at $100,000 or more. The average annual salary is $113,222, and the average bonus among all those reporting a salary is $44,179 (averaging in zero bonuses), for an average total compensation of $157,401 (Exhibit 33). Forty-nine percent of companies reporting a salary for this position also pay it a bonus/commission. The average bonus among only those who actually received a bonus is $90,007 (Appendix B).

As Appendix D shows, the larger the company, the higher the President/CEO's total compensation: $113,658 at firms with 1–10 single-family starts expected in 2017, $165,823 at firms with 11–99 starts, and $294,121 at firms with 100 or more starts expected in 2107 (Exhibit 34).

Exhibit 33. Annual Salary- President/CEO

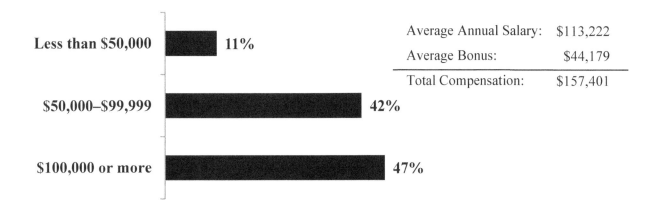

Exhibit 34. Average Total Compensation by Number of 2017 Starts- President/CEO

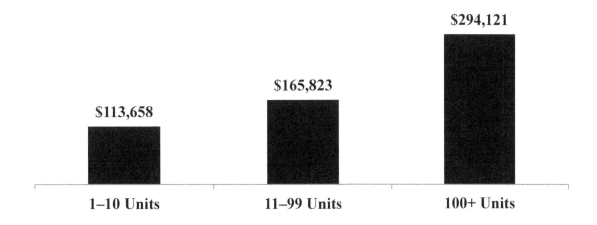

The most common benefit offered to the President/CEO is paid vacation leave—83 percent of respondents who report having a President/CEO offer this benefit to them. Seventy-two percent offer health insurance, 62 percent paid sick leave, 53 percent a 401k plan, 36 percent life insurance, 33 percent dental insurance, and 31 percent offer training. Less than 30 percent offer the following benefits to their President/CEO: prescription program (27 percent), vision program (20 percent), long term disability (17 percent), short term disability (16 percent), tuition reimbursement (13 percent), and flex spending (13 percent). Eight percent offer some other type of benefit to their President/CEO, the most common of which is a company vehicle (Exhibit 35).

Exhibit 35. Fringe Benefits-President/CEO
(Percent of Respondents with Position)

CFO/Head of Finance

Seventy percent of respondents do not have a CFO/Head of Finance. Of the remaining 30 percent, 26 percent have it as a full-time position and four percent as part-time (Exhibit 36). For those firms that have the position full-time, four percent report that the CFO/Head of Finance has an annual salary of less than $50,000, 47 percent between $50,000 and $99,999, and 49 percent report it at $100,000 or more. The average annual salary is $107,758 and the average bonus among all those reporting a salary is $40,825 (averaging in zero bonuses), for an average total compensation of $148,583 (Exhibit 37). Sixty-nine percent of companies reporting a salary for this position also pay it a bonus/commission. The average bonus among only those who actually received a bonus is $58,788 (Appendix B).

Exhibit 36. Does this Position (CFO/Head of Finance) Exist?

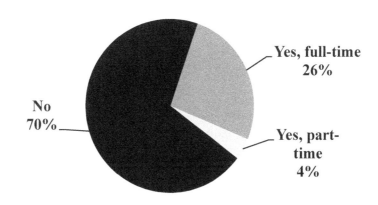

Exhibit 37. Annual Salary- CFO/Head of Finance

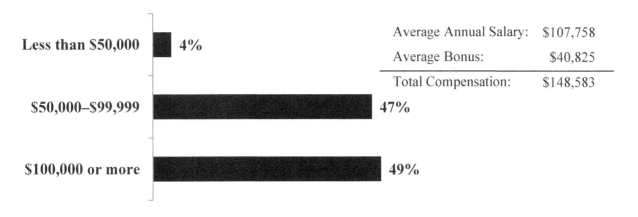

Average Annual Salary:	$107,758
Average Bonus:	$40,825
Total Compensation:	$148,583

Less than $50,000 — 4%

$50,000–$99,999 — 47%

$100,000 or more — 49%

The existence of a full-time CFO/Head of Finance and his/her total compensation are directly correlated with the company's size. Only 11 percent of builders who expect to start 1–10 units in 2017 (small) have a CFO/Head of Finance, compared to 33 percent of those expecting 11–99 starts (medium), and 71 percent of those who will start 100 or more units in 2017 (large) (Exhibit 38). Likewise, total compensation for the CFO/Head of Finance is $86,333, $112,744, and $211,032 at small, medium, and large companies, respectively (Exhibit 39).

Exhibit 38. Percent of Firms who Have Full-Time CFO/Head of Finance by Number of 2017 Starts

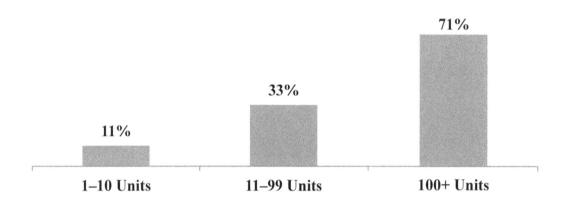

Exhibit 39. Average Total Compensation by Number of 2017 Starts- CFO/Head of Finance

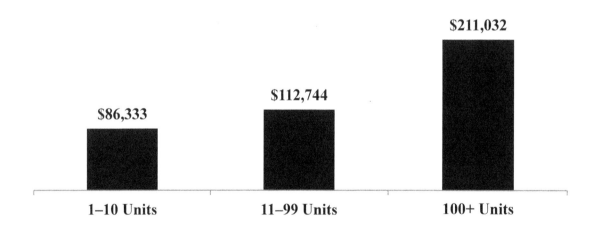

The two most common benefits offered to the CFO/Head of Finance are health insurance (90 percent) and paid vacation leave (87 percent). More than half of the builders who report this position offer it paid sick leave (69 percent), a 401k plan (66 percent), and dental insurance and life insurance (each 53 percent). Forty percent offer each a prescription program and a vision program. The remaining benefits are offered to the CFO/Head of Finance by fewer than 40 percent of builders where the position exists: training (35 percent), long term disability (34 percent), short term disability (31 percent), flex spending (29 percent), and tuition reimbursement (18 percent). Ten percent offer some other type of benefit, including a company vehicle and profit sharing (Exhibit 40).

Exhibit 40. Fringe Benefits- CFO/Head of Finance
(Percent of Respondents with Position)

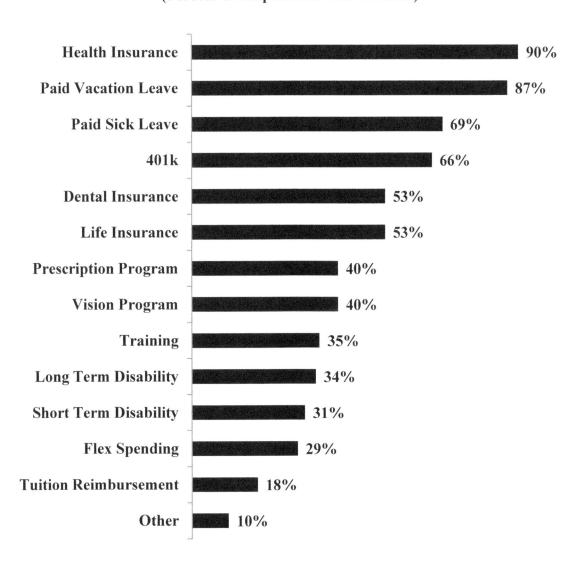

CIO/Head of IT

Only three percent of builders responding to the survey report having a full-time CIO/Head of IT. Another one percent have it on a part-time basis (Exhibit 41). Among the companies where this position exists full-time, 20 percent report its annual salary at less than $50,000, 50 percent at $50,000–$99,999, and 30 percent say their CIO/Head of IT earns $100,000 or more per year (Exhibit 42). The average annual salary is $79,600, and the average bonus among all those reporting a salary is $19,250 (averaging in zero bonuses), for an average total compensation of $98,850. Forty percent of companies reporting a salary for this position also pay it a bonus/commission. The average bonus among only those who reported a bonus (not averaging in zeroes) cannot be reported due to low responses (Appendix B).

Exhibit 41. Does this Position (CIO/Head of IT) Exist?

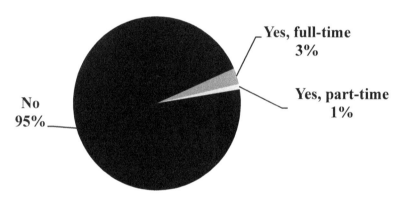

Exhibit 42. Annual Salary- CIO/Head of IT

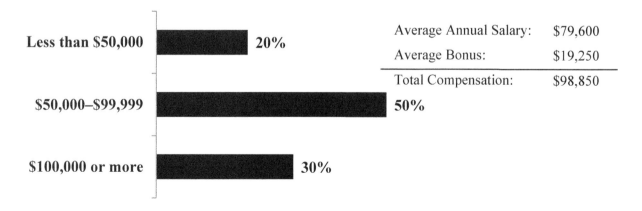

Average Annual Salary:	$79,600
Average Bonus:	$19,250
Total Compensation:	$98,850

Very few single-family builders have a full-time CIO/Head of IT: only one percent of those expecting 1−10 starts in 2017 have this position, the share is three percent among those with 11−99 starts, and six percent among those who will start 100 or more single-family units in 2017 (Exhibit 43).

**Exhibit 43. Percent of Firms who Have a Full-Time CIO/Head of IT
by Number of 2017 Starts**

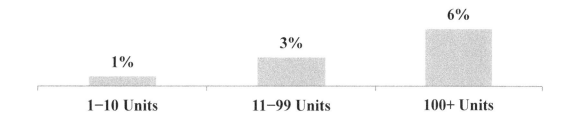

| 1−10 Units | 11−99 Units | 100+ Units |

Fewer than 10 builders reported the benefits offered to the CIO/Head of IT, so the results are not reported.

VP of Construction

Thirty-six percent of respondents report the position of VP of Construction exists in their firm on a full-time basis, while one percent report it is only part-time (Exhibit 44). Nearly all—96 percent—of those who have this position report it is "always" filled by someone with experience in the construction trades. Only two percent say "sometimes" and one percent "never/almost never" (Exhibit 45).

Exhibit 44. Does this Position (VP of Construction) Exist?

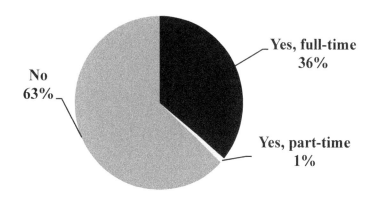

Exhibit 45. Is it Filled by Person with Construction Trades Experience?

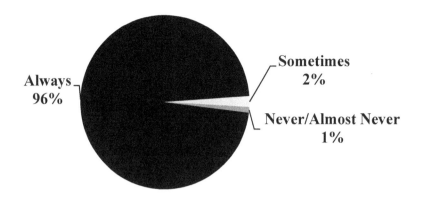

For those firms that have the position full-time, seven percent report an annual salary of less than $50,000, 51 percent between $50,000 and $99,999, and 42 percent report it at $100,000 or more. The average annual salary is $94,293 and the average bonus among all those reporting a salary is $37,625 (averaging in zero bonuses), for an average total compensation of $131,918 (Exhibit 46). Seventy-six percent of companies reporting a salary for this position also pay it a bonus/commission. The average bonus among only those who reported a bonus (not averaging in zeroes) is $49,532 (Appendix B).

Exhibit 46. Annual Salary- VP of Construction

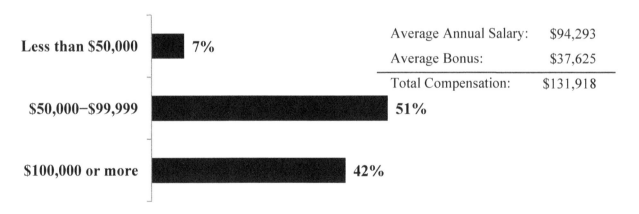

The likelihood that a builder employs a full-time VP of Construction increases with the size of the company: 24 percent of those expecting 1−10 starts in 2017 report this position, compared to 40 percent of those with 11−99 starts, and 81 percent of those who expect to start 100 or more units in 2017 (Exhibit 47). Similarly, average total compensation for this position rises steadily with number of starts: $88,076 at small companies (1−10 units), $128,782 at medium companies (11−99 units), and $179,940 at large companies (100+ units) (Exhibit 48).

Exhibit 47. Percent of Firms who Have a Full-Time VP of Construction by Number of 2017 Starts

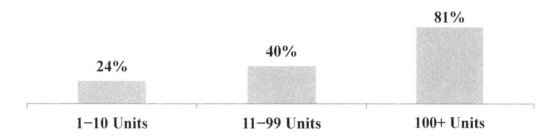

Exhibit 48. Average Total Compensation by Number of 2017 Starts- VP of Construction

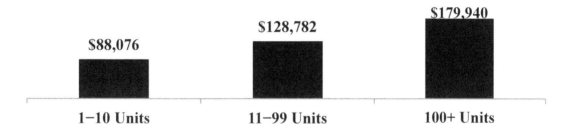

The most common benefit offered to the VP of Construction is paid vacation leave—90 percent of builders who report having a VP of Construction offer this benefit to them. Eighty-eight percent offer health insurance, 73 percent offer paid sick leave, 63 percent a 401k plan, 46 percent dental insurance, and 42 percent life insurance. Less than 40 percent of the responding firms offer the following benefits to their VP of Construction: prescription program (36 percent), training (34 percent), vision program (29 percent), short term disability (27 percent), long term disability (26 percent), flex spending (25 percent), and tuition reimbursement (17 percent). Eleven percent offer some other type of benefit, including a company vehicle and gas allowance (Exhibit 49).

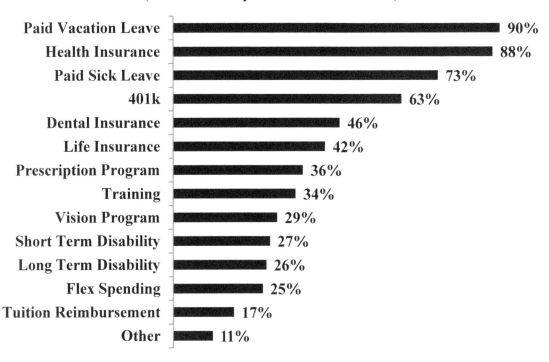

Exhibit 49. Fringe Benefits- VP of Construction (Percent of Respondents with Position)

Paid Vacation Leave	90%
Health Insurance	88%
Paid Sick Leave	73%
401k	63%
Dental Insurance	46%
Life Insurance	42%
Prescription Program	36%
Training	34%
Vision Program	29%
Short Term Disability	27%
Long Term Disability	26%
Flex Spending	25%
Tuition Reimbursement	17%
Other	11%

OPERATIONS JOBS

Head/Director of Purchasing

Seventeen percent of respondents report that the position of Head/Director of Purchasing exists in their firm on a full-time basis, while one percent report it as a part-time job (Exhibit 50). In the majority of cases where position exists (67 percent), it is "always" filled by someone with experience in the construction trades, only "sometimes" in 26 percent of the firms, and "never/almost never" in eight percent (Exhibit 51).

Exhibit 50. Does this Position (Head/Director of Purchasing) Exist?

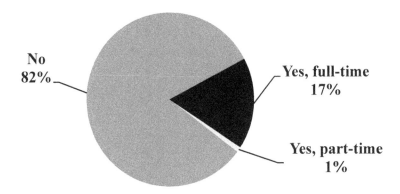

No
82%

Yes, full-time
17%

Yes, part-time
1%

Exhibit 51. Is it Filled by Person with Construction Trades Experience?

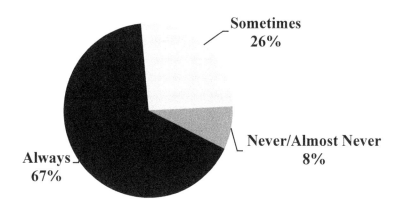

Sometimes
26%

Never/Almost Never
8%

Always
67%

For those firms that have the position full-time, eight percent report that their Head/Director of Purchasing has an annual salary of less than $50,000, 67 percent between $50,000 and $99,999, and 24 percent report it at $100,000 or more. The average annual salary is $80,884 and the average bonus among all those reporting a salary is $20,014 (averaging in zero bonuses), for an average total compensation of $100,898 (Exhibit 52). Seventy-three percent of companies reporting a salary for this position also pay it a bonus/commission. The average bonus among only those who reported a bonus (not averaging in zeroes) is $27,242 (Appendix B).

Exhibit 52. Annual Salary- Head/Director of Purchasing

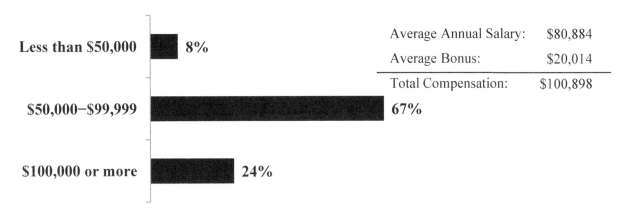

Less than $50,000 8%

$50,000–$99,999 67%

$100,000 or more 24%

Average Annual Salary:	$80,884
Average Bonus:	$20,014
Total Compensation:	$100,898

The more single-family units a firm expects to start in 2017, the more likely it is to have a Head/Director of Purchasing: while only three percent of small builders (1–10 units) have it, the share rises to 22 percent among medium builders (11−99 units), and to 68 percent among large builders (100+ units) (Exhibit 53). Average total compensation for this job is $75,135 at medium builders and $117,014 at large builders (Exhibit 54).

Exhibit 53. Percent of Firms who Have a Full-Time Head/Director of Purchasing by Number of 2017 Starts

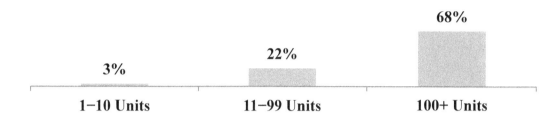

Exhibit 54. Average Total Compensation by Number of 2017 Starts- Head/Director of Purchasing

The most common two benefits offered to the Head/Director of Purchasing are paid vacation leave and health insurance, as 96 percent and 90 percent, respectively, of builders with this position offer it to them. Eighty percent offer paid sick leave, 73 percent a 401k plan, 63 percent dental insurance, and 51 percent life insurance. Less than half of builders that have a Head/Director of Purchasing position offer it the remaining benefits: 49 percent offer each a prescription program and a vision program, 39 percent long term disability, 33 percent each flex spending and short term disability, 29 percent training, and 22 percent tuition reimbursement. Eight percent offer "other" benefits, such as a company vehicle (Exhibit 55).

Exhibit 55. Fringe Benefits- Head/Director of Purchasing
(Percent of Respondents with Position)

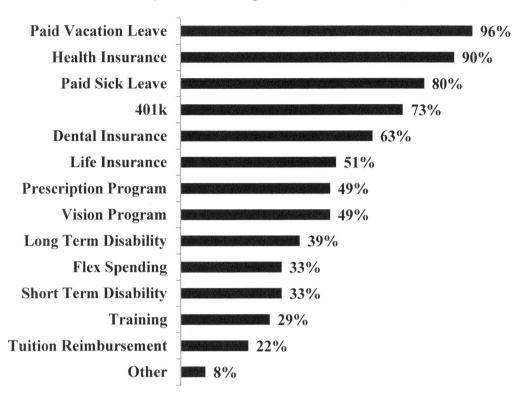

Paid Vacation Leave	96%
Health Insurance	90%
Paid Sick Leave	80%
401k	73%
Dental Insurance	63%
Life Insurance	51%
Prescription Program	49%
Vision Program	49%
Long Term Disability	39%
Flex Spending	33%
Short Term Disability	33%
Training	29%
Tuition Reimbursement	22%
Other	8%

Head/Director of Land Acquisition

The full-time position of Head/Director of Land Acquisition exists only at eight percent of the builders who responded to the survey (Exhibit 56). Of those, the majority (87 percent) report it is "always" filled by a person with experience in the construction trade, while the remaining 13 percent say "never/almost never" (Exhibit 57).

Exhibit 56. Does this Position (Head/Director of Land Acquisition) Exist?

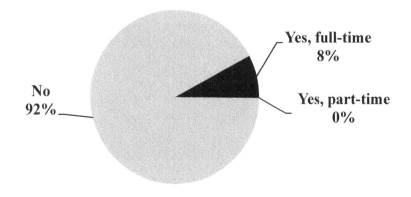

Yes, full-time
8%

Yes, part-time
0%

No
92%

Exhibit 57. Is it Filled by Person with Construction Trades Experience?

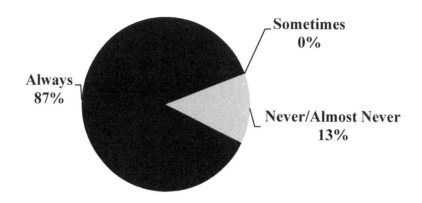

For those firms that have the position, 32 percent report that their Head/Director of Land Acquisition has an annual salary between $50,000 and $99,999 and the other 68 percent report it at $100,000 or more. The average annual salary is $124,114, and the average bonus among all those reporting a salary is $49,352 (averaging in zero bonuses), for an average total compensation of $173,466 (Exhibit 58). Seventy-seven percent of companies reporting a salary for this position also pay it a bonus/commission. The average bonus among only those who reported a bonus (not averaging in zeroes) is $63,868 (Appendix B).

Exhibit 58. Annual Salary- Head/Director of Land Acquisition

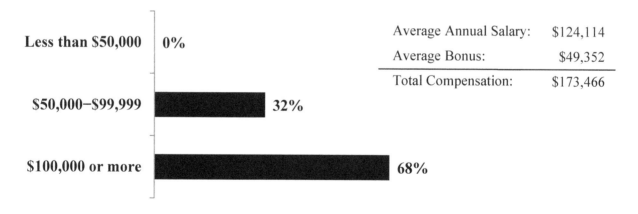

Having a full-time Head/Director of Land Acquisition is rare among small builders—only one percent of those starting 1–10 units in 2017 have it, slightly more common among medium builders—nine

46

percent of those starting 11–99 units have it, and significantly more widespread among large builders—35 percent of those who will start 100 or more units in 2017 have it (Exhibit 59). Because of low response counts, average total compensation cannot be reported for this position at small or medium builders. At large builders, their annual compensation averages $161,682 (Appendix A-28).

Exhibit 59. Percent of Firms who Have a Full-Time Head/Director of Land Acquisition by Number of 2017 Starts

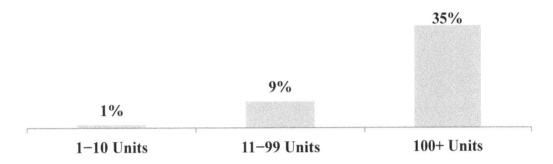

Ninety-five percent of the firms who report having a Head/Director of Land Acquisition offer paid vacation leave to them, 91 percent offer health insurance, and 82 percent offer each a 401k plan and dental insurance. Paid sick leave is offered by 77 percent of firms where job exists, while 59 percent offer each life insurance and a prescription program. Exactly half offer long term disability and a vision program. Fewer than 50 percent of the responding firms offer the following benefits to their Head/Director of Land Acquisition: training and flex spending (41 percent each), short term disability (32 percent), and tuition reimbursement (23 percent). Nine percent offer some other type of benefit, such as a 529 College Saving plan and an auto allowance (Exhibit 60).

Exhibit 60. Fringe Benefits- Head/Director of Land Acquisition
(Percent of Respondents with Position)

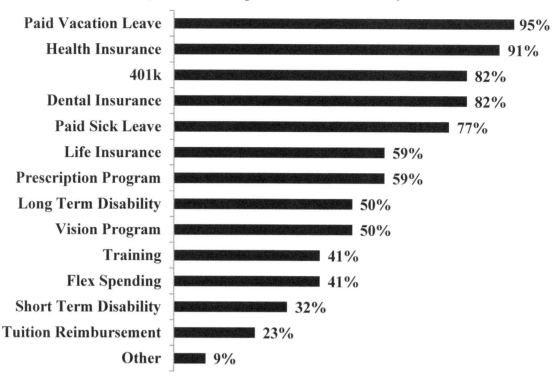

Paid Vacation Leave	95%
Health Insurance	91%
401k	82%
Dental Insurance	82%
Paid Sick Leave	77%
Life Insurance	59%
Prescription Program	59%
Long Term Disability	50%
Vision Program	50%
Training	41%
Flex Spending	41%
Short Term Disability	32%
Tuition Reimbursement	23%
Other	9%

Head/Director of Production

Fourteen percent of single-family builders responding to the survey have a full-time Head/Director of Production on staff. None have it on a part-time basis (Exhibit 61). Having prior experience in the construction trades is important for this position, as 81 percent of builders where it exists say it is "always" filled by a person with such experience, compared to 15 percent who say only "sometimes," and four percent who say "never/almost never" (Exhibit 62).

Exhibit 61. Does this Position (Head/Director of Production) Exist?

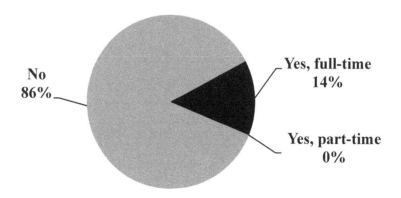

No 86%

Yes, full-time 14%

Yes, part-time 0%

Exhibit 62. Is it Filled by Person with Construction Trades Experience?

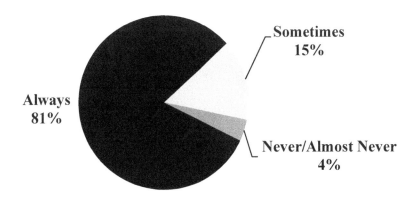

Sometimes
15%

Always
81%

Never/Almost Never
4%

For those firms that have the position, 88 percent report that their Head/Director of Production has an annual salary between $50,000 and $99,999 and 13 percent report it at $100,000 or more. The average annual salary is $74,496, and the average bonus among all those reporting a salary is $26,337 (averaging in zero bonuses), for an average total compensation of $100,833 (Exhibit 63). Sixty-five percent of companies reporting a salary for this position also pay it a bonus/commission. The average bonus among only those who reported a bonus (not averaging in zeroes) is $40,518 (Appendix B).

Exhibit 63. Annual Salary- Head/Director of Production

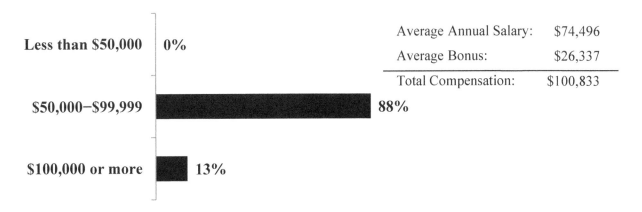

Less than $50,000	0%
$50,000–$99,999	88%
$100,000 or more	13%

Average Annual Salary:	$74,496
Average Bonus:	$26,337
Total Compensation:	$100,833

The chance that a builder has a full-time Head/Director of Production on staff increases with the size of the company. Seven percent of small builders (1–10 starts expected in 2017) have it, compared to 20 percent of medium builders (11–99 starts), and 26 percent of large builders (100 or more starts) (Exhibit 64). Total compensation can only be reported for Head/Director of Production at medium-sized builders, where it averages $78,266 (Appendix A-32).

Exhibit 64. Percent of Firms who Have a Full-Time Head/Director of Production by Number of 2017 Starts

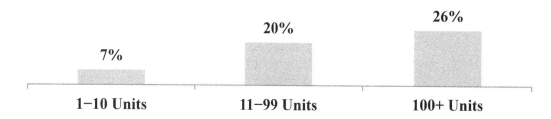

1-10 Units	11-99 Units	100+ Units
7%	20%	26%

Nearly all builders—97 percent—who have the Head/Director of Production position on staff offer it paid vacation leave. Significantly fewer, but still more than half of the companies, offer it health insurance (76 percent), paid sick leave (71 percent), and a 401k plan (66 percent). Dental insurance is offered by 47 percent, long term disability and life insurance each by 34 percent, a prescription program by 32 percent, a vision program by 29 percent, and short term disability by 24 percent. Less than 20 percent of builders offer their Head/Director of Production tuition reimbursement or flex spending. Five percent offer some other type of benefits, such as company equity (Exhibit 65).

Exhibit 65. Fringe Benefits- Head/Director of Production (Percent of Respondents with Position)

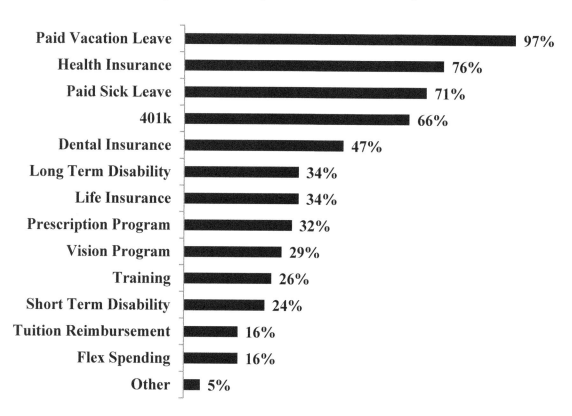

Benefit	Percent
Paid Vacation Leave	97%
Health Insurance	76%
Paid Sick Leave	71%
401k	66%
Dental Insurance	47%
Long Term Disability	34%
Life Insurance	34%
Prescription Program	32%
Vision Program	29%
Training	26%
Short Term Disability	24%
Tuition Reimbursement	16%
Flex Spending	16%
Other	5%

Head/Director of Development and Training

Less than one half of one percent of respondents report the position of Head/Director of Development & Training exists at their firm, either on a full-time or a part-time basis (Exhibit 66). The salary, bonus, and benefits for this position cannot be reported due to its low incidence among builders responding to the survey.

Exhibit 66. Does this Position (Head/Director of Development and Training) Exist?

Yes, full-time
*

Yes, part-time
*

No
99%

*Less than 0.5%

Head/Director of Sales & Marketing

Twenty-one percent of the respondents report the position of Head/Director of Sales & Marketing exists in their firm: 19 percent full-time and two percent part-time (Exhibit 67). Fifty-eight percent of builders say the person in this job "always" has experience in the construction trades, 35 percent say "sometimes," and eight percent "never/almost never" (Exhibit 68).

Exhibit 67. Does this Position (Head/Director of Sales & Marketing) Exist?

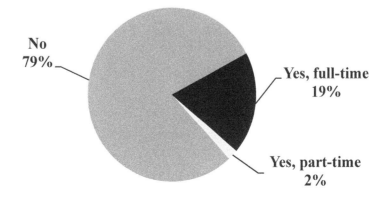

No
79%

Yes, full-time
19%

Yes, part-time
2%

Exhibit 68. Is it Filled by Person with Construction Trades Experience?

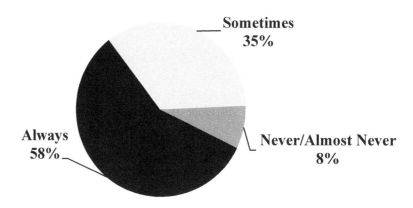

For those firms that have the position full-time, 14 percent report that their Head/Director of Sales & Marketing has an average salary of less than $50,000, 43 percent between $50,000 and $99,999, and another 43 percent report it at $100,000 or more. The average annual salary is $88,027 and the average bonus among all those reporting a salary is $47,863 (averaging in zero bonuses), for an average total compensation of $135,890 (Exhibit 69). Seventy-three percent of companies reporting a salary for this position also pay it a bonus/commission. The average bonus among only those who reported a bonus (not averaging in zeroes) is $65,973 (Appendix B).

Exhibit 69. Annual Salary- Head/Director of Sales & Marketing

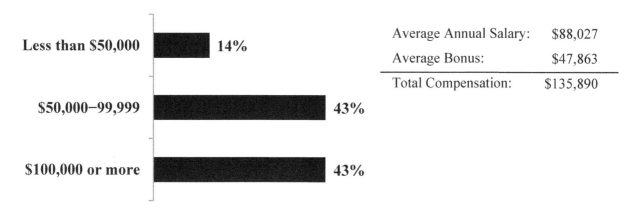

The share of firms with a full-time Head/Director of Sales & Marketing increases significantly with the size of the company. Whereas only five percent of small builders (1–10 starts) report the position exists in their companies, the share goes to 26 percent among medium builders (11–99 units), and to 61 percent among large builders (100 or more starts) (Exhibit 70). Average total compensation for this job is $119,494 at medium builders and $178,438 at large builders (Appendix A-38).

Exhibit 70. Percent of Firms who Have a Full-Time Head/Director of Sales and Marketing by Number of 2017 Starts

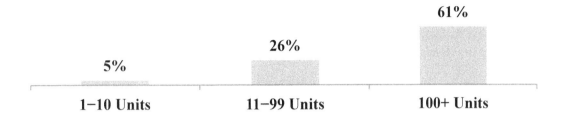

The most common benefit offered to the Head/Director of Sales and Marketing is paid vacation leave—90 percent of firms who report this position offer it to them. More than 80 percent offer health insurance (88 percent) and a 401k plan (82 percent). Paid sick leave is offered by 72 percent of firms where position exists, dental insurance by 56 percent, and life insurance by 52 percent. Less than half offer the remaining benefits: a prescription program and a vision program (each 42 percent), short term disability (34 percent), long term disability (30 percent), training (28 percent), flex spending (24 percent), and tuition reimbursement (16 percent). Six percent offer some other type of benefits to their Head/Director of Sales and Marketing, such as a company vehicle and matching 401k contributions (Exhibit 71).

**Exhibit 71. Fringe Benefits- Head/Director of Sales & Marketing
(Percent of Respondents with Position)**

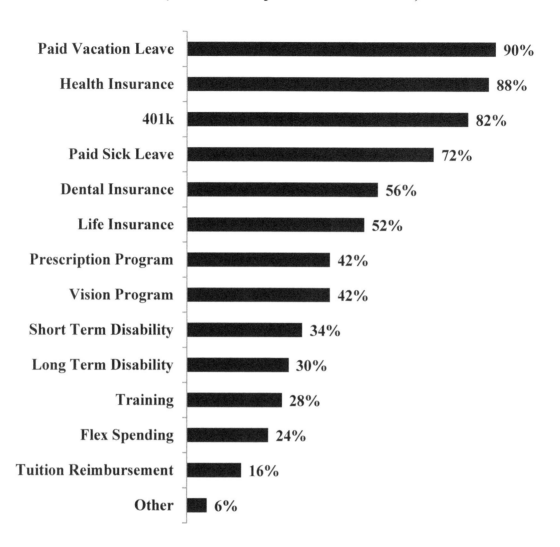

Controller

Eighteen percent of respondents report that the position of Controller exists in their firm full-time, and another five percent say it exists on a part-time basis (Exhibit 72). For those firms that have the position full-time, 14 percent report that the Controller has an annual average salary of less than $50,000, 75 percent between $50,000 and $99,999, and 12 percent report it at $100,000 or more. The average annual salary is $72,002 and the average bonus among all those reporting a salary is $11,697 (averaging in zero bonuses), for an average total compensation of $83,699 (Exhibit 73). Seventy-one percent of companies reporting a salary for this position also pay it a bonus/commission. The average bonus among only those who reported a bonus (not averaging in zeroes) is $16,570 (Appendix B).

Exhibit 72. Does this Position (Controller) Exist?

Exhibit 73. Annual Salary- Controller

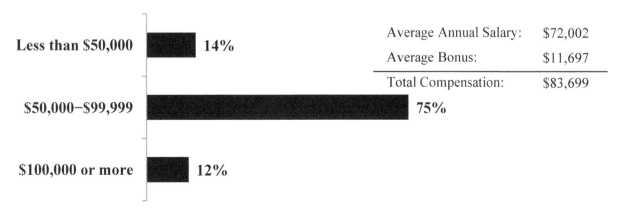

Only five percent of small firms (expecting to start 1–10 units in 2017) have a full-time Controller. In contrast, 26 percent of medium builders (11–99 units) and 55 percent of large builders (100 or more starts in 2017) report this position exists at their companies (Exhibit 74). The Controller's average total compensation is $74,420 in firms with 11–99 starts and $98,220 in firms with 100 or more starts (Exhibit 75).

Exhibit 74. Percent of Firms who Have a Full-Time Controller by Number of 2017 Starts

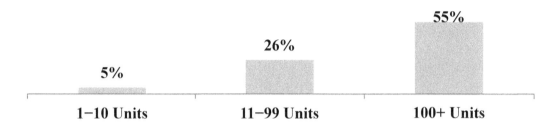

Exhibit 75. Average Total Compensation by Number of 2017 Starts-Controller

Almost all builders—98 percent—offer their Controller paid vacation leave. At least 80 percent offer them health insurance (88 percent), paid sick leave (86 percent), and a 401k plan (80 percent). Sixty-three percent offer them dental insurance and 53 percent life insurance. Less than half of firms with a Controller position offer it the following benefits: a prescription program (45 percent), a vision program (43 percent), flex spending and long term disability (each 37 percent), training (33 percent), short-term disability (31 percent), and tuition reimbursement (20 percent). Ten percent of builders offer their Controller other benefits, such as a vehicle and profit sharing (Exhibit 76).

Exhibit 76. Fringe Benefits-Controller
(Percent of Respondents with Position)

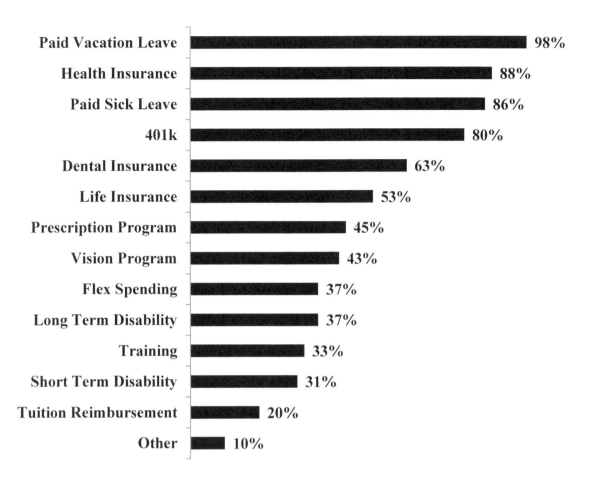

Paid Vacation Leave	98%
Health Insurance	88%
Paid Sick Leave	86%
401k	80%
Dental Insurance	63%
Life Insurance	53%
Prescription Program	45%
Vision Program	43%
Flex Spending	37%
Long Term Disability	37%
Training	33%
Short Term Disability	31%
Tuition Reimbursement	20%
Other	10%

Payroll Manager

The position of full-time Payroll Manager exists at five percent of responding firms, with another two percent reporting it as only part-time (Exhibit 77). For those firms that have the position full-time, 36 percent report that their Payroll Manager has an annual salary of less than $50,000 and the remaining 64 percent report an annual salary between $50,000 and $99,999. The average annual salary is $54,571, and the average bonus among all those reporting a salary is $4,107 (averaging in zero bonuses), for an average total compensation of $58,678 (Exhibit 78). Fifty percent of companies reporting a salary for this position also pay it a bonus/commission. The average bonus among only those who reported a bonus (not averaging in zeroes) cannot be reported due to low responses (Appendix B).

Exhibit 77. Does this Position (Payroll Manager) Exist?

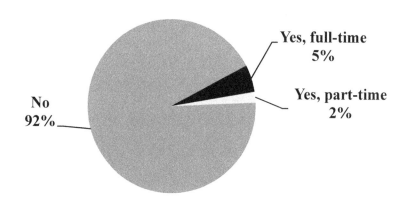

Exhibit 78. Annual Salary- Payroll Manager

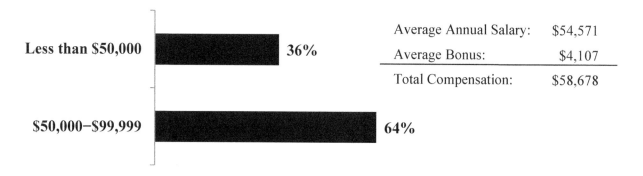

Average Annual Salary:	$54,571
Average Bonus:	$4,107
Total Compensation:	$58,678

The majority of single-family home building companies do not have a full-time Payroll Manager on staff, regardless of company size. While only two percent of firms expecting to start 1−10 units in 2017 have this position, the share is not that much larger among firms starting 11−99 units (6 percent), or those starting 100 or more units (13 percent) (Exhibit 79). Due to low response count, average total compensation for Payroll Managers cannot be reported by company size.

**Exhibit 79. Percent of Firms who Have a Full-Time Payroll Manager
by Number of 2017 Starts**

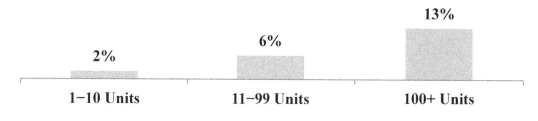

The most common two benefits offered to the Payroll Manager are paid vacation leave and health insurance—79 percent of firms who report this position offer these benefits to them. At least half also offer paid sick leave and life insurance (each 64 percent), a 401k plan (57 percent), and dental insurance (50 percent). Forty-three percent offer their Payroll Manager short term disability, 36 percent offer each training, flex spending, and a vision program, 29 percent a prescription program, 21 percent long term disability, and 14 percent offer tuition reimbursement. Seven percent of the respondents offer some other type of benefit to their Payroll Manager, such as a 529 College Savings Plan (Exhibit 80).

Exhibit 80. Fringe Benefits- Payroll Manager
(Percent of Respondents with Position)

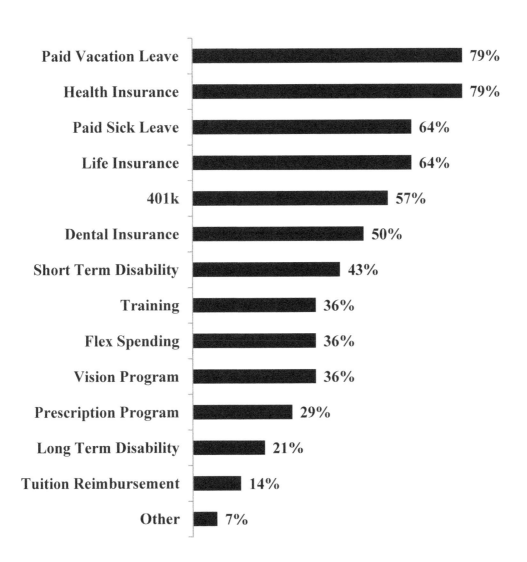

Staff Accountant

Ten percent of builders responding to the survey have a full-time Staff Accountant on staff. Another four percent have the position on a part-time basis (Exhibit 81). For those firms that have the position full-time, 34 percent pay it an annual salary of less than $50,000 and 66 percent pay it between $50,000 and $99,999. The average annual salary is $53,290, and the average bonus among all those reporting a salary is $5,224 (averaging in zero bonuses), for an average total compensation of $58,514 (Exhibit 82). Sixty-six percent of companies reporting a salary for this position also pay it a bonus/commission. The average bonus among only those who reported a bonus (not averaging in zeroes) is $7,974 (Appendix B).

Exhibit 81. Does this Position (Staff Accountant) Exist?

Exhibit 82. Annual Salary- Staff Accountant

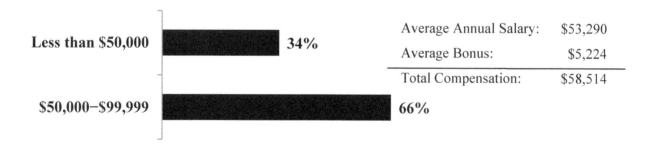

Average Annual Salary:	$53,290
Average Bonus:	$5,224
Total Compensation:	$58,514

Nearly half—48 percent—of the largest builders (100 or more units) employ a full-time Staff Accountant. But the share is significantly lower among smaller builders: only three percent of those expecting to start 1–10 units in 2017 and nine percent of those expecting 11–99 units have this position

(Exhibit 83). Annual compensation for full-time Staff Accountants averages $52,940 at building companies with 11–99 starts and $61,667 at those with 100 or more (Exhibit 84).

Exhibit 83. Percent of Firms who Have a Full-Time Staff Accountant by Number of 2017 Starts

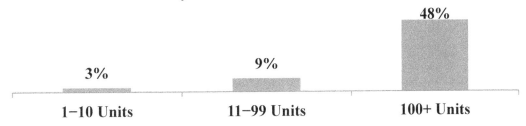

Exhibit 84. Average Total Compensation by Number of 2017 Starts-Staff Accountant

The most common benefit offered to the Staff Accountant is health insurance—93 percent of firms who report this position offer it this benefit. Eighty-six percent offer vacation leave, 79 percent offer paid sick leave, 71 percent offer a 401k plan, 57 percent dental insurance, 54 percent life insurance, and 50 percent a vision program. Less than half of the respondents offer the following benefits to their Staff Accountant: a prescription program (46 percent), training (43 percent), flex spending (32 percent), short term disability (29 percent), tuition reimbursement (25 percent), and long term disability (21 percent). Four percent of the respondents offer some other type of benefit to their Staff Accountant, such as paid bereavement leave (Exhibit 85).

Exhibit 85. Fringe Benefits- Staff Accountant
(Percent of Respondents with Position)

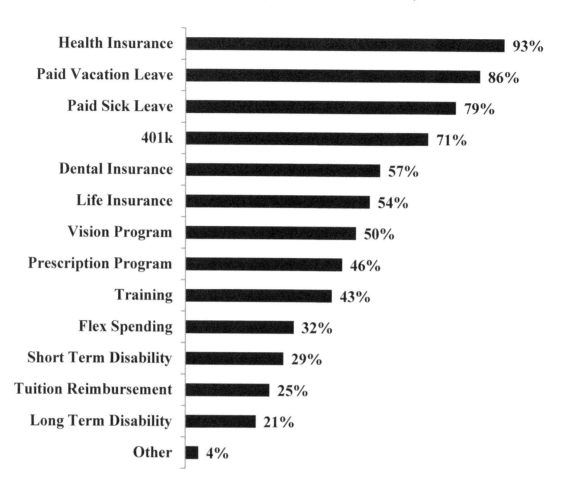

Bookkeeper

Twenty-five percent of the respondents report the position of Bookkeeper exists as a full-time position in their firm, while 20 percent report it on a part-time basis (Exhibit 86). For those firms that have the position full-time, 77 percent pay it an average annual salary of less than $50,000 and the remaining 23 percent between $50,000 and $99,999. The average annual salary is $42,478, and the average bonus among all those reporting a salary is $2,879 (averaging in zero bonuses), for an average total compensation of $45,357 (Exhibit 87). Sixty-three percent of companies reporting a salary for this position also pay it a bonus/commission. The average bonus among only those who reported a bonus (not averaging in zeroes) is $4,543 (Appendix B).

Exhibit 86. Does this Position (Bookkeeper) Exist?

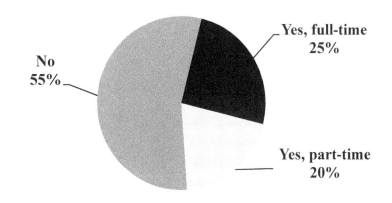

No
55%

Yes, full-time
25%

Yes, part-time
20%

Exhibit 87. Annual Salary- Bookkeeper

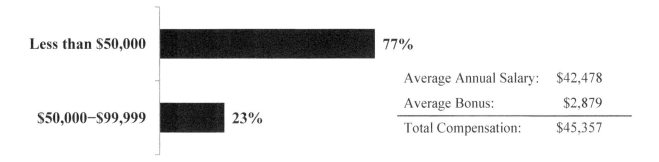

Less than $50,000 — 77%

$50,000−$99,999 — 23%

Average Annual Salary:	$42,478
Average Bonus:	$2,879
Total Compensation:	$45,357

Full-time Bookkeepers become more commonplace as single-family building companies get larger. Among respondents expecting only 1−10 starts in 2017, 16 percent report a full-time Bookkeeper. Twice as many—33 percent—have it at builders starting 11−99 units, as well as nearly half—48 percent—at those starting 100 or more units (Exhibit 88). Total compensation for this position does not vary significantly across different-size builders, averaging $46,712 among small builders, $44,388 among medium builders, and $45,567 among large builders (Exhibit 89).

**Exhibit 88. Percent of Firms who Have a Full-Time Bookkeeper
by Number of 2017 Starts**

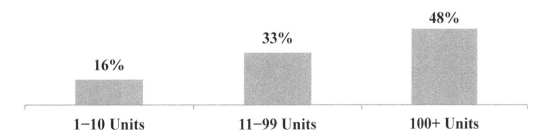

16%
1−10 Units

33%
11−99 Units

48%
100+ Units

Exhibit 89. Average Total Compensation by Number of 2017 Starts- Bookkeeper

$46,712	$44,388	$45,567
1−10 Units	11-99 Units	100+ Units

The most common benefit offered to the Bookkeeper is paid vacation leave—92 percent of firms who report this position offer it to them. Seventy-six percent offer health insurance, 67 percent offer paid sick leave, and 62 percent a 401k plan. Less than half of the respondents offer the remaining nine benefits: dental insurance (44 percent), a prescription program (38 percent), training (35 percent), life insurance (33 percent), a vision program (26 percent), long term and short term disability (each 21 percent), and tuition reimbursement and flex spending (each 17 percent). Six percent of the responding firms offer some other type of benefit to their Bookkeeper, such as a simple IRA (Exhibit 90).

Exhibit 90. Fringe Benefits- Bookkeeper
(Percent of Respondents with Position)

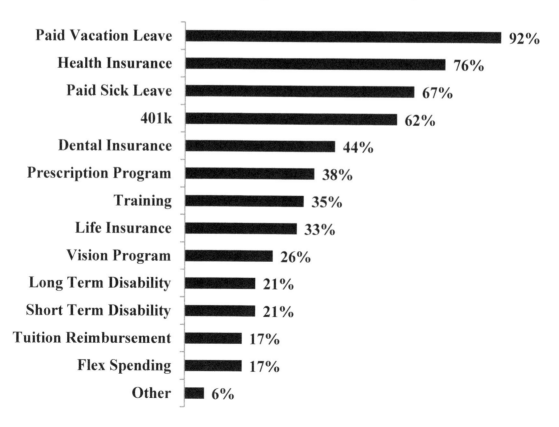

Benefit	Percent
Paid Vacation Leave	92%
Health Insurance	76%
Paid Sick Leave	67%
401k	62%
Dental Insurance	44%
Prescription Program	38%
Training	35%
Life Insurance	33%
Vision Program	26%
Long Term Disability	21%
Short Term Disability	21%
Tuition Reimbursement	17%
Flex Spending	17%
Other	6%

HUMAN RESOURCES JOBS

Director of Human Resources

The vast majority of builders responding to the survey—97 percent—do not employ a Director of Human Resources (Exhibit 91). Large builders, however, are significantly more likely to report this position full-time (16 percent) than small builders (0 percent) or medium builders (1 percent) (Appendix A-58). Due to the low count of responses, the average salary, bonus, and benefits for this position cannot be reliably reported.

Exhibit 91. Does this Position (Director of Human Resources) Exist?

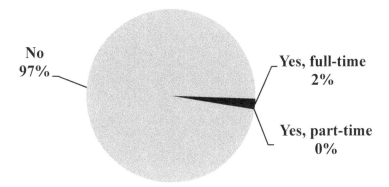

Recruiter

Less than half a percent of builders report having a Recruiter (Exhibit 92). Due to the low count of responses, the average salary, bonus, and benefits for this position cannot be reliably reported.

Exhibit 92. Does this Position (Recruiter) Exist?

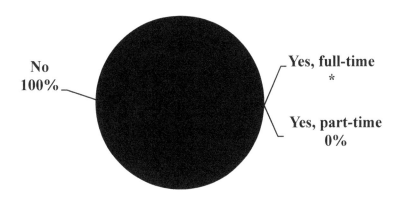

* Less than 0.5%.

In-House Legal Counsel

Ninety-nine percent of the builders in the survey do not have an In-House Legal Counsel position (Exhibit 93). Even large builders expecting to start 100 or more units in 2017 are highly unlikely to report it full-time—only three percent do (Appendix A-58). Due to the low count of responses, the average salary, bonus, and benefits for In-House Legal Counsel cannot be reliably reported.

Exhibit 93. Does this Position (In-House Legal Counsel) Exist?

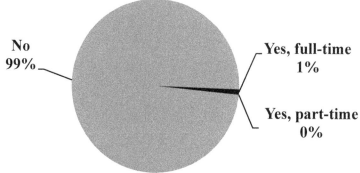

IT JOBS

Director of IT

Only four percent of the respondents report that the position of Director of IT exists in their firm on a full-time basis. Another one percent report it as a part-time job (Exhibit 94). For those firms that have the position full-time, nine percent pay it an average annual salary of less than $50,000, 73 percent between $50,000 and $99,999, and 18 percent $100,000 or more. The average annual salary is $70,491, and the average bonus among all those reporting a salary is $5,773 (averaging in zero bonuses), for an average total compensation of $76,264 (Exhibit 95). Forty-five percent of companies reporting a salary for this position also pay it a bonus/commission. The average bonus among only those who reported a bonus (not averaging in zeroes) cannot be reported due to low responses (Appendix B).

Exhibit 94. Does this Position (Director of IT) Exist?

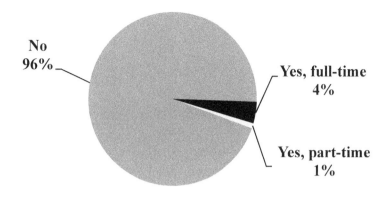

No
96%

Yes, full-time
4%

Yes, part-time
1%

Exhibit 95. Annual Salary- Director of IT

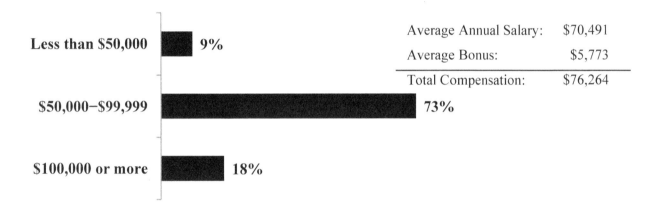

Average Annual Salary:	$70,491
Average Bonus:	$5,773
Total Compensation:	$76,264

Less than $50,000   9%

$50,000−$99,999   73%

$100,000 or more   18%

None of the builders expecting to start 1−10 units in 2017 report having a full-time Director of IT. Among those starting 11−99 units, only five percent do. The position is more common among large builders (100 or more starts), as 19 percent have a full-time Director of IT on staff (Exhibit 96). Due to low response count, average total compensation cannot be reported by company size.

Exhibit 96. Percent of Firms who Have a Full-Time Director of IT by Number of 2017 Starts

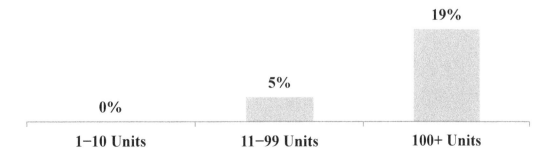

0%   1−10 Units

5%   11−99 Units

19%   100+ Units

All firms who report having a Director of IT offer paid vacation leave to that position. Ninety percent offer the following three benefits: paid sick leave, a 401k plan, and health insurance. Eighty percent offer dental insurance, 70 percent life insurance, 60 percent each long term disability and a vision program, and 50 percent flex spending. Forty percent offer each training, short term disability, and a prescription program, while only 30 percent offer tuition reimbursement. Twenty percent of respondents offer some other type of benefit, such as ownership shares (Exhibit 97).

Exhibit 97. Fringe Benefits- Director of IT

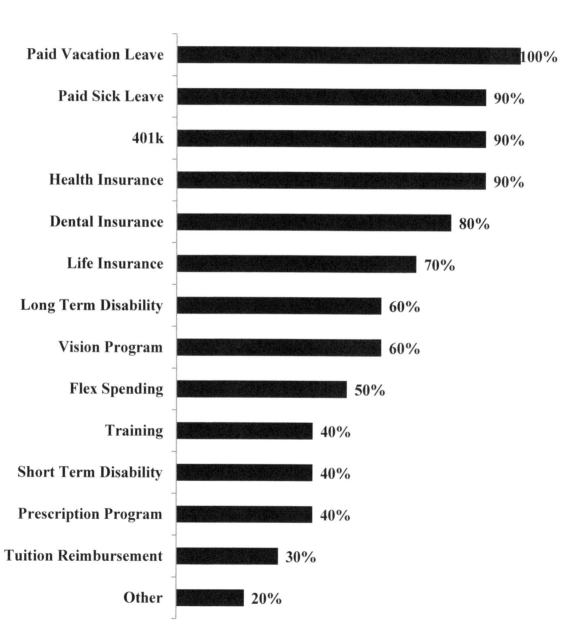

Network Engineer

Only one percent of respondents report that the position of full-time Network Engineer exists in their firm (Exhibit 98). None of the small builders have this position on staff. It is uncommon even among the large builders (100 or more starts), as only six percent of that group report it (Appendix A-64). Due to the low count of responses, the average salary, bonus, and benefits for this position cannot be reliably reported.

Exhibit 98. Does this Position (Network Engineer) Exist?

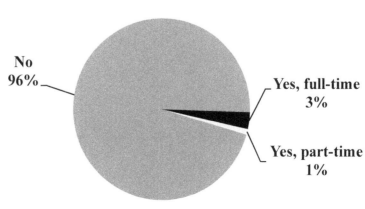

Web Design Specialist

Overall, only four percent of respondents report that the position of Web Design Specialist exits at their firm: three percent on a full-time basis and one percent as part-time (Exhibit 99). For those firms that have the position full-time, 44 report it pays an annual salary of less than $50,000, 44 percent between $50,000 and $99,999, and 11 percent pay $100,000 or more. The average annual salary is $56,222 (Exhibit 100). Due to the low count of responses, the average bonus and benefits for this position cannot be reliably reported.

Exhibit 99. Does this Position (Web Design Specialist) Exist?

No
96%

Yes, full-time
3%

Yes, part-time
1%

Exhibit 100. Annual Salary- Web Design Specialist

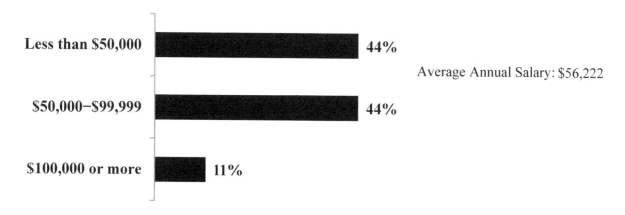

Less than $50,000   44%

Average Annual Salary: $56,222

$50,000–$99,999   44%

$100,000 or more   11%

None of the small builders report having a full-time Web Design Specialist. The position is only slightly more common among medium builders (5 percent have it) and large builders (10 percent) (Appendix A-64).

ADMINISTRATIVE JOBS

Executive Assistant

The Executive Assistant position exists as a full-time job at 11 percent of the companies responding to the survey, and as a part-time job at another one percent. (Exhibit 101). For those firms that have the position full-time, 70 percent report paying an annual salary of less than $50,000 and 30 percent between $50,000 and $99,999. The average annual salary is $44,732, and the average bonus among all those reporting a salary is $3,955 (averaging in zero bonuses), for an average total compensation of $48,687 (Exhibit 102). Sixty-one percent of companies reporting a salary for this position also pay it a bonus/commission. The average bonus among only those who reported a bonus (not averaging in zeroes) is $6,525 (Appendix B).

Exhibit 101. Does this Position (Executive Assistant) Exist?

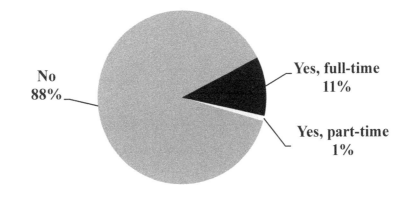

No
88%

Yes, full-time
11%

Yes, part-time
1%

Exhibit 102. Annual Salary- Executive Assistant

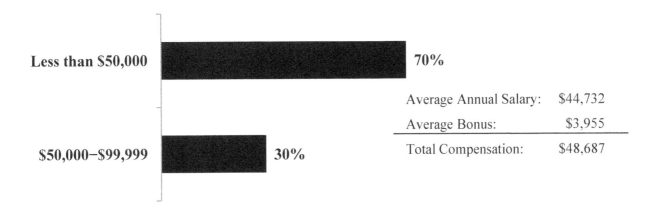

Less than $50,000   70%

$50,000−$99,999   30%

Average Annual Salary:	$44,732
Average Bonus:	$3,955
Total Compensation:	$48,687

The likelihood that a builder employs a full-time Executive Assistant increases with company size. While only five percent of small builders report having this position, the share grows to 12 percent among medium builders, and to 40 percent among large builders (Exhibit 103). Annual total compensation for Executive Assistants averages $44,931 and $50,958, respectively, at medium and large builders (Exhibit 104).

Exhibit 103. Percent of Firms who Have a Full-Time Executive Assistant by Number of 2017 Starts

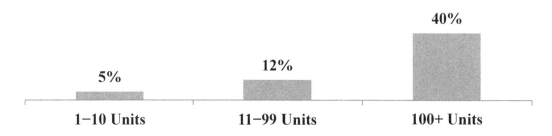

1−10 Units	11−99 Units	100+ Units
5%	12%	40%

Exhibit 104. Average Total Compensation by Number of 2017 Starts-Executive Assistant

11−99 Units	100+ Units
$44,931	$50,958

Over 90 percent of firms with an Executive Assistant offer that person paid vacation leave (94 percent) and health insurance (91 percent). More than half also offer paid sick leave (76 percent), a 401k plan (70 percent), and life insurance, a prescription program, and dental insurance (all 52 percent). Less common benefits to Executive Assistants include a vision program (offered by 45 percent), flex spending (39 percent), training (36 percent), short term disability (33 percent), long term disability (30 percent), and tuition reimbursement (15 percent). Nine percent of respondents offered some other type of benefit, such as an auto allowance (Exhibit 105).

Exhibit 105. Fringe Benefits- Executive Assistant
(Percent of Respondents with Position)

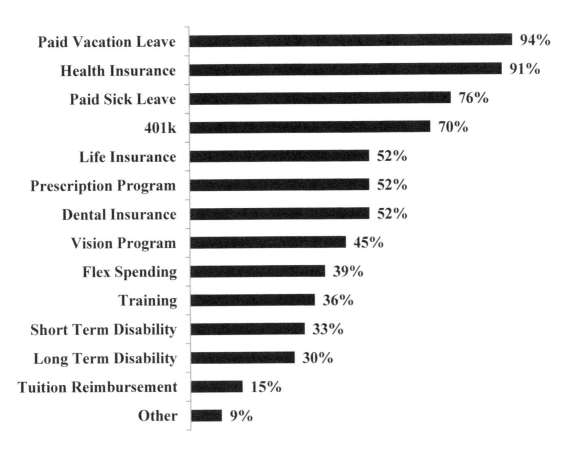

Office Manager

The position of Office Manager exists on a full-time basis at 17 percent of the companies responding to the survey, and at three percent on a part-time basis (Exhibit 106). For those firms that have the position full-time, 56 percent report paying an annual salary of less than $50,000, 40 percent between $50,000 and $99,999, and four percent $100,000 or more. The average annual salary is $50,287, and the average bonus among all those reporting a salary is $5,430 (averaging in zero bonuses), for an average total compensation of $55,717 (Exhibit 107). Sixty-three percent of companies reporting a salary for this position also pay it a bonus/commission. The average bonus among only those who reported a bonus (not averaging in zeroes) is $8,688 (Appendix B).

Exhibit 106. Does this Position (Office Manager) Exist?

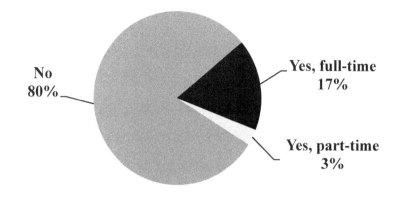

No
80%

Yes, full-time
17%

Yes, part-time
3%

Exhibit 107. Annual Salary- Office Manager

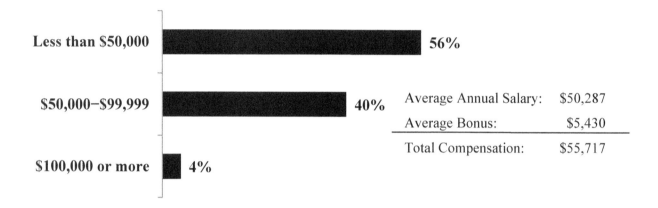

Less than $50,000	56%
$50,000–$99,999	40%
$100,000 or more	4%

Average Annual Salary:	$50,287
Average Bonus:	$5,430
Total Compensation:	$55,717

Twenty-three percent of companies expecting to start more than 10 single-family units in 2017 have a full-time Office Manager. The position is more unlikely to exist at small builders—only 10 percent of whom report it (Exhibit 108). Total compensation for a full-time Office Manager averages $44,499 and $60,584, respectively, at small and medium builders (Exhibit 109).

Exhibit 108. Percent of Firms who Have a Full-Time Office Manager by Number of 2017 Starts

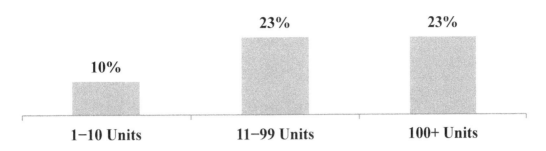

10%   23%   23%

1−10 Units   11−99 Units   100+ Units

Exhibit 109. Average Total Compensation by Number of 2017 Starts-Office Manager

$44,499 $60,584

1−10 Units   11−99 Units

Nearly all respondents who have an Office Manager on staff offer this person paid vacation leave—98 percent. More than half also offer paid sick leave (84 percent), health insurance (70 percent), and a 401k plan (64 percent). Most of the benefits, however, are offered by a minority of the respondents: dental insurance, life insurance, a prescription program, and training (all 36 percent), a vision program (30 percent), long term disability (23 percent), tuition reimbursement (20 percent), short term disability (18 percent), and flex spending (11 percent). Seven percent of respondents offered some other type of benefit, such as flexible hours (Exhibit 110).

Exhibit 110. Fringe Benefits- Office Manager
(Percent of Respondents with Position)

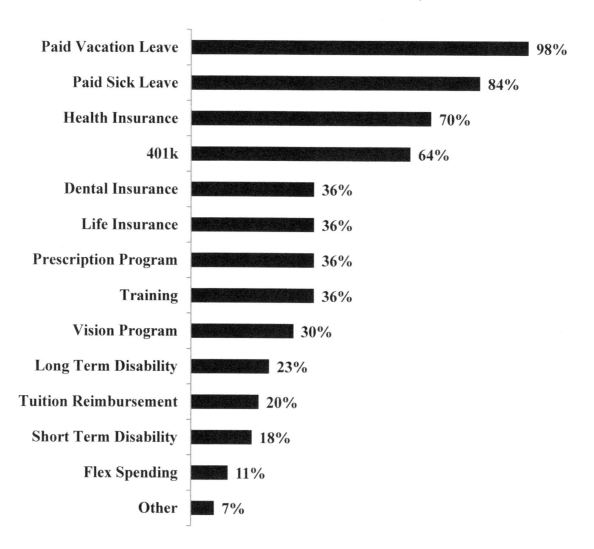

Paid Vacation Leave	98%
Paid Sick Leave	84%
Health Insurance	70%
401k	64%
Dental Insurance	36%
Life Insurance	36%
Prescription Program	36%
Training	36%
Vision Program	30%
Long Term Disability	23%
Tuition Reimbursement	20%
Short Term Disability	18%
Flex Spending	11%
Other	7%

Administrative Assistant

Nine percent of respondents have full-time Administrative Assistants on staff and another six percent have them part-time (Exhibit 111). For those firms that have the position full-time, 88 percent report paying an annual salary of less than $50,000 and 12 percent between $50,000 and $99,999. The average annual salary is $38,473, and the average bonus among all those reporting a salary is $2,278 (averaging in zero bonuses), for an average total compensation of $40,751 (Exhibit 112). Only 36 percent of companies reporting a salary for this position also pay it a bonus/commission. The average bonus among only those who reported a bonus (not averaging in zeroes) cannot be reported due to low responses (Appendix B).

Exhibit 111. Does this Position (Administrative Assistant) Exist?

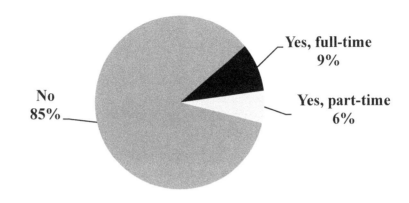

Yes, full-time
9%

Yes, part-time
6%

No
85%

Exhibit 112. Annual Salary- Administrative Assistant

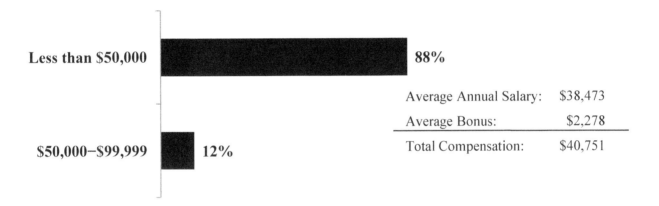

Less than $50,000 — 88%

$50,000–$99,999 — 12%

Average Annual Salary:	$38,473
Average Bonus:	$2,278
Total Compensation:	$40,751

The number of units builders expect to start in 2017 is directly related to the existence of a full-time Administrative Assistant on staff. While only two percent of small builders have this position, the share is 14 percent among medium builders, and 27 percent among large builders (Exhibit 113). Average total compensation can only be reliably reported for Administrative Assistants at medium builders: $38,356 (Appendix A-74).

Exhibit 113. Percent of Firms who Have a Full-Time Administrative Assistant by Number of 2017 Starts

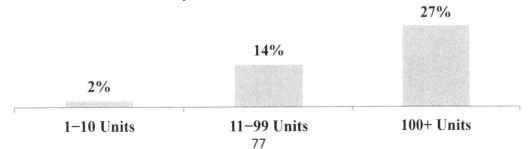

27%

14%

2%

1–10 Units   11–99 Units   100+ Units

The most common benefit offered to the Administrative Assistant is paid vacation leave—96 percent of firms who report this position offer it to them. Eighty-four percent offer each a 401k plan and health insurance, 76 percent offer paid sick leave, 56 percent each training and life insurance, and 52 percent dental insurance. Less than half offer a prescription program (44 percent), a vision program (40 percent), flex spending and short term disability (each 32 percent), long term disability (20 percent), and tuition reimbursement (16 percent). Eight percent offer some other type of benefit to their Administrative Assistant, such as paid holidays (Exhibit 114).

Exhibit 114. Fringe Benefits- Administrative Assistant
(Percent of Respondents with Position)

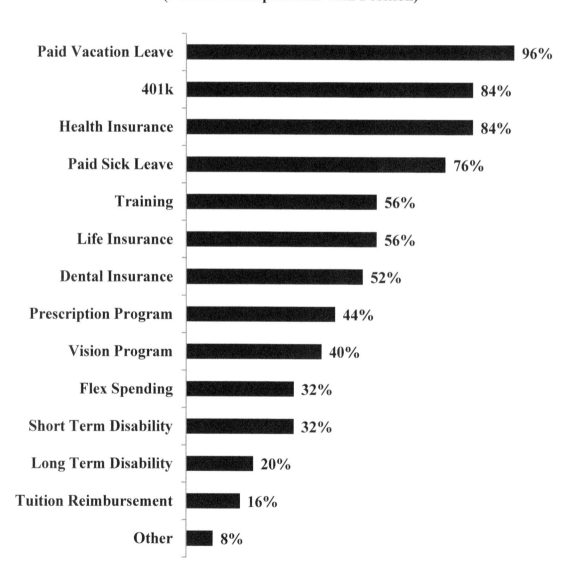

Receptionist

Only eight percent of respondents report having a full-time Receptionist position, while two percent have it part-time (Exhibit 115). All the firms where the position exists full-time report paying an annual salary of less than $50,000. The average annual salary is $32,464, and the average bonus among all those reporting a salary is $2,341 (averaging in zero bonuses), for an average total compensation of $34,805 (Exhibit 116). Fifty-nine percent of companies reporting a salary for this position also pay it a bonus/commission. The average bonus among only those who reported a bonus (not averaging in zeroes) is $3,962 (Appendix B).

Exhibit 115. Does this Position (Receptionist) Exist?

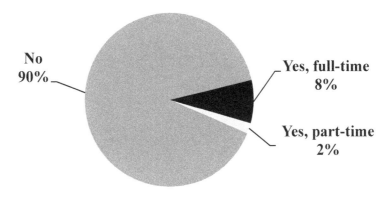

Exhibit 116. Annual Salary- Receptionist

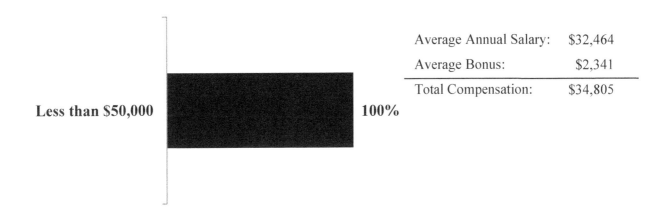

Average Annual Salary:	$32,464
Average Bonus:	$2,341
Total Compensation:	$34,805

The more single-family units a firm starts, the more likely it is to have a Receptionist: only one percent of firms starting 1–10 units have a Receptionist, compared to 10 percent of those starting 11–99 units, and 35 percent of those firms who expect to start 100 or more units (Exhibit 117). Total compensation for a Receptionist at medium builders averages $33,862, not much different than at large builders: $34,508 (Exhibit 118).

Exhibit 117. Percent of Firms who Have a Full-Time Receptionist by Number of 2017 Starts

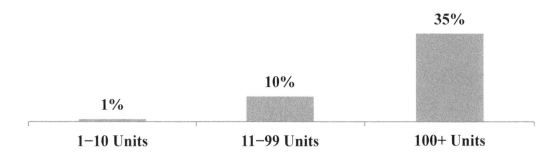

Exhibit 118. Average Total Compensation by Number of 2017 Starts-Receptionist

All firms with a Receptionist offer that person paid vacation leave. Ninety percent offer them health insurance, 80 percent a 401k plan, 75 percent dental insurance, 70 percent paid sick leave, 60 percent a vision program, and 55 percent life insurance. Less than half of respondents offer a prescription program (45 percent), short term disability (40 percent), training, flex spending, and long term disability (all 35 percent), and tuition reimbursement (30 percent) (Exhibit 119).

Exhibit 119. Fringe Benefits- Receptionist
(Percent of Respondents with Position)

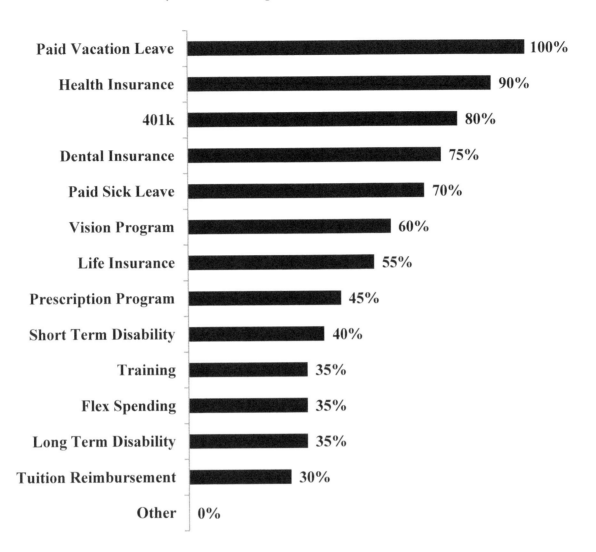

Benefit	Percent
Paid Vacation Leave	100%
Health Insurance	90%
401k	80%
Dental Insurance	75%
Paid Sick Leave	70%
Vision Program	60%
Life Insurance	55%
Prescription Program	45%
Short Term Disability	40%
Training	35%
Flex Spending	35%
Long Term Disability	35%
Tuition Reimbursement	30%
Other	0%

Settlement Coordinator

A Settlement Coordinator exists as a full-time position at eight percent of builders responding to the survey (Exhibit 120). The majority of those builders—59 percent—pay this person an annual salary of less than $50,000, 36 percent pay between $50,000 and $99,999, and the remaining five percent pay $100,000 or more. The average annual salary is $51,486, and the average bonus among all those reporting a salary is $7,459 (averaging in zero bonuses), for an average total compensation of $58,945 (Exhibit 121). Fifty-five percent of companies reporting a salary for this position also pay it a bonus/commission. The average bonus among only those who reported a bonus (not averaging in zeroes) is $13,675 (Appendix B).

Exhibit 120. Does this Position (Settlement Coordinator) Exist?

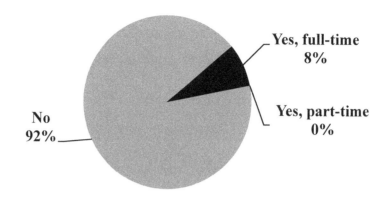

Yes, full-time
8%

Yes, part-time
0%

No
92%

Exhibit 121. Annual Salary- Settlement Coordinator

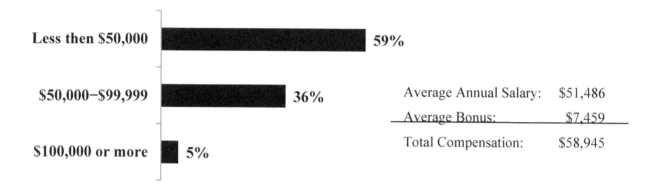

Less then $50,000 — 59%

$50,000–$99,999 — 36%

$100,000 or more — 5%

Average Annual Salary:	$51,486
Average Bonus:	$7,459
Total Compensation:	$58,945

The more single-family units a firm starts, the more likely it is to have a Settlement Coordinator: one percent of firms starting 1–10 units have a Settlement Coordinator, compared to 10 percent of those starting 11–99 units, and 42 percent of those expecting to start 100 or more units (Exhibit 122). Total compensation for Settlement Coordinators averages $65,100 at large (100 or more units) home building companies (Appendix A-82).

Exhibit 122. Percent of Firms who Have a Full-Time Settlement Coordinator by Number of 2017 Starts

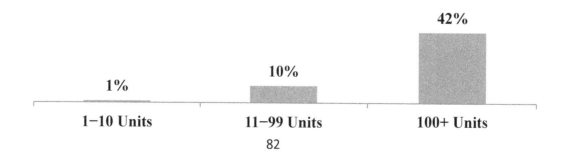

1% 1–10 Units

10% 11–99 Units

42% 100+ Units

The most common benefit Settlement Coordinators receive is health insurance (offered by 91 percent of builders who have this position on staff), followed by paid vacation leave (86 percent), paid sick leave (77 percent), a 401k plan (68 percent), and dental insurance (55 percent). Forty-five percent offer each life insurance and a prescription program, 41 percent long term disability, 36 percent each training and short term disability, 32 percent a vision program, and 18 percent each tuition reimbursement and flex spending. Five percent offer some other type of benefit to the Settlement Coordinator, such as paid holidays (Exhibit 123).

Exhibit 123. Fringe Benefits- Settlement Coordinator (Percent of Respondents with Position)

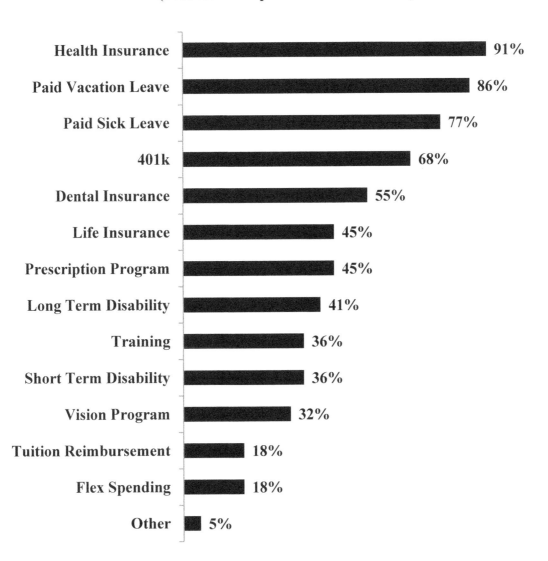

Production Manager

Fifteen percent of respondents report having a full-time Production Manager on staff (Exhibit 124). More than three-quarters (78 percent) of those that do say this position is "always" filled by someone with experience in the construction trades, while the other 22 percent say only "sometimes" (Exhibit 125).

Exhibit 124. Does this Position (Production Manager) Exist?

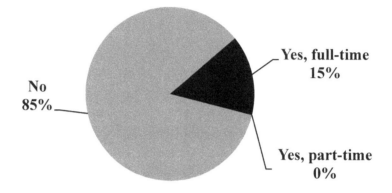

Exhibit 125. Is it Filled by Person with Construction Trades Experience?

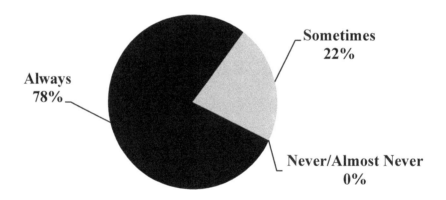

For those firms that have a full-time Production Manager, 16 percent report paying an annual salary of less than $50,000, 74 percent between $50,000 and $99,999, and nine percent $100,000 or more. The average annual salary is $69,520, and the average bonus among all those reporting a salary is $11,137 (averaging in zero bonuses), for an average total compensation of $80,657 (Exhibit 126). The majority of

companies reporting a salary for this position—79 percent—also pay it a bonus/commission. The average

bonus among only those who reported a bonus (not averaging in zeroes) is $14,085 (Appendix B).

Exhibit 126. Annual Salary- Production Manager

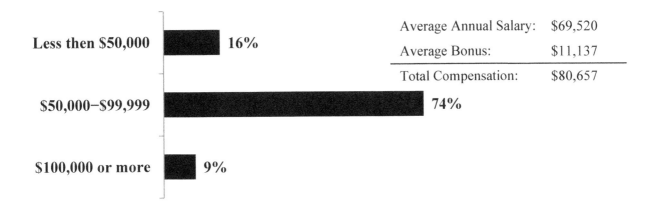

Average Annual Salary:	$69,520
Average Bonus:	$11,137
Total Compensation:	$80,657

Small single-family home building companies are less likely than their larger counterparts to have

a full-time Production Manager on staff. As Exhibit 127 shows, eight percent of those starting 1−10 units

report the existence of this job, compared to 17 percent among medium builders, and 29 percent among

large builders (100 or more units). Average total compensation also increases with company size, from

$67,259 at small builders to $75,804 at medium builders (Exhibit 128).

**Exhibit 127. Percent of Firms who Have a Full-Time Production Manager
by Number of 2017 Starts**

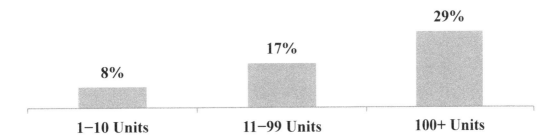

Exhibit 128. Average Total Compensation by Number of 2017 Starts- Production Manager

$67,259 $75,804

1−10 Units   11−99 Units

All companies with a Production Manager on staff offer that person paid vacation leave. Most also offer paid sick leave (77 percent), health insurance (72 percent), and a 401k plan (64 percent). The other nine benefits are offered by a minority of these builders: 46 percent offer training, 44 percent offer each dental insurance and life insurance, 36 percent offer a prescription program, 33 percent each short term disability and a vision program, 28 percent flex spending, 26 percent long term disability, and 18 percent tuition reimbursement. Ten percent of the responding firms offer their Production Manager some other type of benefit, such as all vehicle expenses paid (Exhibit 129).

Exhibit 129. Fringe Benefits- Production Manager
(Percent of Respondents with Position)

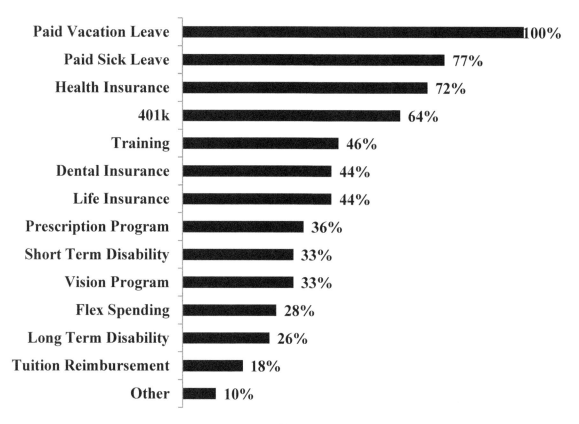

Paid Vacation Leave	100%
Paid Sick Leave	77%
Health Insurance	72%
401k	64%
Training	46%
Dental Insurance	44%
Life Insurance	44%
Prescription Program	36%
Short Term Disability	33%
Vision Program	33%
Flex Spending	28%
Long Term Disability	26%
Tuition Reimbursement	18%
Other	10%

Land Manager

Only two percent of respondents report the existence of a full-time Land Manager at their companies (Exhibit 130). Among those few where the position exists, 67 percent pay between $50,000 and $99,999 in salary and 33 percent pay $100,000 or more. The average annual salary is $87,500 (Exhibit 131). Due to the low count of responses, the average bonus and benefits for this position cannot be reliably reported.

Exhibit 130. Does this Position (Land Manager) Exist?

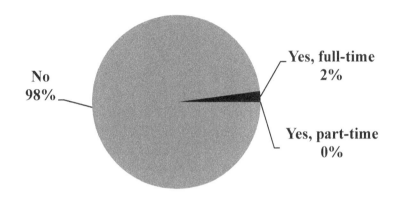

Exhibit 131. Annual Salary- Land Manager

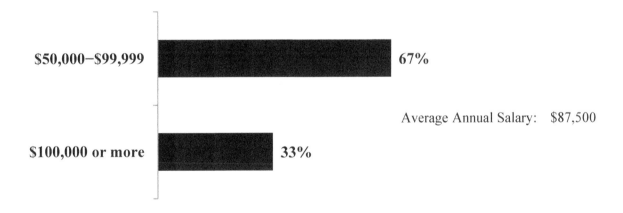

None of the small builders in the survey have a full-time Land Manager, and the position is practically non-existent at medium builders as well (only one percent report it). It is rare even among large builders, only 13 percent of whom report having a full-time Land Manager on staff (Appendix A-90).

Purchasing Manager

The position of Purchasing Manager only exists on a full-time basis at five percent of the companies in the survey, while none have it as a part-time job (Exhibit 132). Among builders that do have the position, 70 percent say that it is "always" filled by someone with experience in the construction trades, 20 percent say "sometimes," and 10 percent say "never/almost never" (Exhibit 133).

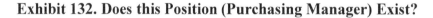

Exhibit 132. Does this Position (Purchasing Manager) Exist?

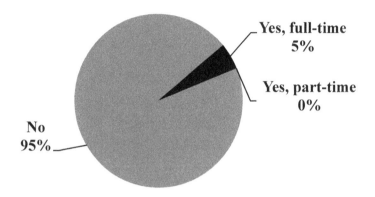

Yes, full-time
5%

Yes, part-time
0%

No
95%

Exhibit 133. Is it Filled by Person with Construction Trades Experience?

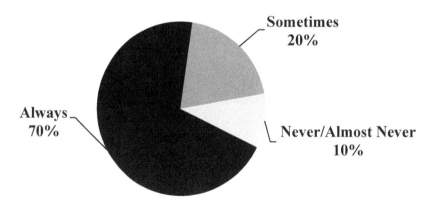

Sometimes
20%

Always
70%

Never/Almost Never
10%

For those firms that have a full-time Purchasing Manager, six percent report paying an annual salary of less than $50,000, 81 percent between $50,000 and $99,999, and 13 percent $100,000 or more. The average annual salary is $69,875, and the average bonus among all those reporting a salary is $12,031 (averaging in zero bonuses), for an average total compensation of $81,906 (Exhibit 134). The majority of

companies reporting a salary for this position—81 percent—also pay it a bonus/commission. The average

bonus among only those who reported a bonus (not averaging in zeroes) is $14,808 (Appendix B).

Exhibit 134. Annual Salary- Purchasing Manager

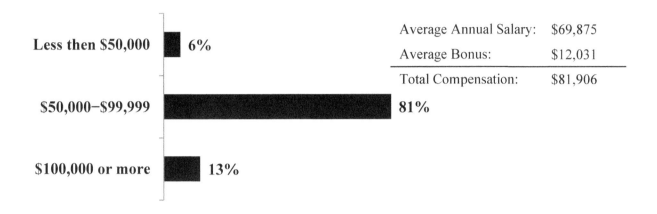

None of the small builders in the survey have a full-time Purchasing Manager, and the position is

uncommon even among medium builders (only five percent have it) (Exhibit 135). In contrast, 32 percent

of large builders report the existence of a full-time Purchasing Manager, with an average total compensation

of $75,500 a year (Appendix A-92).

**Exhibit 135. Percent of Firms who Have a Full-Time Purchasing Manager
by Number of 2017 Starts**

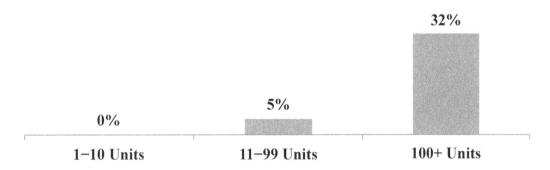

All builders who employ a Purchasing Manager offer that person paid vacation leave. More than

half also offer health insurance (93 percent), paid sick leave (87 percent), a 401k plan (80 percent), dental

insurance (73 percent), and life insurance and a vision program (each 53 percent). Forty-seven percent offer each of these benefits: flex spending, long term disability, a prescription program, and short term disability. Forty percent offer each training and tuition reimbursement. Thirteen percent of respondents offer some other type of benefit, such as paid bereavement leave (Exhibit 136).

Exhibit 136. Fringe Benefits- Purchasing Manager
(Percent of Respondents with Position)

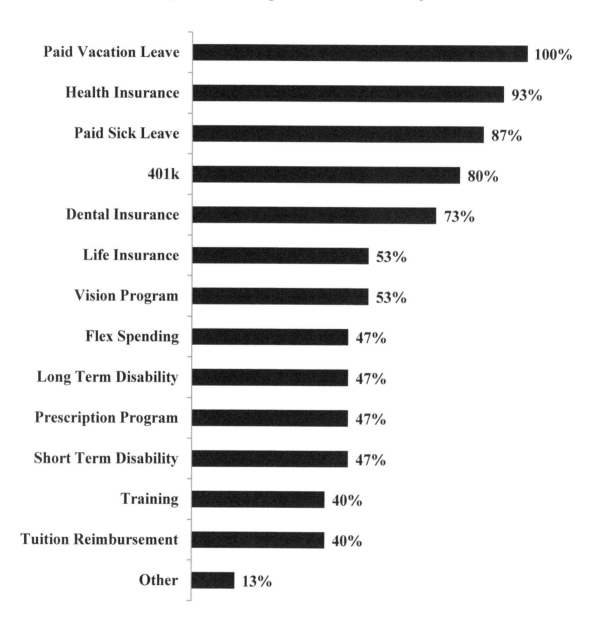

Home Services/Warranty Manager

Twenty percent of respondents have a Home Services/Warranty Manager on staff: 16 percent as a full-time employee and two percent on a part-time basis (Exhibit 137). The majority of builders—70 percent—who have this position report it is "always" filled by someone with construction trades experience, while the other 30 percent say that is the case "sometimes" (Exhibit 138).

Exhibit 137. Does this Position (Home Services/Warranty Manager) Exist?

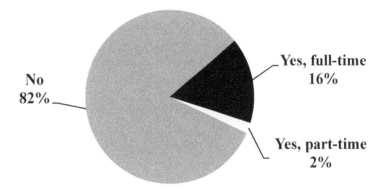

Exhibit 138. Is it Filled by Person with Construction Trades Experience?

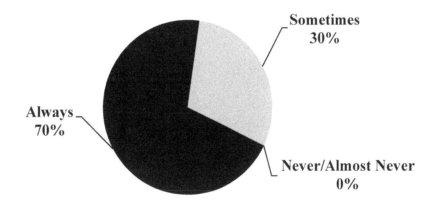

For those firms that have a full-time Home Services/Warranty Manager, 31 percent report paying an annual salary of less than $50,000 and 69 percent pay between $50,000 and $99,999. The average annual salary is $53,373, and the average bonus among all those reporting a salary is $6,938 (averaging in zero bonuses), for an average total compensation of $60,311 (Exhibit 139). The majority of companies reporting a salary for this position—76 percent—also pay it a bonus/commission. The average bonus among only those who reported a bonus (not averaging in zeroes) is $9,182 (Appendix B).

Exhibit 139. Annual Salary- Home Services/Warranty Manager

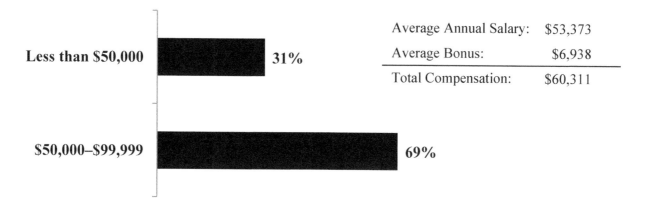

Average Annual Salary:	$53,373
Average Bonus:	$6,938
Total Compensation:	$60,311

The likelihood that a builder employs a full-time Home Services/Warranty Manager increases significantly with company size. Whereas only five percent of builders expecting 1–10 starts in 2017 have the position, the share rises to 18 percent among those starting 11–99 units, and to 58 percent of those who expect 100 or more starts (Exhibit 140). Total annual compensation varies by the size of the company as well, going from an average of $56,680 at medium builders to $64,595 at large builders (Exhibit 141).

Exhibit 140. Percent of Firms who Have a Full-Time Home Services/Warranty Manager by Number of 2017 Starts

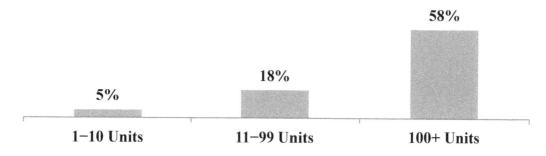

Exhibit 141. Average Total Compensation by Number of 2017 Starts-Home Services/Warranty Manager

$56,680 $64,595

11-99 Units   100+ Units

Nearly all companies—98 percent—offer their Home Services/Warranty Manager paid vacation leave. At least 80 percent also offer health insurance, paid sick leave, and a 401k plan, while 66 percent offer dental insurance. Less than half offer the other nine benefits: life insurance (48 percent), a prescription program (45 percent), a vision program (41 percent), short term disability (32 percent), training and flex spending (each 30 percent), long term disability (27 percent) and tuition reimbursement (18 percent). Nine percent offer some other type of benefit to their Home Services/Warranty Manager, such as an auto allowance (Exhibit 142).

Exhibit 142. Fringe Benefits- Home Services/Warranty Manager
(Percent of Respondents with Position)

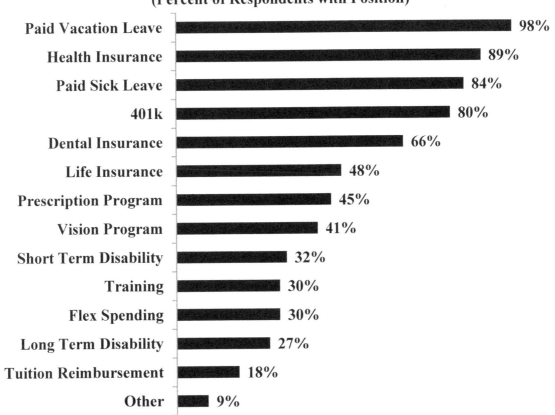

Benefit	Percent
Paid Vacation Leave	98%
Health Insurance	89%
Paid Sick Leave	84%
401k	80%
Dental Insurance	66%
Life Insurance	48%
Prescription Program	45%
Vision Program	41%
Short Term Disability	32%
Training	30%
Flex Spending	30%
Long Term Disability	27%
Tuition Reimbursement	18%
Other	9%

Contract Manager

Only three percent of respondents report the existence of a full-time Contract Manager at their companies (Exhibit 143). For those firms that have the position, 44 percent report that their Contract Manager has an annual salary of less than $50,000, 33 percent between $50,000 and $99,000, and 22 percent report an annual salary of $100,000 or more. The average annual salary is $62,222 (Exhibit 144). Due to the low count of responses, the average bonus and benefits for this position cannot be reliably reported.

Exhibit 143. Does this Position (Contract Manager) Exist?

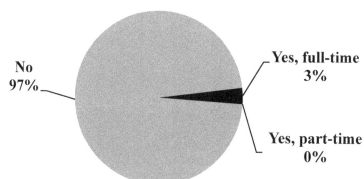

Exhibit 144. Annual Salary- Contract Manager

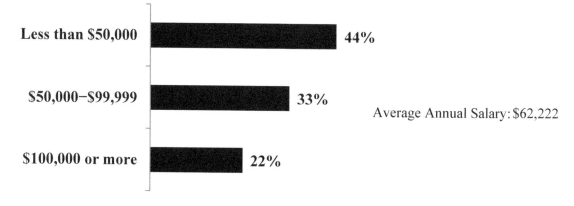

Only one percent of builders starting fewer than 100 single-family units in 2017 have a full-time Contract Manager. The share is much larger—19 percent—among those starting 100 or more units (Appendix A-100).

Project Manager

Thirty percent of respondents report that the position of Project Manager exists in their firm on a full-time basis. No one reports it as a part-time job (Exhibit 145). For those firms that have the position, 16 percent report that their Project Manager has an annual salary of less than $50,000, 77 percent between $50,000 and $99,999, while seven percent report it at $100,000 or more. The average annual salary is $67,247 and the average bonus among all those reporting a salary is $11,670 (averaging in zero bonuses), for an average total compensation of $78,917 (Exhibit 146). The majority of companies reporting a salary for this position—74 percent—also pay it a bonus/commission. The average bonus among only those who reported a bonus (not averaging in zeroes) is $15,864 (Appendix B).

Exhibit 145. Does this Position (Project Manager) Exist?

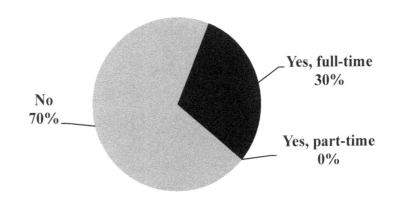

Exhibit 146. Annual Salary- Project Manager

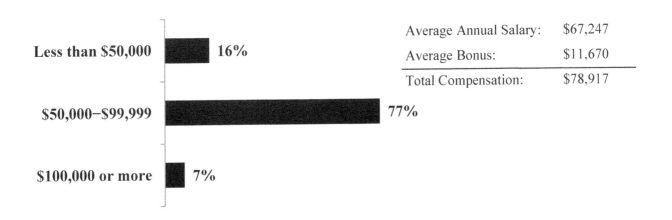

Average Annual Salary:	$67,247	
Average Bonus:	$11,670	
Total Compensation:	$78,917	

Between a quarter and slightly more than a third of all respondents have a full-time Project Manager on staff regardless of company size, varying from 25 percent of small builders (1–10 units) to around 35 percent of those starting 11 or more units (Exhibit 147). Total annual compensation for Project Managers averages $72,038 at small builders, $78,321 at medium builders, and $100,021 at large builders (Exhibit 148).

Exhibit 147. Percent of Firms who Have a Full-Time Project Manager by Number of 2017 Starts

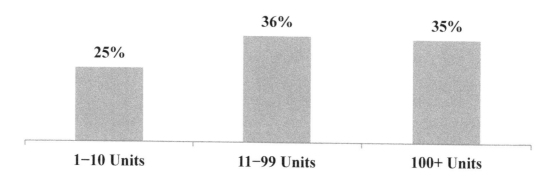

Exhibit 148. Average Total Compensation by Number of 2017 Starts- Project Manager

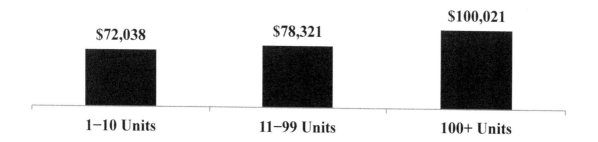

Only four benefits are offered by a majority of builders to their Project Manager: 92 percent offer paid vacation leave to that position, 73 percent offer health insurance, 70 percent paid sick leave, and 69 percent a 401k plan. Less than 40 percent offer dental insurance (39 percent), training (35 percent), a prescription program (29 percent), life insurance and a vision program (each 27 percent), short term disability (23 percent), tuition reimbursement and long term disability (each 17 percent), and flex spending

(12 percent). Seven percent offer some other type of benefit, such as a company vehicle and a cell phone (Exhibit 149).

Exhibit 149. Fringe Benefits- Project Manager
(Percent of Respondents with Position)

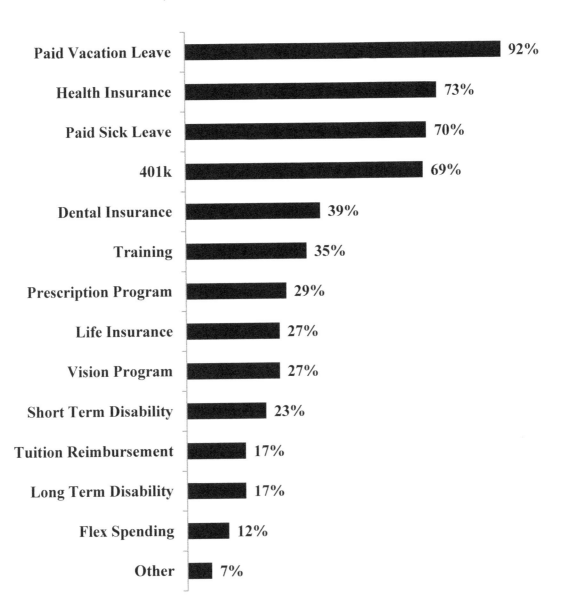

Architect

Ten percent of builders have a full-time architect on staff. One percent have the position on a part-time basis (Exhibit 150). For those firms that have the position full-time, 21 percent report paying it an annual salary of less than $50,000, 68 percent between $50,000 and $99,999, and 11 percent $100,000 or more. The average annual salary is $80,858 and the average bonus among all those reporting a salary is $10,461 (averaging in zero bonuses), for an average total compensation of $91,319 (Exhibit 151). The majority of companies reporting a salary for this position—68 percent—also pay it a bonus/commission. The average bonus among only those who reported a bonus (not averaging in zeroes) is $15,416 (Appendix B).

Exhibit 150. Does this Position (Architect) Exist?

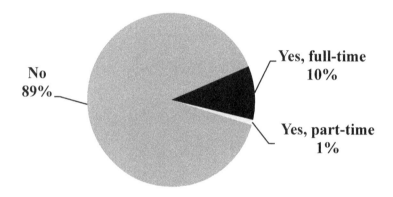

Exhibit 151. Annual Salary- Architect

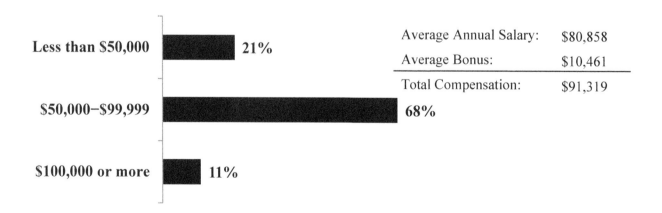

The more single-family units a firm starts, the more likely it is to have an Architect: only four percent of firms expecting to start 1−10 units in 2017 report having a full-time Architect, compared to 13 percent of those starting 11−99 units, and 29 percent of those firms who expect to start 100 or more units in 2017 (Exhibit 152). Total annual compensation for full-time Architects at medium builders averages $75,951 (Appendix A-106).

Exhibit 152. Percent of Firms who Have a Full-Time Architect
by Number of 2017 Starts

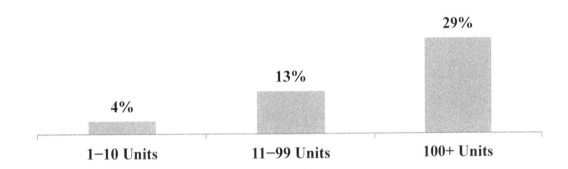

The three most common benefits firms offer to their Architects are health insurance (88 percent offer it), paid vacation leave (85 percent), and a 401k plan (81 percent). Sixty-two percent offer dental insurance and 58 percent paid sick leave. Less than 40 percent offer the remaining eight benefits: 38 percent offer each life insurance and a prescription program, 35 percent each training and a vision program, 27 percent short term disability, 23 percent each flex spending and long term disability, and 19 percent tuition reimbursement (Exhibit 153).

Exhibit 153. Fringe Benefits- Architect
(Percent of Respondents with Position)

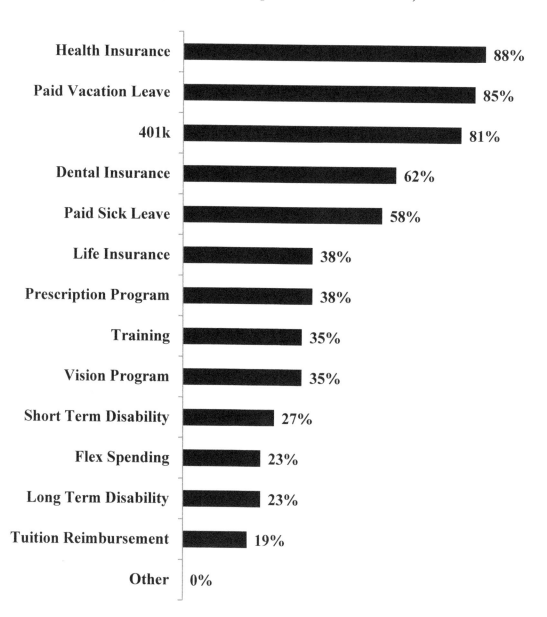

Health Insurance	88%
Paid Vacation Leave	85%
401k	81%
Dental Insurance	62%
Paid Sick Leave	58%
Life Insurance	38%
Prescription Program	38%
Training	35%
Vision Program	35%
Short Term Disability	27%
Flex Spending	23%
Long Term Disability	23%
Tuition Reimbursement	19%
Other	0%

Estimator

Estimators exist as full-time positions at 15 percent of respondents' firms and as part-time at another two percent (Exhibit 154). For those firms that have the position full-time, 21 percent report paying an annual salary of less than $50,000 and the remaining 79 percent between $50,000 and $99,999. The average annual salary is $55,306 and the average bonus among all those reporting a salary is $5,466 (averaging in zero bonuses), for an average total compensation of $60,772 (Exhibit 155). The majority of companies reporting a salary for this position—70 percent—also pay it a bonus/commission. The average bonus among only those who reported a bonus (not averaging in zeroes) is $7,835 (Appendix B).

Exhibit 154. Does this Position (Estimator) Exist?

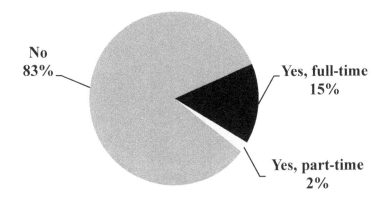

Exhibit 155. Annual Salary- Estimator

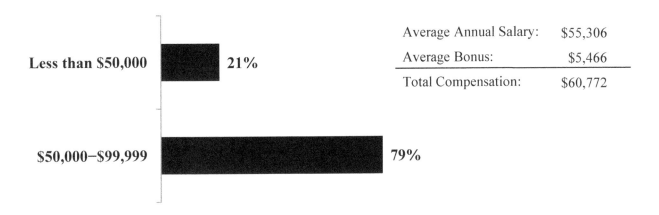

Average Annual Salary:	$55,306
Average Bonus:	$5,466
Total Compensation:	$60,772

The likelihood of having a full-time Estimator is dramatically higher for companies starting 100 or more units a year than for their smaller counterparts: whereas only 10–12 percent of builders starting 99 or fewer units in 2017 have a full-time Estimator, the share is four times larger among builder starting 100 or

more units, at 45 percent (Exhibit 156). Full-time estimators at small and medium companies average less

than $60,000 as total annual compensation, compared to $65,960 at large companies (Exhibit 157).

**Exhibit 156. Percent of Firms who Have a Full-Time Estimator
by Number of 2017 Starts**

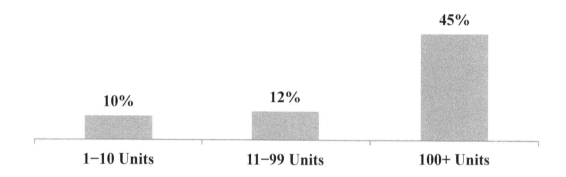

**Exhibit 157. Average Total Compensation by Number of 2017 Starts-
Estimator**

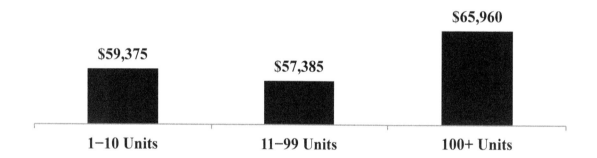

The two most common benefits builders offer their Estimators are paid vacation leave (88 percent)

and health insurance (81 percent). A majority of respondents that have this position also offer it a 401k plan

(79 percent), paid sick leave (70 percent), and training (51 percent). Most benefits, however, are offered by

less than 50 percent of respondents: life insurance and dental insurance (each 49 percent), a prescription

and a vision program (each 40 percent), short term disability (35 percent), long term disability (30 percent),

tuition reimbursement and flex spending (each 26 percent). Seven percent of respondents offer some other

type of benefit, such as a simple IRA (Exhibit 158).

Exhibit 158. Fringe Benefits- Estimator
(Percent of Respondents with Position)

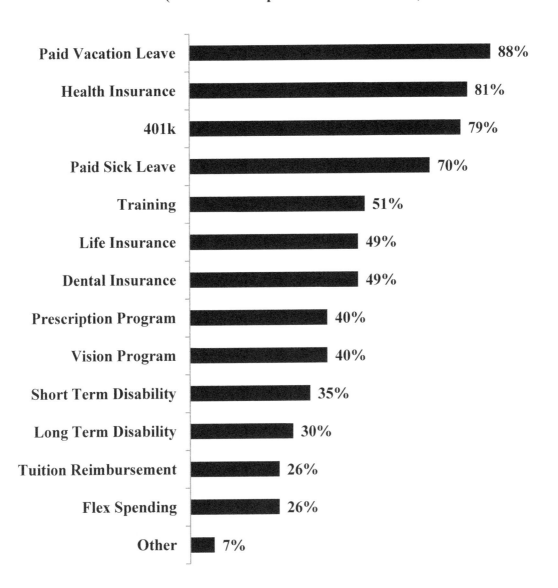

Benefit	Percent
Paid Vacation Leave	88%
Health Insurance	81%
401k	79%
Paid Sick Leave	70%
Training	51%
Life Insurance	49%
Dental Insurance	49%
Prescription Program	40%
Vision Program	40%
Short Term Disability	35%
Long Term Disability	30%
Tuition Reimbursement	26%
Flex Spending	26%
Other	7%

Superintendent

Nearly half of all respondents have a Superintendent on staff: 44 percent as a full-time job and one percent as part-time (Exhibit 159). For those firms that have the position full-time, 20 percent report an annual salary of less than $50,000, 78 percent between $50,000 and $99,999, and two percent at $100,000 or more. The average annual salary is $59,888 and the average bonus among all those reporting a salary is $7,818 (averaging in zero bonuses), for an average total compensation of $67,706 (Exhibit 160). The majority of

companies reporting a salary for this position—67 percent—also pay it a bonus/commission. The average

bonus among only those who reported a bonus (not averaging in zeroes) is $11,588 (Appendix B).

Exhibit 159. Does this Position (Superintendent) Exist?

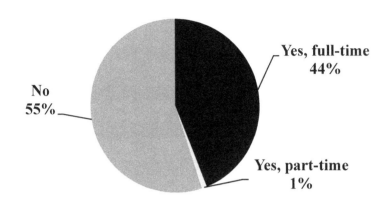

Exhibit 160. Annual Salary- Superintendent

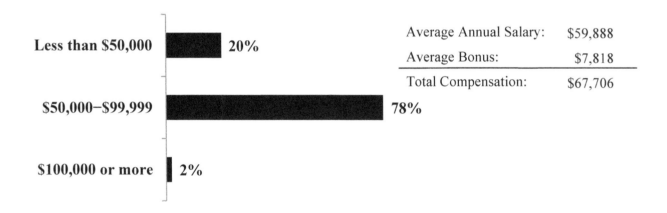

The position of full-time Superintendent exists at most large builders (100 or more starts), as 84

percent of that group report having it on staff. It also exists at 45 percent of medium builders (11−99 units),

and at 35 percent of small builders responding to the survey (1−10 units) (Exhibit 161). The

Superintendent's average total compensation is $63,824 at small firms, $64,673 at medium firms, and

$82,021 at large single-family home building firms (Exhibit 162).

Exhibit 161. Percent of Firms who Have a Full-Time Superintendent by Number of 2017 Starts

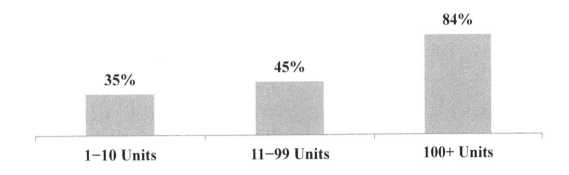

35%   45%   84%

1–10 Units   11–99 Units   100+ Units

Exhibit 162. Average Total Compensation by Number of 2017 Starts-Superintendent

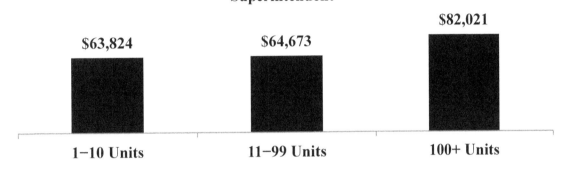

$63,824 $64,673 $82,021

1–10 Units   11–99 Units   100+ Units

Only one benefit is offered by more than 90 percent of builders to their Superintendents: paid vacation leave (94 percent). Paid sick leave and health insurance are each offered by 73 percent, and a 401k plan by 63 percent. Less than half of builders where the position exists offer Superintendents the remaining nine benefits: dental insurance (42 percent), training (37 percent), a prescription program (32 percent), life insurance (31 percent), a vision program (25 percent), short term disability (22 percent), flex spending (18 percent), long term disability (17 percent), and tuition reimbursement (15 percent). Six percent of the responding firms offer their Superintendent some other type of benefit, such as a company vehicle (Exhibit 163).

Exhibit 163. Fringe Benefits- Superintendent
(Percent of Respondents with Position)

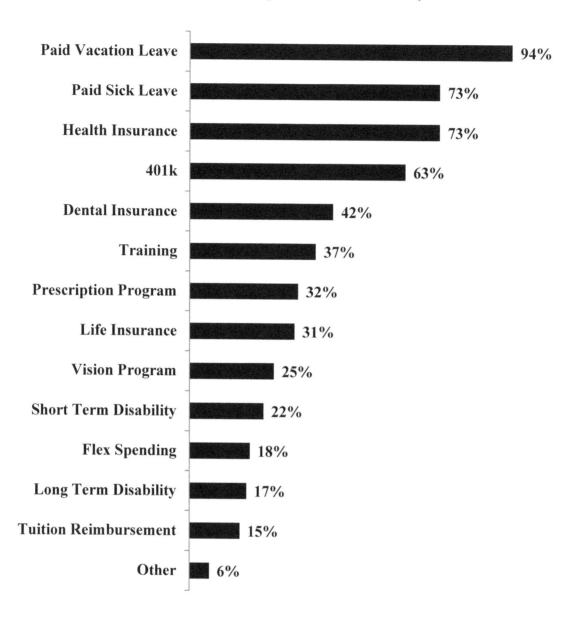

Sales Manager

Seven percent of respondents have a full-time Sales Manager on staff. One percent have the position on a part-time basis (Exhibit 164). For those firms that have the position full-time, one-third pay an annual salary of less than $50,000, half pay between $50,000 and $99,999, and 17 percent $100,000 or more. The average annual salary is $65,142 and the average bonus among all those reporting a salary is $48,444 (averaging in zero bonuses), for an average total compensation of $113,586 (Exhibit 165). A large majority of companies reporting a salary for this position—83 percent—also pay it a bonus/commission. The average bonus among only those who reported a bonus (not averaging in zeroes) is $58,133 (Appendix B).

Exhibit 164. Does this Position (Sales Manager) Exist?

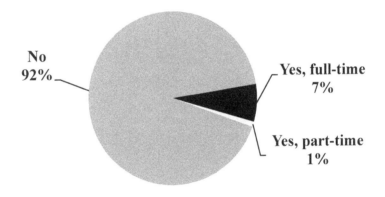

Exhibit 165. Annual Salary- Sales Manager

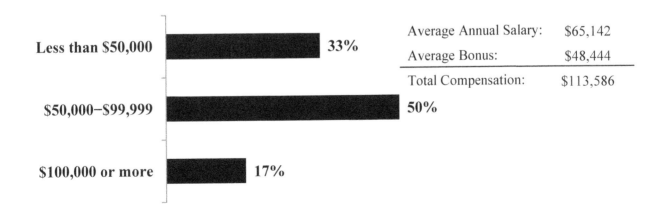

Average Annual Salary:	$65,142
Average Bonus:	$48,444
Total Compensation:	$113,586

Less than $50,000 — 33%

$50,000–$99,999 — 50%

$100,000 or more — 17%

Few builders starting under 100 units a year have a full-time Sales Manager: only three percent of those starting 1–10 units and six percent of those starting 11–99 units report it. In contrast, more than a quarter of builders with 100 or more starts a year have this position on staff (Exhibit 166).

Exhibit 166. Percent of Firms who Have a Full-Time Sales Manager by Number of 2017 Starts

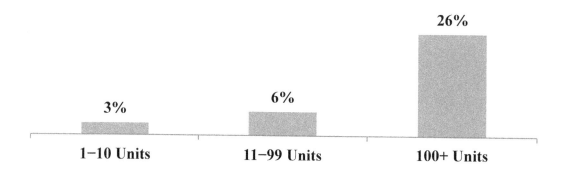

The most common benefit builders offer their Sales Managers is paid vacation leave—95 percent offer it. A 401k plan and health insurance are each offered by 86 percent, paid sick leave by 81 percent, dental insurance by 62 percent, and short term disability and life insurance each by 52 percent. Less than half of respondents where position exists offer the remaining benefits: training and vision program (each 48 percent), long term disability and a prescription program (each 43 percent), tuition reimbursement (38 percent), and flex spending (33 percent). Ten percent of respondents offer the Sales Manager some other type of benefit, such as paid bereavement leave (Exhibit 167).

Exhibit 167. Fringe Benefits- Sales Manager
(Percent of Respondents with Position)

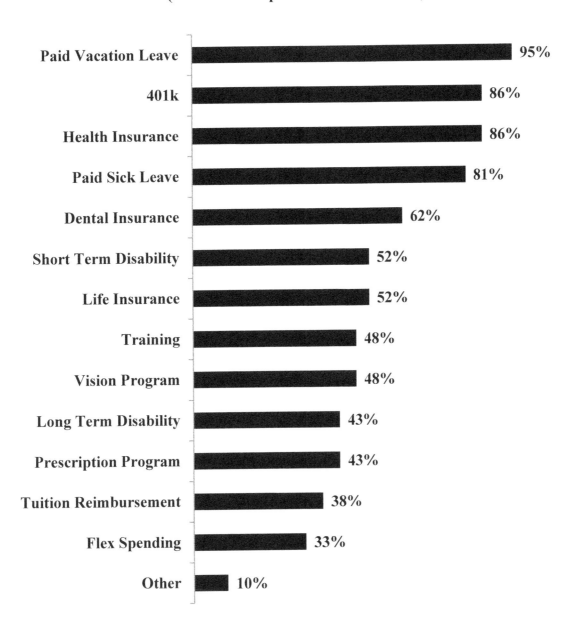

Benefit	Percent
Paid Vacation Leave	95%
401k	86%
Health Insurance	86%
Paid Sick Leave	81%
Dental Insurance	62%
Short Term Disability	52%
Life Insurance	52%
Training	48%
Vision Program	48%
Long Term Disability	43%
Prescription Program	43%
Tuition Reimbursement	38%
Flex Spending	33%
Other	10%

Model Home Host

Only eight percent of respondents report having a Model Home Host: three percent as a full-time job and five percent as part-time (Exhibit 168). All firms that have a full-time Model Home Host report paying an annual salary of less than $50,000. The average annual salary is $33,938 (Exhibit 169). Due to the low count of responses, the average bonus and benefits for this position cannot be reliably reported.

Exhibit 168. Does this Position (Model Home Host) Exist?

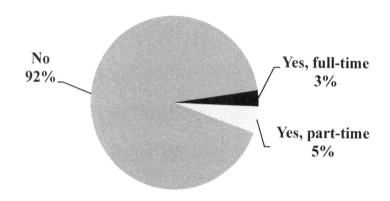

Exhibit 169. Annual Salary- Model Home Host

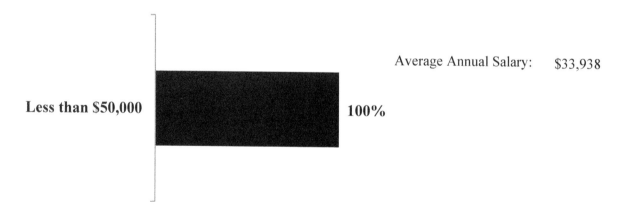

None of the builders with 1–10 starts report having a full-time Model Home Host on staff. Among those starting 11–99 units, the chance of having one is not that much better—only three percent do. In contrast, 19 percent of builders starting 100 or more units report the existence of this position at their companies (Appendix A-120).

Salesperson

Sixteen percent of respondents report having a full-time Salesperson in their firm (Exhibit 170). For those firms that have the position, 72 percent report paying an annual salary of less than $50,000, 22 percent between $50,000 and $99,999, and seven percent $100,000 or more. The average annual salary is $34,050 and the average bonus among all those reporting a salary is $64,365 (averaging in zero bonuses), for an average total compensation of $98,415 (Exhibit 171). The majority of companies reporting a salary for this position—76 percent—also pay it a bonus/commission. The average bonus among only those who reported a bonus (not averaging in zeroes) is $84,594 (Appendix B).

Exhibit 170. Does this Position (Salesperson) Exist?

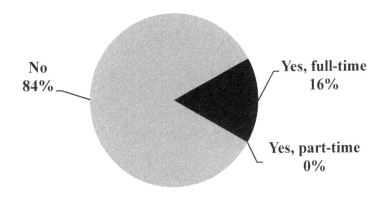

Exhibit 171. Annual Salary- Salesperson

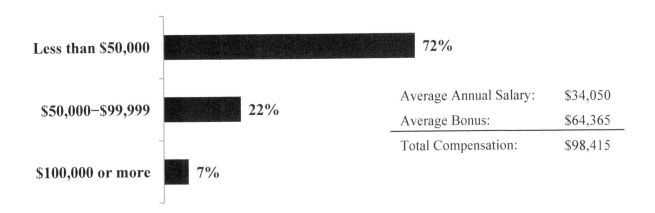

Average Annual Salary:	$34,050
Average Bonus:	$64,365
Total Compensation:	$98,415

Full-time Salespersons are almost non-existent among small builders—only one percent of that group reports having the position. In contrast, it is more common among medium builders (23 percent report it), and even more widespread among large builders (68 percent) (Exhibit 172). Total compensation for a salesperson averages $94,684 at companies with 11−99 starts and $108,105 at those with 100 or more starts (Exhibit 173).

Exhibit 172. Percent of Firms who Have a Full-Time Salesperson by Number of 2017 Starts

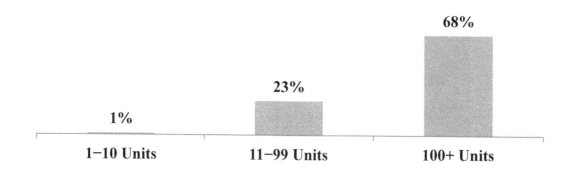

Exhibit 173. Average Total Compensation by Number of 2017 Starts- Salesperson

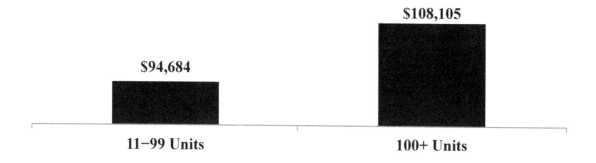

The two most common benefits offered by builders to their Salesperson are paid vacation leave (86 percent offer it) and health insurance (83 percent). More than 70 percent offer paid sick leave and a 401k plan. Fifty-two percent offer dental insurance. The remaining eight benefits are offered by less than half of respondents: life insurance (45 percent), a prescription program (43 percent), a vision program (38 percent), short term disability (31 percent), flex spending and long term disability (each 29 percent), training (26 percent), and tuition reimbursement (19 percent). Five percent of respondents offer some other type of benefit to the Salesperson, such as an IRA and licensing reimbursement (Exhibit 174).

Exhibit 174. Fringe Benefits- Salesperson
(Percent of Respondents with Position)

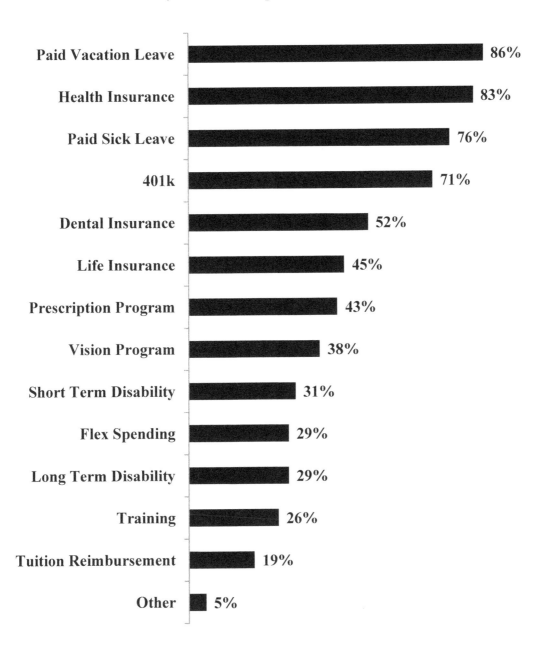

113

Design Center Manager

Seven percent of respondents report that the position of Design Center Manager exists in their firm full-time, while one percent report it part-time (Exhibit 175). For those firms that have the position full-time, 32 percent pay an annual salary of less than $50,000 and 68 percent pay between $50,000 and $99,999. The average annual salary is $57,701 and the average bonus among all those reporting a salary is $7,852 (averaging in zero bonuses), for an average total compensation of $65,553 (Exhibit 176). Just above half of companies reporting a salary for this position—59 percent—also pay it a bonus/commission. The average bonus among only those who reported a bonus (not averaging in zeroes) is $13,288 (Appendix B).

Exhibit 175. Does this Position (Design Center Manager) Exist?

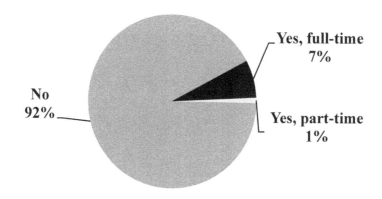

Exhibit 176. Annual Salary- Design Center Manager

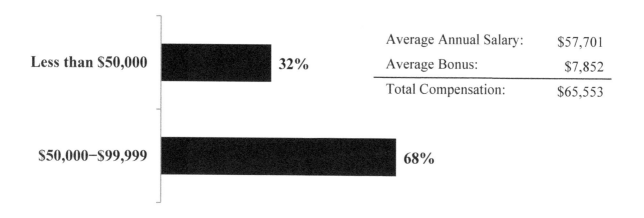

Full-time Design Center Managers are rare at small and medium single-family building companies, as only two percent and six percent, respectively, report having this position. They are, however, much more common at large companies with 100 or more starts a year, 35 percent of whom report their existence on staff (Exhibit 177). Total annual compensation for full-time Design Center Managers averages $70,682 at large companies, the only group for which it can be reliably reported (Appendix A-126).

Exhibit 177. Percent of Firms who Have a Full-Time Design Center Manager by Number of 2017 Starts

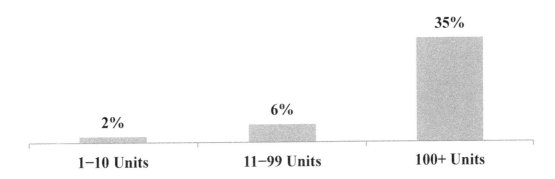

Most builders do not have a Design Center Manager on staff, but among the few that do, most offer them multiple benefits. In fact, at least half of builders with this position offer it the following eight benefits: paid vacation leave (86 percent), health insurance (82 percent), a 401k plan (77 percent), paid sick leave (73 percent), life insurance and dental insurance (each 59 percent), and short term disability and a prescription program (each 50 percent). Less than half but more than a quarter offer training and flex spending (each 45 percent), long term disability (36 percent), a vision program (32 percent), and tuition reimbursement (27 percent). Nine percent offer the Design Center Manager some other type of benefit, such as an auto allowance (Exhibit 178).

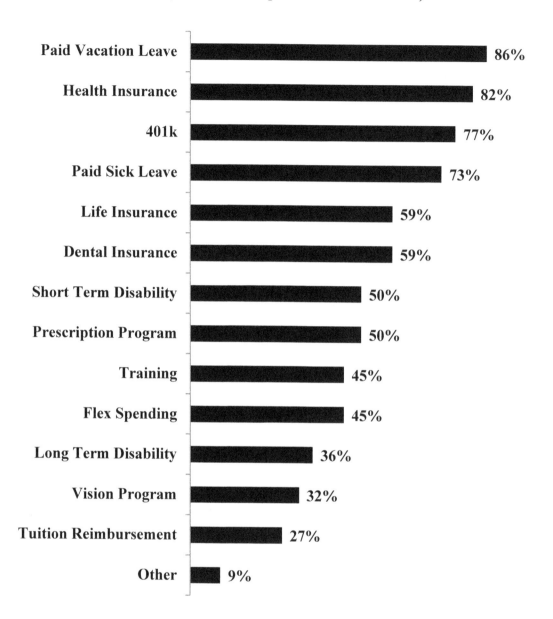

Exhibit 178. Fringe Benefits- Design Center Manager
(Percent of Respondents with Position)

Benefit	Percent
Paid Vacation Leave	86%
Health Insurance	82%
401k	77%
Paid Sick Leave	73%
Life Insurance	59%
Dental Insurance	59%
Short Term Disability	50%
Prescription Program	50%
Training	45%
Flex Spending	45%
Long Term Disability	36%
Vision Program	32%
Tuition Reimbursement	27%
Other	9%

Selections Coordinator

Ten percent of respondents report that the position of Settlement Coordinator exists in their firm as a full-time job and three percent report it exists part-time (Exhibit 179). For those firms that have the position full-time, 63 percent report paying an annual salary of less than $50,000 and 37 percent between $50,000 and $99,999. The average annual salary is $47,285 and the average bonus among all those reporting a salary is $6,393 (averaging in zero bonuses), for an average total compensation of $53,678 (Exhibit 180). The majority of companies reporting a salary for this position—63 percent—also pay it a bonus/commission. The average bonus among only those who reported a bonus (not averaging in zeroes) is $10,153 (Appendix B).

Exhibit 179. Does this Position (Selections Coordinator) Exist?

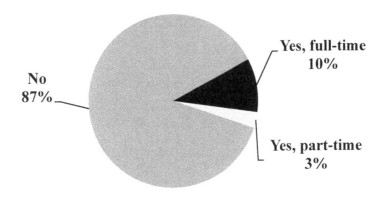

Exhibit 180. Annual Salary- Selections Coordinator

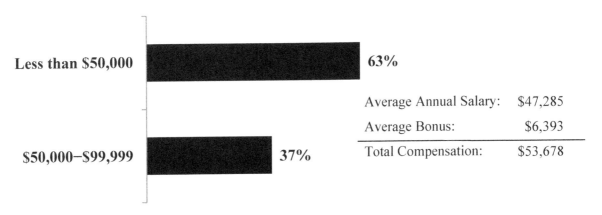

The existence of a full-time Selections Coordinator at single-family building companies increases with size: while only two percent of small builders who start 1–10 units have it, the share goes to 15 percent of those with 11–99 starts, and to 29 percent of large builders who start at least 100 units a year (Exhibit 181). Average total compensation can only be reliably reported for Selection Coordinators at medium builders: $49,925 (Appendix A-130).

Exhibit 181. Percent of Firms who Have a Full-Time Selections Coordinator by Number of 2017 Starts

2%	15%	29%
1−10 Units	11−99 Units	100+ Units

Ninety-three percent of builders that have Selections Coordinators on staff offer them health insurance. More than half also offer paid vacation leave (89 percent), a 401k plan (85 percent), paid sick leave (74 percent), dental insurance (67 percent), life insurance (63 percent), and long term disability (52 percent). Training, short term disability, and a prescription program are each offered by 48 percent, a vision program by 41 percent, flex spending by 37 percent, and tuition reimbursement by 33 percent. Seven percent of the respondents offer the Selections Coordinator some other type of benefit, such as vehicle mileage (Exhibit 182).

Exhibit 182. Fringe Benefits- Selections Coordinator (Percent of Respondents with Position)

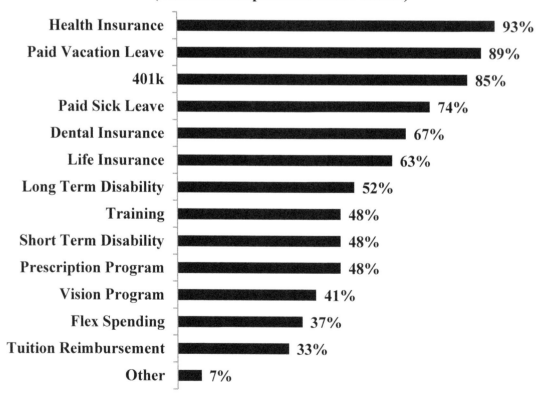

Benefit	Percent
Health Insurance	93%
Paid Vacation Leave	89%
401k	85%
Paid Sick Leave	74%
Dental Insurance	67%
Life Insurance	63%
Long Term Disability	52%
Training	48%
Short Term Disability	48%
Prescription Program	48%
Vision Program	41%
Flex Spending	37%
Tuition Reimbursement	33%
Other	7%

Customer Service Manager

Customer Service Manager is not a common position at single-family building companies—only three percent have it on a full-time basis and one percent as part-time (Exhibit 183). For those firms that have the position full-time, a quarter report an annual salary of less than $50,000 and the remaining 75 percent report it between $50,000 and $99,999. The average annual salary is $53,913 (Exhibit 184). Due to the low count of responses, the average bonus and benefits for this position cannot be reliably reported.

Exhibit 183. Does this Position (Customer Service Manager) Exist?

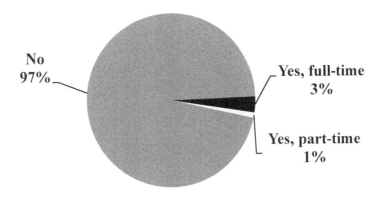

Exhibit 184. Annual Salary- Customer Service Manager

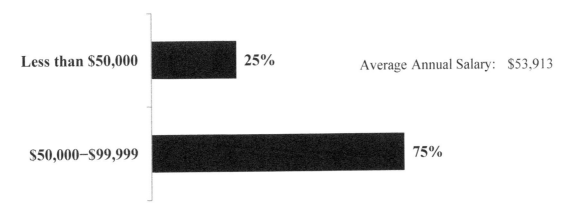

None of the builders with 1–10 starts report having a full-time Customer Service Manager on staff. The share is just slightly higher—five percent—among builders with 11–99 starts, and reaches only 10 percent among large builders with 100 or starts a year (Appendix A-132).

OTHER POSITIONS

Builders were also asked to list any additional positions in their companies that were not included in the survey, providing a description of their duties. Some of the most commonly mentioned include carpenter, general laborer, and drafter. Exhibit 185 shows builders' exact responses.

Exhibit 185. Other Positions in the Company

- **Assistant to Director of Design**. Provides support for Design Studio, entering selections into computer system, general support.
- **Marketing Assistant**. Produces marketing collateral, updates website, blogs, etc. Supports Director of Sales and Marketing.
- **Assistant Construction Manager**. Provides support to construction managers.
- **Home Designer**. Produces CAD based designs, details, etc.
- **Associate**. Performs duties as required by the CEO for the processing of all cost tracking and customer related documents, contract follow through, lien waiver processing.
- **Carpenters (4)**
- **Carpenter**. Onsite construction
- **Carpenter**. Full-time, paid vacation and 401k
- **Carpenter**. 2 employees.
- **Carpenter**. General carpentry duties to facilitate the completion of projects
- **Carpenters**. General carpentry and construction, paid vacation, 401k match, sick pay
- **Carpenters**.
- **Laborers**.
- **Carpenters**.
- **Clean up guys**.
- **Construction Coordinator**. Coordinates the start process of construction and in house scheduling of rough-in walks and quality control visits etc.
- **COO**. Operations Officer
- **Data / Bill processing**. Inputs bills and data for payables.
- **Designer** (not an Architect). Part time, paid time off, retirement plan, paid training
- **Detail Carpenter**. Details and prepares home for settlement performing duties associated with required carpentry work.
- **Marketing Manager**. Drives marketing activities that lead to direct sales.
- **Creative Director**. Drives creative direction for sales and marketing by developing and maintaining content and overall branding vision to implement marketing plans and strengthen overall brand identity.
- **Graphic Designer**. Creates and maintains packaging design and sales support tools to ensure continuity with the company's marketing messaging.
- **Warranty Customer Care Representative**. Provides customer and administrative support to the warranty department. First point of contact for all warranty communications.
- **Chief Compliance Officer**. Responsible for risk management, legal structures, contracts, and bank & investor compliance.

- **Building and Grounds Maintenance Coordinator.** Ensures the corporate office and model homes are properly maintained.
- **Director of Drafting.** Oversees new home plans with designing, scheduling, value engineering to ensure cost effectiveness for all models built.
- **Architectural Technician.** Creates lot-specific customer home plans using CAD system, creates new model bidsets as well as maintaining current bidsets.

- **Draftsman.** Creates construction documents in CAD or Revit format.
- **General Laborer.** Perform a variety of tasks at all kinds of construction sites.

- **Draftsman.** Part-time.

- **Field Workers.** Daily Labor to complete construction requirements at each job site. No benefits.

- **Framers.** 4.

- **General Construction workers.** Interior/exterior/cabinetry.

- **General helper/job site overseer.** Provides cleanup and protection for all jobs.

- **General Laborer.** Job clean up, punch list completion.

- **Handyman.** Knows how to perform all trade activities and can do warranty and punch list). Bonus based on profitability, single insurance fully paid by company.
- **Intern.** Working in Production Paperwork (estimating/purchasing).

- **Intern.**
- **Laborer.**
- **Laborer.**
- **Laborer.** Performs non-skilled labor.
- **Labor.** General laborer
- **Lead Carpenter.** Lead, coordinate, and help with scheduling jobs and projects.
- **Lead Carpenter.** Manage Crews, and install products.
- **Carpenter.** Install products
- **Marketing Coordinator.**
- **Drafting Manager.**
- **Drafter.**
- **Operations Manager.** Performs the duties of an office manager, human resources, IT, and marketing of the company.
- **Production Staff.** Carpenter, Lead Carpenter
- **Skilled labor, carpenter.** Builds our specialty.
- **Staff carpenter.** Misc. carpentry, clean up
- **Summer Intern.** Assists with all areas of the business.

- **Systems Manager.** Manages company software.
- **Framing Foreman.** Manages framing crew.
- **Carpenters.** Rough and finished carpenters
- **Operation Managers.** Mill Manager and Excavation manager
- **Mill Operators.** Operators in the company mill that produces Doors, Cabinets and Moldings.

- **VP of Sales and Marketing.**
- **Planner.** Land entitlements

Appendix A. Detailed Tables by Region, Dollar Volume, Starts, & Employees

Q1. What is your company's principal operation?
(Percent of Respondents)

| | Total | Region | | | | 2017 Expected Dollar Volume | | | | |
		Northeast	Midwest	South	West	Less than $1 million	$1 million to $4,999,999	$5 million to $9,999,999	$10 million to $14,999,999	$15 million or over
Single-Family Spec/Tract Builder	27	24	22	25	38	10	11	25	30	67
Single-Family Custom Builder	56	52	55	64	39	61	69	66	48	21
Single-Family General Contractor	16	20	22	11	23	26	20	8	18	11
Other	1	4	2	1		3		2	3	
Responses	311	25	60	162	64	31	123	61	33	61

Q2. How many single-family units did your company start in 2016?
(Percent of Respondents)

| | Total | Region | | | | 2017 Expected Dollar Volume | | | | |
		Northeast	Midwest	South	West	Less than $1 million	$1 million to $4,999,999	$5 million to $9,999,999	$10 million to $14,999,999	$15 million or over
Zero Units	4	4	4	3	8	20	6			4
1-10 Units	55	63	49	61	44	80	83	49	34	5
11-25 Units	17	8	23	15	22		9	42	38	5
26-99 Units	15	21	18	12	17		2	8	25	49
100-499 Units	7	4	5	9	6				3	37
500 Units or more	1		2	1	2					5
Mean	31	23	34	29	38	3	6	13	28	122
Median	8	8	10	7	10	1	4	12	19	80
Responses	300	24	57	156	63	30	121	59	32	57

Notes:
1) Results were suppressed in most cells where the number of responses was below 10. This process eliminated most tabulations for several of the 39 jobs.

2) Throughout this and all appendices, the character "*" means less than 0.5%.

A-1

Q1. What is your company's principal operation?
(Percent of Respondents)

	2017 Expected Single-Family Starts			Number of Employees			
	1 to 10	11 to 99	100 or more	0 to 2	3 to 4	5 to 9	10 or more
Single-Family Spec/Tract Builder	7	41	72	18	17	16	46
Single-Family Custom Builder	75	44	13	65	63	72	34
Single-Family General Contractor	17	14	16	15	19	13	19
Other	1	1		2			2
Responses	156	111	32	55	63	88	101

Q2. How many single-family units did your company start in 2016?
(Percent of Respondents)

	2017 Expected Single-Family Starts			Number of Employees			
	1 to 10	11 to 99	100 or more	0 to 2	3 to 4	5 to 9	10 or more
Zero Units	7			13	3	3	1
1-10 Units	91	22		79	75	63	23
11-25 Units	2	45		6	19	24	16
26-99 Units		34	22	2	3	9	34
100-499 Units			69				23
500 Units or more			9				3
Mean	4	27	182	5	8	12	80
Median	3	20	135	3	5	7	50
Responses	155	110	32	52	63	87	97

Q2. How many do you expect to start in 2017?
(Percent of Respondents)

		Region				2017 Expected Dollar Volume				
	Total	Northeast	Midwest	South	West	Less than $1 million	$1 million to $4,999,999	$5 million to $9,999,999	$10 million to $14,999,999	$15 million or over
Zero Units	1	4	4	1		3	2			
1-10 Units	52	54	42	56	49	90	77	39	31	4
11-25 Units	21	13	26	21	17	7	18	47	22	4
26-99 Units	16	29	19	11	21		3	14	44	39
100-499 Units	10	4	7	11	11				3	49
500 Units or more	1		2	1	2					5
Mean	38	33	40	36	45	4	8	16	33	148
Median	10	9	13	10	12	2	6	14	23	100
Responses	300	24	57	156	63	30	121	59	32	57

Q3. Approximately, what will be the company's total dollar volume of business in 2017?
(Percent of Respondents)

		Region				2017 Expected Dollar Volume				
	Total	Northeast	Midwest	South	West	Less than $1 million	$1 million to $4,999,999	$5 million to $9,999,999	$10 million to $14,999,999	$15 million or over
Less than $500,000	2		2	1	3	17				
$500,000 - $999,999	8	13	10	8	6	83				
$1 million - $4,999,999	40	54	34	44	30		100			
$5 million - $9,999,999	20	8	25	21	16			100		
$10 million - $14,999,999	10	8	12	9	14				100	
$15 million or over	20	17	17	18	30					100
Median	$4,999,998	$3,769,229	$5,833,332	$4,718,308	$8,249,998	$699,999				
Responses	306	24	59	160	63	30	123	60	32	61

Q2. How many do you expect to start in 2017?
(Percent of Respondents)

	2017 Expected Single-Family Starts			Number of Employees			
	1 to 10	11 to 99	100 or more	0 to 2	3 to 4	5 to 9	10 or more
Zero Units				2	2	1	22
1-10 Units	100			87	63	55	11
11-25 Units		56		10	30	31	36
26-99 Units		44		2	5	10	28
100-499 Units			91			2	3
500 Units or more			9				
Mean	5	33	221	6	9	15	96
Median	5	24	155	6	6	10	55
Responses	155	110	32	52	63	87	97

Q3. Approximately, what will be the company's total dollar volume of business in 2017?
(Percent of Respondents)

	2017 Expected Single-Family Starts			Number of Employees			
	1 to 10	11 to 99	100 or more	0 to 2	3 to 4	5 to 9	10 or more
Less than $500,000	3			4	3	1	1
$500,000 - $999,999	15	2		17	17	5	5
$1 million - $4,999,999	60	24		67	57	44	12
$5 million - $9,999,999	15	33		11	19	33	13
$10 million - $14,999,999	6	19	3	2	3	14	17
$15 million or over	1	22	97			3	57
Median	$3,172,041	$8,680,554		$2,777,776	$3,055,554	$5,086,206	
Responses	155	109	32	54	63	87	99

Q4. How long has your company been in business?
(Percent of Respondents)

	Total	Region				2017 Expected Dollar Volume				
		Northeast	Midwest	South	West	Less than $1 million	$1 million to $4,999,999	$5 million to $9,999,999	$10 million to $14,999,999	$15 million or over
Less then 5 years	5		4	7	5	7	7	3		5
5 to 10	18	17	12	21	16	23	16	18	16	18
11 to 15	14	17	4	19	11	7	18	12	16	13
16 to 20	12	4	16	14	6	20	10	17	10	8
More than 20 years	51	63	65	39	63	43	49	50	58	55
Mean (years)	24	27	31	20	24	22	22	25	25	25
Median (years)	21	30	25	17	25	20	20	21	25	23
Responses	305	24	57	160	64	30	123	60	31	60

Q5. How many employees were on your payroll as of June 30, 2017? (Include Owner/President/CEO)

	Total	Region				2017 Expected Dollar Volume				
		Northeast	Midwest	South	West	Less than $1 million	$1 million to $4,999,999	$5 million to $9,999,999	$10 million to $14,999,999	$15 million or over
Zero	1		2	2		2	2			
1 to 2	17	4	8	23	14	37	28	8	3	
3 to 4	21	17	22	22	17	43	30	20	6	
5 to 9	29	33	32	30	22	17	31	48	38	5
10 or more	33	46	37	23	46	3	10	22	53	95
Mean	14	12	25	10	15	3	5	7	14	45
Median	6	8	7	5	8	3	4	6	10	23
Responses	308	24	59	161	64	30	123	60	32	61
Did not report	1			2	2		1			3

Q4. How long has your company been in business?
(Percent of Respondents)

	2017 Expected Single-Family Starts			Number of Employees			
	1 to 10	11 to 99	100 or more	0 to 2	3 to 4	5 to 9	10 or more
Less then 5 years	6	4	6	13	8	2	2
5 to 10	14	22	22	17	24	17	15
11 to 15	18	12	9	11	13	16	16
16 to 20	11	15	6	9	17	11	9
More than 20 years	51	48	56	50	38	53	57
Mean (years)	24	23	25	21	19	25	27
Median (years)	21	20	24	21	17	25	23
Responses	154	109	32	54	63	88	97

Q5. How many employees were on your payroll as of June 30, 2017? (Include Owner/President/CEO)

	2017 Expected Single-Family Starts			Number of Employees			
	1 to 10	11 to 99	100 or more	0 to 2	3 to 4	5 to 9	10 or more
Zero	1			6			
1 to 2	28	5		94			
3 to 4	26	20			100		
5 to 9	31	33	6			100	
10 or more	14	42	94				100
Mean	6	11	40	2	3	7	34
Median	4	8	30	2	3	6	18
Responses	155	110	32	54	63	88	99
Did not report	1						

A-6

Q6. What was your total payroll as of June 30, 2017? (Include Owner/President/CEO).

	Total	Region				2017 Expected Dollar Volume				
		Northeast	Midwest	South	West	Less than $1 million	$1 million to $4,999,999	$5 million to $9,999,999	$10 million to $14,999,999	$15 million or over
Less than $50,000	4			6	6		7	3		
$50,000 to $99,999	7			9	9		14	3		
$100,000 to $499,999	54	38	67	56	48	83	73	61	53	11
$500,000 to $999,999	16	38	14	14	15	17	7	27	24	21
$1,000,000 to $1,999,999	13	15	14	10	21			6	24	42
$2,000,000 to $4,999,999	6	8	5	5	9					26
Mean	$577,689	$768,804	$547,092	$494,551	$773,806	$295,833	$219,304	$403,600	$626,459	$1,440,034
Median	$330,000	$510,000	$325,000	$268,180	$465,000	$200,000	$200,000	$340,000	$480,000	$1,337,000
Responses	308	24	59	161	64	30	123	60	32	61
Did not report	*46*	*46*	*64*	*38*	*48*	*80*	*41*	*45*	*47*	*38*

Q6. What was your total payroll as of June 30, 2017? (Include Owner/President/CEO).

	2017 Expected Single-Family Starts			Number of Employees			
	1 to 10	11 to 99	100 or more	0 to 2	3 to 4	5 to 9	10 or more
Less then $50,000	6			16			
$50,000 to $99,999	14			32	3		
$100,000 to $499,999	62	63	5	52	95	69	12
$500,000 to $999,999	14	20	9		3	31	22
$1,000,000 to $1,999,999	3	16	45				45
$2,000,000 to $4,999,999		2	41				20
Mean	$281,155	$552,367	$1,743,393	$118,528	$203,437	$400,659	$1,339,496
Median	$220,000	$360,000	$1,562,500	$105,000	$174,000	$369,000	$1,200,000
Responses	155	110	32	54	63	88	99
Did not report	*50*	*42*	*31*	*43*	*41*	*44*	*51*

	Total	Region				2017 Expected Dollar Volume				
		Northeast	Midwest	South	West	Less than $1 million	$1 million to $4,999,999	$5 million to $9,999,999	$10 million to $14,999,999	$15 million or over
Does Position Exist?										
Yes, full-time	95	96	93	95	95	93	94	97	100	93
Yes, part-time	3	4	5	2	2	3	3	3		2
No	2		2	3	3	3	2			5
Responses	301	24	59	155	63	30	121	58	32	59
Is it filled by person(s) with experience in construction trades?										
Always	89	95	85	91	86	100	95	83	93	75
Sometimes	4		7	3	4		1	9		8
Never/Almost never	7	5	7	6	11		4	8	7	17
Responses	269	22	54	136	57	28	105	53	30	52
Salary										
Less then $50,000	11	9	15	9	12	26	16	4	3	6
$50,000 to $99,999	42	43	45	38	47	61	52	40	40	15
$100,000 or more	47	48	40	52	41	13	32	56	57	80
Mean	$113,222	$96,306	$102,361	$116,289	$122,398	$61,287	$84,108	$113,788	$133,793	$184,814
Median	$90,000	$96,000	$80,000	$100,000	$85,000	$50,000	$78,000	$100,000	$105,400	$163,720
Responses	273	23	53	138	59	23	113	52	30	54
Bonus/Commissions										
Yes	49	35	49	46	61	22	38	56	60	70
No	51	65	51	54	39	78	62	44	40	30
Responses	273	23	53	138	59	23	113	52	30	54
Bonus (among all with salary)										
Zero	51	65	51	54	39	78	62	44	40	30
$1,000 to $4,999	1	4	4	1		4	3			
$5,000 to $9,999	1		2	2	2			2		
$10,000 or more	47	30	43	46	59	17	35	54	60	69
Mean	$44,179	$58,543	$42,326	$37,239	$56,478	$7,174	$16,283	$37,154	$56,167	$119,056
Median	$0	$0	$0	$0	$15,000	$0	$0	$17,500	$22,500	$60,000
Responses	273	23	53	138	59	23	113	52	30	54

EXECUTIVE JOBS
Q7. President/CEO
(Percent of Respondents)

	2017 Expected Single-Family Starts			Number of Employees			
	1 to 10	11 to 99	100 or more	0 to 2	3 to 4	5 to 9	10 or more
Does Position Exist?							
Yes, full-time	96	93	97	92	95	95	96
Yes, part-time	3	4		4	3	3	1
No	1	4	3	4	2	1	3
Responses	153	109	31	51	63	87	97
Is it filled by person(s) with experience in construction trades?							
Always	94	89	64	95	91	90	84
Sometimes	2	3	14		4	4	6
Never/Almost never	4	8	21	5	5	6	10
Responses	138	96	28	41	56	80	89
Salary							
Less then $50,000	14	8	10	14	18	12	4
$50,000 to $99,999	50	41	10	47	54	45	30
$100,000 or more	36	51	79	40	28	43	65
Mean	$90,581	$114,752	$187,362	$90,674	$80,549	$105,533	$149,613
Median	$80,000	$100,000	$180,000	$80,000	$75,000	$89,200	$120,000
Responses	137	99	29	43	57	82	89
Bonus/Commissions							
Yes	39	57	66	35	35	43	70
No	61	43	34	65	65	57	30
Responses	137	99	29	43	57	82	89
Bonus (among all with salary)							
Zero	61	43	34	65	65	57	30
$1,000 to $4,999	2	1		2	2	2	1
$5,000 to $9,999	1						2
$10,000 or more	36	56	66	35	33	40	66
Mean	$23,077	$51,071	$106,759	$23,116	$16,789	$29,354	$83,180
Median	$0	$20,000	$60,000	$0	$0	$0	$35,000
Responses	137	99	29	43	57	82	89

Q7. President/CEO
(Percent of Respondents) - continued

	Total	Region				2017 Expected Dollar Volume				
		Northeast	Midwest	South	West	Less than $1 million	$1 million to $4,999,999	$5 million to $9,999,999	$10 million to $14,999,999	$15 million or over
Bonus (among only those who actually got bonuses)										
$1,000 to $4,999	3		8	2			7			3
$5,000 to $9,999	1		4		3			3		3
$10,000 or more	96		88	98	97		93	97	100	97
Mean	$90,007		$86,281	$80,297	$92,561		$42,791	$66,621	$93,611	$169,184
Median	$50,000		$50,000	$52,500	$50,000		$40,000	$50,000	$85,000	$100,000
Responses	134		26	64	36		43	29	18	38
Benefits										
Health Insurance	72	82	71	69	75	50	59	76	93	87
Dental Insurance	33	36	29	33	36	11	17	35	39	67
Vision Program	20	23	16	21	22	11	4	24	25	48
Prescription Program	27	27	31	28	22	17	11	31	39	54
Life Insurance	36	50	39	33	36	28	25	33	39	63
Short Term Disability	16	27	20	15	13	17	5	20	18	33
Long Term Disability	17	27	18	15	18	11	5	18	25	39
Flex Spending	13	9	20	8	18	0	7	9	11	33
401 K	53	59	71	40	62	39	38	53	61	81
Paid Vacation Leave	83	86	82	86	76	72	77	87	82	96
Paid Sick Leave	62	55	55	65	65	50	56	60	50	85
Tuition Reimbursement	13	14	16	10	16	11	7	18	18	17
Training	31	41	27	31	29	28	30	29	29	35
Other	8	14	8	7	7	11	8	9	0	9
Responses	259	22	51	131	55	18	103	55	28	54

Q7. President/CEO
(Percent of Respondents) - continued

	2017 Expected Single-Family Starts			Number of Employees			
	1 to 10	11 to 99	100 or more	0 to 2	3 to 4	5 to 9	10 or more
Bonus (among only those who actually got bonuses)							
$1,000 to $4,999	6					6	2
$5,000 to $9,999	2	2			5		3
$10,000 or more	92	98	100	100	95	94	95
Mean	$59,651	$90,286	$162,947	$66,267	$47,850	$68,771	$119,403
Median	$50,000	$50,000	$150,000	$50,000	$40,000	$50,000	$65,000
Responses	53	56	19	15	20	35	62
Benefits							
Health Insurance	60	81	93	58	55	70	88
Dental Insurance	20	37	75	26	12	25	53
Vision Program	8	22	61	11	4	19	32
Prescription Program	15	34	61	26	8	20	44
Life Insurance	24	41	68	29	14	33	53
Short Term Disability	9	17	39	5	6	14	27
Long Term Disability	6	20	50	3	10	11	31
Flex Spending	4	13	39	5	8	8	21
401 K	43	56	79	29	41	51	69
Paid Vacation Leave	78	85	100	66	76	84	94
Paid Sick Leave	57	64	82	45	59	55	78
Tuition Reimbursement	10	10	25	8	8	11	18
Training	31	26	46	26	29	29	36
Other	7	8	7	5	6	8	10
Responses	124	100	28	38	49	80	90

Q7. CFO/Head of Finance
(Percent of Respondents)

	Total	Region				2017 Expected Dollar Volume				
		Northeast	Midwest	South	West	Less than $1 million	$1 million to $4,999,999	$5 million to $9,999,999	$10 million to $14,999,999	$15 million or over
Does Position Exist?										
Yes, full-time	26	33	25	21	35	7	13	19	38	63
Yes, part-time	4	4	7	3	5	7	3	7	3	2
No	70	63	68	76	60	87	83	74	59	36
Responses	300	24	59	154	63	30	121	57	32	59
Salary										
Less then $50,000	4			10			14			3
$50,000 to $99,999	47		46	48	50		71		83	22
$100,000 or more	49		54	41	50		14		17	76
Mean	$107,758		$116,232	$97,165	$116,445		$70,357		$86,960	$134,759
Median	$93,500		$100,000	$80,000	$94,400		$67,500		$80,000	$125,000
Responses	72		13	29	22		14		12	37
Bonus/Commissions										
Yes	69		46	66	82		57		50	84
No	31		54	34	18		43		50	16
Responses	72		13	29	22		14		12	37
Bonus (among all with salary)										
Zero	31		54	34	18		43		50	16
$1,000 to $4,999	6			3	9		14		8	3
$5,000 to $9,999	8			17	5		7		8	8
$10,000 or more	56		46	45	68		36		33	73
Mean	$40,825		$52,377	$32,000	$55,773		$12,214		$11,750	$66,281
Median	$15,000		$0	$5,000	$22,500		$2,000		$500	$35,000
Responses	72		13	29	22		14		12	37
Bonus (among only those who actually got bonuses)										
$1,000 to $4,999	8			5	11					3
$5,000 to $9,999	12			26	6					10
$10,000 or more	80			68	83					87
Mean	$58,788			$48,842	$68,167					$79,110
Median	$32,500			$30,000	$42,500					$60,000
Responses	50			19	18					31

Q7. CFO/Head of Finance
(Percent of Respondents)

	2017 Expected Single-Family Starts			Number of Employees			
	1 to 10	11 to 99	100 or more	0 to 2	3 to 4	5 to 9	10 or more
Does Position Exist?							
Yes, full-time	11	33	71		14	20	52
Yes, part-time	5	5				8	1
No	84	62	29	92	86	72	47
Responses	152	109	31	51	63	87	96
Salary							
Less then $50,000		9				6	4
$50,000 to $99,999	87	56	14			75	32
$100,000 or more	13	34	86			19	64
Mean	$75,933	$87,463	$144,809			$79,688	$121,992
Median	$75,000	$82,000	$134,644			$75,000	$110,000
Responses	15	32	22			16	47
Bonus/Commissions							
Yes	60	63	82			44	81
No	40	38	18			56	19
Responses	15	32	22			16	47
Bonus (among all with salary)							
Zero	40	38	18			56	19
$1,000 to $4,999	13	6				13	4
$5,000 to $9,999	7	9	9			6	9
$10,000 or more	40	47	73			25	68
Mean	$10,400	$25,281	$66,223			$7,156	$53,189
Median	$2,500	$5,000	$55,000			$0	$25,000
Responses	15	32	22			16	47
Bonus (among only those who actually got bonuses)							
$1,000 to $4,999		10	11				5
$5,000 to $9,999		15					11
$10,000 or more		75	89				84
Mean		$40,450	$80,939				$65,787
Median		$22,500	$64,200				$35,000
Responses		20	18				38

Q7. CFO/Head of Finance
(Percent of Respondents) - continued

Benefits	Total	Region				2017 Expected Dollar Volume				
		Northeast	Midwest	South	West	Less than $1 million	$1 million to $4,999,999	$5 million to $9,999,999	$10 million to $14,999,999	$15 million or over
Benefits										
Health Insurance	90		75	96	86		77		91	91
Dental Insurance	53		50	56	52		23		55	69
Vision Program	40		33	44	38		15		36	51
Prescription Program	40		25	44	33		15		27	57
Life Insurance	53		50	52	52		23		45	66
Short Term Disability	31		42	30	29		0		27	37
Long Term Disability	34		33	30	38		0		36	49
Flex Spending	29		42	19	33		8		27	43
401 K	66		58	63	67		15		64	83
Paid Vacation Leave	87		92	93	81		85		64	97
Paid Sick Leave	69		58	74	71		62		45	83
Tuition Reimbursement	18		42	7	14		8		18	20
Training	35		33	33	38		23		0	49
Other	10		8	11	10		15		0	11
Responses	68		12	27	21		13		11	35

A-15

Q7. CFO/Head of Finance
(Percent of Respondents) - continued

	2017 Expected Single-Family Starts			Number of Employees				
	1 to 10	11 to 99	100 or more	0 to 2	3 to 4	5 to 9	10 or more	
Benefits								
Health Insurance	80	86	100			93	89	
Dental Insurance	27	41	81			36	62	
Vision Program	13	31	62			36	44	
Prescription Program	20	31	62			29	49	
Life Insurance	20	52	71			50	58	
Short Term Disability	20	24	38			21	33	
Long Term Disability	0	28	57			7	44	
Flex Spending	7	17	52			29	31	
401 K	40	62	86			57	76	
Paid Vacation Leave	80	79	100			86	91	
Paid Sick Leave	53	72	76			64	76	
Tuition Reimbursement	13	7	29			14	18	
Training	27	21	57			21	38	
Other	7	14	5			14	9	
Responses	15	29	21			14	45	

	Total	Region				2017 Expected Dollar Volume				
		Northeast	Midwest	South	West	Less than $1 million	$1 million to $4,999,999	$5 million to $9,999,999	$10 million to $14,999,999	$15 million or over
Does Position Exist?										
Yes, full-time	3	4	3	3	5	3	1	1		14
Yes, part-time	1	1	2	1	3		1	3		2
No	95	96	95	97	92	97	98	97	100	85
Responses	301	24	59	155	63	30	121	58	32	59
Is it filled by person(s) with experience in construction trades?										
Always										
Sometimes										
Never/Almost never										
Responses										
Salary										
Less then $50,000	20									
$50,000 to $99,999	50									
$100,000 or more	30									
Mean	$79,600									
Median	$67,500									
Responses	10									
Bonus/Commissions										
Yes	40									
No	60									
Responses	10									
Bonus (among all with salary)										
Zero	60									
$10,000 or more	40									
Mean	$19,250									
Median	$0									
Responses	10									

Q7. CIO/Head of IT
(Percent of Respondents)

	2017 Expected Single-Family Starts			Number of Employees			
	1 to 10	11 to 99	100 or more	0 to 2	3 to 4	5 to 9	10 or more
Does Position Exist?							
Yes, full-time	1	3	6		2	1	6
Yes, part-time	1	3				3	1
No	98	94	94	100	98	95	93
Responses	153	109	31	51	63	87	97
Is it filled by person(s) with experience in construction trades?							
Always							
Sometimes							
Never/Almost never							
Responses							
Salary							
Less then $50,000							
$50,000 to $99,999							
$100,000 or more							
Mean							
Median							
Responses							
Bonus/Commissions							
Yes							
No							
Responses							
Bonus (among all with salary)							
Zero							
$10,000 or more							
Mean							
Median							
Responses							

Q7. VP of Construction
(Percent of Respondents)

	Total	Region				2017 Expected Dollar Volume				
		Northeast	Midwest	South	West	Less than $1 million	$1 million to $4,999,999	$5 million to $9,999,999	$10 million to $14,999,999	$15 million or over
Does Position Exist?										
Yes, full-time	36	42	29	34	46	30	21	26	44	75
Yes, part-time	1		2	1	2		2		3	2
No	63	58	69	65	52	70	78	74	53	24
Responses	300	24	58	155	63	30	121	57	32	59
Is it filled by person(s) with experience in construction trades?										
Always	96	100	100	97	90		94		100	97
Sometimes	2			3	10		6			3
Never/Almost never	1									
Responses	81	10	14	37	20		18		13	38
Salary										
Less then $50,000	7	10	6	8	4		13		7	7
$50,000 to $99,999	51	40	53	53	50		75	64	64	28
$100,000 or more	42	50	41	39	46		13	36	29	72
Mean	$94,293	$98,260	$92,382	$88,724	$103,779		$70,275	$86,500	$85,393	$119,589
Median	$85,000	$97,500	$85,000	$80,000	$89,250		$70,000	$85,000	$85,000	$108,000
Responses	104	10	17	49	28		24	14	14	43
Bonus/Commissions										
Yes	76	50	65	82	82		58	86	79	88
No	24	50	35	18	18		42	14	21	12
Responses	104	10	17	49	28		24	14	14	43
Bonus (among all with salary)										
Zero	24	50	35	18	18		42	14	14	12
$1,000 to $4,999	3		6	7	7					2
$5,000 to $9,999	3		6	4	4				14	2
$10,000 or more	70	50	59	78	71		58	71	71	84
Mean	$37,625	$37,500	$34,176	$34,480	$45,268		$21,208	$21,857	$49,821	$54,709
Median	$20,000	$5,000	$20,000	$20,000	$27,500		$10,000	$15,000	$20,000	$35,000
Responses	104	10	17	49	28		24	14	14	43

Q7. VP of Construction
(Percent of Respondents)

	2017 Expected Single-Family Starts			Number of Employees			
	1 to 10	11 to 99	100 or more	0 to 2	3 to 4	5 to 9	10 or more
Does Position Exist?							
Yes, full-time	24	40	81	12	27	31	57
Yes, part-time		4			2	1	2
No	76	56	19	88	71	68	41
Responses	152	109	31	51	63	87	96
Is it filled by person(s) with experience in construction trades?							
Always	96	97	95			100	98
Sometimes	4	3	5				2
Never/Almost never							
Responses	25	31	22			21	47
Salary							
Less then $50,000	15	5			13	15	
$50,000 to $99,999	65	60	24		75	62	37
$100,000 or more	21	36	76		13	23	63
Mean	$72,900	$88,472	$124,680		$68,563	$74,792	$112,737
Median	$72,500	$85,000	$108,000		$67,500	$77,500	$102,161
Responses	34	42	25		16	26	54
Bonus/Commissions							
Yes	56	83	88		63	69	87
No	44	17	12		38	31	13
Responses	34	42	25		16	26	54
Bonus (among all with salary)							
Zero	44	17	12		38	31	13
$1,000 to $4,999	3	5			6		4
$5,000 to $9,999	3	2	4			4	4
$10,000 or more	50	76	84		56	65	80
Mean	$15,176	$40,310	$55,260		$24,750	$26,231	$47,130
Median	$7,500	$20,000	$50,000		$10,000	$15,000	$30,000
Responses	34	42	25		16	26	54

Q7. VP of Construction
(Percent of Respondents) - continued

	Total	Region				2017 Expected Dollar Volume				
		Northeast	Midwest	South	West	Less than $1 million	$1 million to $4,999,999	$5 million to $9,999,999	$10 million to $14,999,999	$15 million or over
Bonus (among only those who actually got bonuses)										
$1,000 to $4,999	4		9		9				9	3
$5,000 to $9,999	4			5	4			17		3
$10,000 or more	92		91	95	87		100	83	91	95
Mean	$49,532		$52,818	$42,238	$55,109		$36,357	$25,500	$63,409	$61,908
Median	$30,000		$35,000	$30,000	$30,000		$25,000	$20,000	$35,000	$50,000
Responses	79		11	40	23		14	12	11	38
Benefits										
Health Insurance	88	100	81	83	96		63	86	100	100
Dental Insurance	46	30	44	47	54		8	29	46	79
Vision Program	29	20	19	30	38		0	21	31	52
Prescription Program	36	40	38	36	35		8	21	54	55
Life Insurance	42	40	50	45	35		17	29	31	64
Short Term Disability	27	50	31	23	23		13	14	23	43
Long Term Disability	26	40	38	19	27		17	7	38	38
Flex Spending	25	20	38	19	31		13	7	23	43
401 K	63	60	81	51	73		46	50	54	83
Paid Vacation Leave	90	90	94	89	88		88	86	85	93
Paid Sick Leave	73	60	75	77	69		79	57	54	81
Tuition Reimbursement	17	20	31	11	19		13	7	31	21
Training	34	40	31	26	50		38	21	8	43
Other	11	20	13	11	8		13	21	0	10
Responses	99	10	16	47	26		24	14	13	42

Q7. VP of Construction
(Percent of Respondents) - continued

	2017 Expected Single-Family Starts			Number of Employees			
	1 to 10	11 to 99	100 or more	0 to 2	3 to 4	5 to 9	10 or more
Bonus (among only those who actually got bonuses)							
$1,000 to $4,999	5	6	5		10		4
$5,000 to $9,999	5	3				6	4
$10,000 or more	89	91	95		90	94	91
Mean	$27,158	$48,371	$62,795		$39,600	$37,889	$54,149
Median	$15,000	$25,000	$51,750		$30,500	$15,000	$35,000
Responses	19	35	22		10	18	47
Benefits							
Health Insurance	71	93	100		63	83	100
Dental Insurance	13	49	79		0	29	70
Vision Program	3	24	63		0	21	42
Prescription Program	19	34	58		0	38	49
Life Insurance	16	39	75		19	38	53
Short Term Disability	10	27	42		6	25	34
Long Term Disability	6	22	50		13	13	36
Flex Spending	10	20	46		6	17	34
401 K	48	63	75		38	54	77
Paid Vacation Leave	87	90	92		88	88	91
Paid Sick Leave	68	73	79		75	58	77
Tuition Reimbursement	16	7	29		6	13	21
Training	35	24	46		38	25	36
Other	10	15	4		13	13	11
Responses	31	41	24		16	24	53

OPERATIONS JOBS
Q7. Head/Director of Purchasing
(Percent of Respondents)

	Total	Region				2017 Expected Dollar Volume				
		Northeast	Midwest	South	West	Less than $1 million	$1 million to $4,999,999	$5 million to $9,999,999	$10 million to $14,999,999	$15 million or over
Does Position Exist?										
Yes, full-time	17	21	17	17	16		1	16	22	58
Yes, part-time	1	1		1			1	2		
No	82	79	83	82	84	100	98	83	78	42
Responses	301	24	59	155	63	30	121	58	32	59
Is it filled by person(s) with experience in construction trades?										
Always	67			62						78
Sometimes	26			33						19
Never/Almost never	8			5						4
Responses	39			21						27
Salary										
Less then $50,000	8			12						
$50,000 to $99,999	67			76	50					71
$100,000 or more	24			12	50					29
Mean	$80,884			$74,360	$90,200					$86,903
Median	$70,000			$70,000	$90,000					$75,500
Responses	49			25	10					34
Bonus/Commissions										
Yes	73			80	70					79
No	27			20	30					21
Responses	49			25	10					34
Bonus (among all with salary)										
Zero	27			20	30					21
$1,000 to $4,999	4			4						3
$5,000 to $9,999	12			16	20					12
$10,000 or more	57			60	50					65
Mean	$20,014			$15,600	$28,550					$24,976
Median	$10,000			$10,000	$12,500					$17,500
Responses	49			25	10					34

OPERATIONS JOBS
Q7. Head/Director of Purchasing
(Percent of Respondents)

	2017 Expected Single-Family Starts			Number of Employees			
	1 to 10	11 to 99	100 or more	0 to 2	3 to 4	5 to 9	10 or more
Does Position Exist?							
Yes, full-time	3	22	68	2	2	10	41
Yes, part-time	1	1				1	
No	97	77	32	98	98	89	59
Responses	153	109	31	51	63	87	97
Is it filled by person(s) with experience in construction trades?							
Always		63	76				77
Sometimes		26	18				13
Never/Almost never		11	6				10
Responses		19	17				31
Salary							
Less then $50,000		13					
$50,000 to $99,999		79	67				74
$100,000 or more		8	33				26
Mean		$67,760	$88,743				$83,727
Median		$62,500	$85,000				$75,000
Responses		24	21				39
Bonus/Commissions							
Yes		63	86				77
No		38	14				23
Responses		24	21				39
Bonus (among all with salary)							
Zero		38	14				23
$1,000 to $4,999		4					3
$5,000 to $9,999		17	10				13
$10,000 or more		42	76				62
Mean		$7,375	$28,271				$21,236
Median		$5,000	$25,000				$15,000
Responses		24	21				39

Q7. Head/Director of Purchasing
(Percent of Respondents) - continued

	Total	Region				2017 Expected Dollar Volume				
		Northeast	Midwest	South	West	Less than $1 million	$1 million to $4,999,999	$5 million to $9,999,999	$10 million to $14,999,999	$15 million or over
Bonus (among only those who actually got bonuses)										
$1,000 to $4,999	6			5						4
$5,000 to $9,999	17			20						15
$10,000 or more	78			75						81
Mean	$27,242			$19,500						$31,452
Median	$20,000			$12,500						$20,000
Responses	36			20						27
Benefits										
Health Insurance	90			100	90					91
Dental Insurance	63			64	80					76
Vision Program	49			52	60					59
Prescription Program	49			64	30					50
Life Insurance	51			60	30					65
Short Term Disability	33			28	20					35
Long Term Disability	39			36	30					41
Flex Spending	33			20	50					38
401 K	73			72	80					82
Paid Vacation Leave	96			96	90					94
Paid Sick Leave	80			76	90					85
Tuition Reimbursement	22			12	20					24
Training	29			16	40					38
Other	8			4	0					6
Responses	49			25	10					34

Q7. Head/Director of Purchasing
(Percent of Respondents) - continued

	2017 Expected Single-Family Starts			Number of Employees			
	1 to 10	11 to 99	100 or more	0 to 2	3 to 4	5 to 9	10 or more
Bonus (among only those who actually got bonuses)							
$1,000 to $4,999		7					3
$5,000 to $9,999		27	11				17
$10,000 or more		67	89				80
Mean		$11,800	$32,983				$27,607
Median		$10,000	$29,750				$20,000
Responses		15	18				30
Benefits							
Health Insurance		79	100				90
Dental Insurance		50	81				74
Vision Program		33	67				54
Prescription Program		42	62				51
Life Insurance		29	76				59
Short Term Disability		21	43				36
Long Term Disability		25	52				44
Flex Spending		17	48				38
401 K		67	81				77
Paid Vacation Leave		96	95				95
Paid Sick Leave		88	71				82
Tuition Reimbursement		13	29				23
Training		8	48				33
Other		8	5				8
Responses		24	21				39

A-26

Q7. Head /Director of Land Acquisition
(Percent of Respondents)

	Total	Region				2017 Expected Dollar Volume				
		Northeast	Midwest	South	West	Less than $1 million	$1 million to $4,999,999	$5 million to $9,999,999	$10 million to $14,999,999	$15 million or over
Does Position Exist?										
Yes, full-time	8	17	7	6	8		1	2	3	34
No	92	83	93	94	92	100	99	98	97	66
Responses	301	24	59	155	63	30	121	58	32	59
Is it filled by person(s) with experience in construction trades?										
Always	87									85
Never/Almost never	13									15
Responses	15									13
Salary										
$50,000 to $99,999	32									21
$100,000 or more	68									79
Mean	$124,114									$130,816
Median	$120,255									$125,000
Responses	22									19
Bonus/Commissions										
Yes	77									79
No	23									21
Responses	22									19
Bonus (among all with salary)										
Zero	23									21
$1,000 to $4,999	5									5
$5,000 to $9,999	5									5
$10,000 or more	68									68
Mean	$49,352									$52,671
Median	$35,000									$35,000
Responses	22									19

Q7. Head /Director of Land Acquisition
(Percent of Respondents)

	2017 Expected Single-Family Starts			Number of Employees			
	1 to 10	11 to 99	100 or more	0 to 2	3 to 4	5 to 9	10 or more
Does Position Exist?							
Yes, full-time	1	9	35			2	22
No	99	91	65	100	100	98	78
Responses	153	109	31	51	63	87	97
Is it filled by person(s) with experience in construction trades?							
Always							86
Never/Almost never							14
Responses							14
Salary							
$50,000 to $99,999			27				25
$100,000 or more			73				75
Mean			$114,727				$128,276
Median			$120,000				$122,755
Responses			11				20
Bonus/Commissions							
Yes			82				80
No			18				20
Responses			11				20
Bonus (among all with salary)							
Zero			18				20
$1,000 to $4,999							5
$5,000 to $9,999							5
$10,000 or more			82				70
Mean			$46,955				$53,788
Median			$48,000				$37,500
Responses			11				20

Q7. Head /Director of Land Acquisition
(Percent of Respondents) - continued

		Region				2017 Expected Dollar Volume				
	Total	Northeast	Midwest	South	West	Less than $1 million	$1 million to $4,999,999	$5 million to $9,999,999	$10 million to $14,999,999	$15 million or over
Bonus (among only those who actually got bonuses)										
$1,000 to $4,999	6									7
$5,000 to $9,999	6									7
$10,000 or more	88									87
Mean	$63,868									$66,717
Median	$48,000									$48,000
Responses	17									15
Benefits										
Health Insurance	91									95
Dental Insurance	82									84
Vision Program	50									47
Prescription Program	59									58
Life Insurance	59									63
Short Term Disability	32									37
Long Term Disability	50									53
Flex Spending	41									42
401 K	82									89
Paid Vacation Leave	95									95
Paid Sick Leave	77									79
Tuition Reimbursement	23									26
Training	41									47
Other	9									11
Responses	22									19

Q7. Head /Director of Land Acquisition
(Percent of Respondents) - continued

	2017 Expected Single-Family Starts			Number of Employees			
	1 to 10	11 to 99	100 or more	0 to 2	3 to 4	5 to 9	10 or more
Bonus (among only those who actually got bonuses)							
$1,000 to $4,999							6
$5,000 to $9,999							6
$10,000 or more							88
Mean							$67,234
Median							$49,000
Responses							16
Benefits							
Health Insurance			100				95
Dental Insurance			91				85
Vision Program			64				50
Prescription Program			64				60
Life Insurance			73				65
Short Term Disability			36				35
Long Term Disability			64				55
Flex Spending			55				45
401 K			91				90
Paid Vacation Leave			100				95
Paid Sick Leave			73				80
Tuition Reimbursement			27				25
Training			64				45
Other			9				10
Responses			11				20

Q7. Head /Director of Production
(Percent of Respondents)

	Total	Region				2017 Expected Dollar Volume				
		Northeast	Midwest	South	West	Less than $1 million	$1 million to $4,999,999	$5 million to $9,999,999	$10 million to $14,999,999	$15 million or over
Does Position Exist?										
Yes, full-time	14	13	20	12	14	3	9	17	16	25
No	86	88	80	88	86	97	91	83	84	75
Responses	301	24	59	155	63	30	121	58	32	59
Is it filled by person(s) with experience in construction trades?										
Always	81			83						100
Sometimes	15			17						
Never/Almost never	4									
Responses	26			12						10
Salary										
$50,000 to $99,999	88		100	82			91			73
$100,000 or more	13			18			9			27
Mean	$74,496		$71,273	$79,765			$65,545			$87,733
Median	$65,500		$70,000	$70,000			$60,000			$82,000
Responses	40		11	17			11			15
Bonus/Commissions										
Yes	65		45	65			45			80
No	35		55	35			55			20
Responses	40		11	17			11			15
Bonus (among all with salary)										
Zero	35		55	35			55			20
$1,000 to $4,999	3			6			9			13
$5,000 to $9,999	15		27				9			
$10,000 or more	48		18	59			27			67
Mean	$26,337		$4,943	$39,476			$6,964			$54,625
Median	$8,688		$0	$11,100			$0			$10,000
Responses	40		11	17			11			15

Q7. Head /Director of Production
(Percent of Respondents)

	2017 Expected Single-Family Starts			Number of Employees			
	1 to 10	11 to 99	100 or more	0 to 2	3 to 4	5 to 9	10 or more
Does Position Exist?							
Yes, full-time	7	20	26		8	17	22
No	93	80	74	100	92	83	78
Responses	153	109	31	51	63	87	97
Is it filled by person(s) with experience in construction trades?							
Always		80				70	85
Sometimes		13				30	8
Never/Almost never		7					8
Responses		15				10	13
Salary							
$50,000 to $99,999		100				100	85
$100,000 or more							15
Mean		$66,403				$68,490	$77,100
Median		$60,000				$65,500	$67,500
Responses		22				14	20
Bonus/Commissions							
Yes		68				43	85
No		32				57	15
Responses		22				14	20
Bonus (among all with salary)							
Zero		32				57	15
$1,000 to $4,999		18					5
$5,000 to $9,999						7	25
$10,000 or more		50				36	55
Mean		$11,863				$7,857	$40,119
Median		$9,688				$0	$10,000
Responses		22				14	20

Q7. Head /Director of Production
(Percent of Respondents) - continued

	Total	Region				2017 Expected Dollar Volume				
		Northeast	Midwest	South	West	Less than $1 million	$1 million to $4,999,999	$5 million to $9,999,999	$10 million to $14,999,999	$15 million or over
Bonus (among only those who actually got bonuses)										
$1,000 to $4,999	4									
$5,000 to $9,999	23			9						17
$10,000 or more	73			91						83
Mean	$40,518			$61,009						$68,281
Median	$17,500			$25,000						$25,000
Responses	26			11						12
Benefits										
Health Insurance	76		70	75			40			93
Dental Insurance	47		40	50			10			67
Vision Program	29		20	38			10			40
Prescription Program	32		10	44			10			40
Life Insurance	34		40	38			10			47
Short Term Disability	24		20	19			0			27
Long Term Disability	34		30	38			10			40
Flex Spending	16		10	19			0			27
401 K	66		60	56			20			100
Paid Vacation Leave	97		90	100			100			100
Paid Sick Leave	71		40	94			60			87
Tuition Reimbursement	16		20	13			10			13
Training	26		10	19			10			33
Other	5		0	6			0			7
Responses	38		10	16			10			15

Q7. Head /Director of Production
(Percent of Respondents) - continued

	2017 Expected Single-Family Starts			Number of Employees			
	1 to 10	11 to 99	100 or more	0 to 2	3 to 4	5 to 9	10 or more
Bonus (among only those who actually got bonuses)							
$1,000 to $4,999							6
$5,000 to $9,999		27					29
$10,000 or more		73					65
Mean		$17,398					$47,199
Median		$11,100					$10,000
Responses		15					17
Benefits							
Health Insurance		86				77	85
Dental Insurance		52				46	55
Vision Program		33				31	30
Prescription Program		43				31	40
Life Insurance		33				15	45
Short Term Disability		24				23	25
Long Term Disability		38				38	35
Flex Spending		5				8	20
401 K		62				54	85
Paid Vacation Leave		95				92	100
Paid Sick Leave		76				62	80
Tuition Reimbursement		10				23	10
Training		24				23	30
Other		10				8	5
Responses		21				13	20

Q7. Head /Director of Development and Training
(Percent of Respondents)

	Total	Region				2017 Expected Dollar Volume				
		Northeast	Midwest	South	West	Less than $1 million	$1 million to $4,999,999	$5 million to $9,999,999	$10 million to $14,999,999	$15 million or over
Does Position Exist?										
Yes, full-time	*		2							2
Yes, part-time	*			1				2		
No	99	100	98	99	100	100	100	98	100	98
Responses	301	24	59	155	63	30	121	58	32	59

A-35

Q7. Head /Director of Development and Training
(Percent of Respondents)

	2017 Expected Single-Family Starts			Number of Employees				
	1 to 10	11 to 99	100 or more	0 to 2	3 to 4	5 to 9	10 or more
Does Position Exist?							
Yes, full-time			3				1
Yes, part-time	1					1	
No	99	100	97	100	100	99	99
Responses	153	109	31	51	63	87	97

Q7. Head /Director of Sales & Marketing
(Percent of Respondents)

	Region					2017 Expected Dollar Volume				
	Total	Northeast	Midwest	South	West	Less than $1 million	$1 million to $4,999,999	$5 million to $9,999,999	$10 million to $14,999,999	$15 million or over
Does Position Exist?										
Yes, full-time	19	17	22	18	17		6	9	38	54
Yes, part-time	2	13	3	3	3		3	3	3	
No	79	71	75	82	79	100	91	88	59	46
Responses	301	24	59	155	63	30	121	58	32	59
Is it filled by person(s) with experience in construction trades?										
Always	58			58						47
Sometimes	35			25						47
Never/Almost never	8			17						7
Responses	26			12						15
Salary										
Less then $50,000	14	14	17	16	10				8	3
$50,000 to $99,999	43	43	42	40	40				58	34
$100,000 or more	43	43	42	44	50				33	62
Mean	$88,027		$92,125	$85,640	$89,286				$84,833	$101,155
Median	$80,000		$82,000	$80,000	$87,500				$75,000	$100,000
Responses	51		12	25	10				12	29
Bonus/Commissions										
Yes	73		92	64	80				67	83
No	27		8	36	20				33	17
Responses	51		12	25	10				12	29
Bonus (among all with salary)										
Zero	27		8	36	20				33	17
$1,000 to $4,999	6		8	4	10				8	3
$5,000 to $9,999	4		17							3
$10,000 or more	63		67	60	70				58	76
Mean	$47,863		$33,542	$41,880	$91,650				$44,833	$62,500
Median	$15,000		$18,750	$10,000	$76,750				$10,000	$50,000
Responses	51		12	25	10				12	29

Q7. Head /Director of Sales & Marketing
(Percent of Respondents)

	2017 Expected Single-Family Starts			Number of Employees			
	1 to 10	11 to 99	100 or more	0 to 2	3 to 4	5 to 9	10 or more
Does Position Exist?							
Yes, full-time	5	26	61		10	11	41
Yes, part-time	4	1			2	2	4
No	92	73	39	100	89	86	55
Responses	153	109	31	51	63	87	97
Is it filled by person(s) with experience in construction trades?							
Always		75	30				50
Sometimes		17	70				40
Never/Almost never		8					10
Responses		12	10				20
Salary							
Less then $50,000		15					5
$50,000 to $99,999		48	38				41
$100,000 or more		37	63				54
Mean		$77,661	$106,219				$97,473
Median		$74,000	$100,000				$100,000
Responses		27	16				37
Bonus/Commissions							
Yes		70		88			81
No		30		13			19
Responses		27		16			37
Bonus (among all with salary)							
Zero		30	13				19
$1,000 to $4,999		4	6				5
$5,000 to $9,999		4	6				5
$10,000 or more		63	75				70
Mean		$41,833	$72,219				$59,014
Median		$10,000	$56,750				$30,000
Responses		27	16				37

Q7. Head /Director of Sales & Marketing
(Percent of Respondents) - continued

		Region				2017 Expected Dollar Volume				
	Total	Northeast	Midwest	South	West	Less than $1 million	$1 million to $4,999,999	$5 million to $9,999,999	$10 million to $14,999,999	$15 million or over
Bonus (among only those who actually got bonuses)										
$1,000 to $4,999	8		9	6						4
$5,000 to $9,999	5		18							4
$10,000 or more	86		73	94						92
Mean	$65,973		$36,591	$65,438						$75,521
Median	$50,000		$22,500	$40,000						$51,750
Responses	37		11	16						24
Benefits										
Health Insurance	88		83	88	90				100	93
Dental Insurance	56		58	50	80				50	72
Vision Program	42		33	42	60				42	52
Prescription Program	42		25	42	60				42	55
Life Insurance	52		42	58	50				42	66
Short Term Disability	34		33	38	30				42	38
Long Term Disability	30		33	29	30				42	31
Flex Spending	24		33	13	40				8	38
401 K	82		100	71	90				75	93
Paid Vacation Leave	90		83	92	100				83	93
Paid Sick Leave	72		75	67	80				50	83
Tuition Reimbursement	16		25	8	10				17	17
Training	28		33	17	40				0	41
Other	6		8	0	10				0	10
Responses	50		12	24	10				12	29

Q7. Head /Director of Sales & Marketing
(Percent of Respondents) - continued

	2017 Expected Single-Family Starts			Number of Employees			
	1 to 10	11 to 99	100 or more	0 to 2	3 to 4	5 to 9	10 or more
Bonus (among only those who actually got bonuses)							
$1,000 to $4,999		5	7				7
$5,000 to $9,999		5	7				7
$10,000 or more		89	86				87
Mean		$59,447	$82,536				$72,783
Median		$24,000	$60,000				$50,000
Responses		19	14				30
Benefits							
Health Insurance		85	94				92
Dental Insurance		48	75				68
Vision Program		33	63				49
Prescription Program		41	50				54
Life Insurance		41	81				62
Short Term Disability		26	44				43
Long Term Disability		19	50				38
Flex Spending		11	50				32
401 K		81	88				89
Paid Vacation Leave		85	94				92
Paid Sick Leave		70	69				76
Tuition Reimbursement		7	31				16
Training		11	56				32
Other		4	6				8
Responses		27	16				37

FINANCE JOBS
Q7. Controller
(Percent of Respondents)

	Total	Region				2017 Expected Dollar Volume				
		Northeast	Midwest	South	West	Less than $1 million	$1 million to $4,999,999	$5 million to $9,999,999	$10 million to $14,999,999	$15 million or over
Does Position Exist?										
Yes, full-time	18	25	22	15	19		5	10	28	56
Yes, part-time	5	4	2	5	6	3	5	7	6	2
No	77	71	76	80	75	97	90	83	66	42
Responses	301	24	59	155	63	30	121	58	32	59
Salary										
Less then $50,000	14		25	18						6
$50,000 to $99,999	75		58	77	82					78
$100,000 or more	12		17	5	18					16
Mean	$72,002		$70,000	$67,631	$80,295					$76,493
Median	$72,000		$67,500	$71,000	$75,000					$75,000
Responses	51		12	22	11					32
Bonus/Commissions										
Yes	71		75	73	91					75
No	29		25	27	9					25
Responses	51		12	22	11					32
Bonus (among all with salary)										
Zero	29		25	27	9					25
$1,000 to $4,999	6		8		18					6
$5,000 to $9,999	25		17	36	27					28
$10,000 or more	39		50	36	45					41
Mean	$11,697		$11,111	$14,614	$11,973					$13,647
Median	$7,500		$9,250	$7,750	$8,500					$8,000
Responses	51		12	22	11					32

FINANCE JOBS
Q7. Controller
(Percent of Respondents)

	2017 Expected Single-Family Starts			Number of Employees			
	1 to 10	11 to 99	100 or more	0 to 2	3 to 4	5 to 9	10 or more
Does Position Exist?							
Yes, full-time	5	26	55	2	5	9	42
Yes, part-time	6	4	3	2	6	7	3
No	90	71	42	96	89	84	55
Responses	153	109	31	51	63	87	97
Salary							
Less then $50,000		11	6				5
$50,000 to $99,999		85	71				79
$100,000 or more		4	24				15
Mean		$67,621	$80,941				$76,567
Median		$70,000	$80,000				$75,000
Responses		27	17				39
Bonus/Commissions							
Yes		56	82				72
No		44	18				28
Responses		27	17				39
Bonus (among all with salary)							
Zero		44	18				28
$1,000 to $4,999		11	29				5
$5,000 to $9,999		19	29				28
$10,000 or more		26	53				38
Mean		$6,799	$17,279				$12,044
Median		$2,750	$10,000				$8,000
Responses		27	17				39

Q7. Controller
(Percent of Respondents) - continued

	Total	Region				2017 Expected Dollar Volume				
		Northeast	Midwest	South	West	Less than $1 million	$1 million to $4,999,999	$5 million to $9,999,999	$10 million to $14,999,999	$15 million or over
Bonus (among only those who actually got bonuses)										
$1,000 to $4,999	8				20					8
$5,000 to $9,999	36			50	30					38
$10,000 or more	56			50	50					54
Mean	$16,570			$20,094	$13,170					$18,196
Median	$10,000			$11,500	$9,250					$10,000
Responses	36			16	10					24
Benefits										
Health Insurance	88		64	95	100					94
Dental Insurance	63		55	52	91					72
Vision Program	43		36	43	45					44
Prescription Program	45		36	48	45					50
Life Insurance	53		36	57	55					63
Short Term Disability	31		36	14	45					38
Long Term Disability	37		36	24	45					41
Flex Spending	37		45	19	55					38
401 K	80		91	71	91					81
Paid Vacation Leave	98		91	100	100					100
Paid Sick Leave	86		82	76	100					91
Tuition Reimbursement	20		27	0	45					25
Training	33		27	10	64					38
Other	10		9	10	0					6
Responses	49		11	21	11					32

Q7. Controller
(Percent of Respondents) - continued

	2017 Expected Single-Family Starts			Number of Employees			
	1 to 10	11 to 99	100 or more	0 to 2	3 to 4	5 to 9	10 or more
Bonus (among only those who actually got bonuses)							
$1,000 to $4,999		20					7
$5,000 to $9,999		33	36				39
$10,000 or more		47	64				54
Mean		$12,239	$20,982				$16,775
Median		$8,000	$16,250				$10,000
Responses		15	14				28
Benefits							
Health Insurance		81	100				95
Dental Insurance		58	76				69
Vision Program		38	53				41
Prescription Program		38	59				51
Life Insurance		42	76				56
Short Term Disability		23	41				33
Long Term Disability		27	59				44
Flex Spending		23	53				38
401 K		81	71				79
Paid Vacation Leave		96	100				100
Paid Sick Leave		92	76				90
Tuition Reimbursement		12	29				23
Training		19	41				33
Other		4	6				8
Responses		26	17				39

Q7. Payroll Manager
(Percent of Respondents)

	Total	Region				2017 Expected Dollar Volume				
		Northeast	Midwest	South	West	Less than $1 million	$1 million to $4,999,999	$5 million to $9,999,999	$10 million to $14,999,999	$15 million or over
Does Position Exist?										
Yes, full-time	5	8	3	5	6	7	3	3	3	17
Yes, part-time	2		5	1	3		2	2	2	
No	92	92	92	94	90	93	94	95	97	83
Responses	301	24	59	155	63	30	121	58	32	59
Salary										
Less then $50,000	36									
$50,000 to $99,999	64									
Mean	$54,571									
Median	$54,000									
Responses	14									
Bonus/Commissions										
Yes	50									
No	50									
Responses	14									
Bonus (among all with salary)										
Zero	50									
$5,000 to $9,999	36									
$10,000 or more	14									
Mean	$4,107									
Median	$2,500									
Responses	14									

Q7. Payroll Manager
(Percent of Respondents)

	2017 Expected Single-Family Starts			Number of Employees			
	1 to 10	11 to 99	100 or more	0 to 2	3 to 4	5 to 9	10 or more
Does Position Exist?							
Yes, full-time	2	6	13	2		3	11
Yes, part-time	4	1			3	5	1
No	94	94	87	98	97	92	88
Responses	153	109	31	51	63	87	97
Salary							
Less then $50,000							30
$50,000 to $99,999							70
Mean							$56,900
Median							$54,000
Responses							10
Bonus/Commissions							
Yes							60
No							40
Responses							10
Bonus (among all with salary)							
Zero							40
$5,000 to $9,999							40
$10,000 or more							20
Mean							$5,250
Median							$5,000
Responses							10

Q7. Payroll Manager
(Percent of Respondents) - continued

	Total	Region				2017 Expected Dollar Volume				
		Northeast	Midwest	South	West	Less than $1 million	$1 million to $4,999,999	$5 million to $9,999,999	$10 million to $14,999,999	$15 million or over
Bonus (among only those who actually got bonuses)										
$5,000 to $9,999										
$10,000 or more										
Mean										
Median										
Responses										
Benefits										
Health Insurance	79									
Dental Insurance	50									
Vision Program	36									
Prescription Program	29									
Life Insurance	64									
Short Term Disability	43									
Long Term Disability	21									
Flex Spending	36									
401 K	57									
Paid Vacation Leave	79									
Paid Sick Leave	64									
Tuition Reimbursement	14									
Training	36									
Other	7									
Responses	14									

Q7. Payroll Manager
(Percent of Respondents) - continued

	2017 Expected Single-Family Starts			Number of Employees			
	1 to 10	11 to 99	100 or more	0 to 2	3 to 4	5 to 9	10 or more
Bonus (among only those who actually got bonuses)							
$5,000 to $9,999							
$10,000 or more							
Mean							
Median							
Responses							
Benefits							
Health Insurance							90
Dental Insurance							60
Vision Program							40
Prescription Program							40
Life Insurance							70
Short Term Disability							50
Long Term Disability							30
Flex Spending							40
401 K							70
Paid Vacation Leave							90
Paid Sick Leave							70
Tuition Reimbursement							10
Training							40
Other							10
Responses							10

Q7. Staff Accountant
(Percent of Respondents)

	Total	Region				2017 Expected Dollar Volume				
		Northeast	Midwest	South	West	Less than $1 million	$1 million to $4,999,999	$5 million to $9,999,999	$10 million to $14,999,999	$15 million or over
Does Position Exist?										
Yes, full-time	10	13	8	10	11		2	12	6	33
Yes, part-time	4	9	3	1	8	3	2	5	3	5
No	86	78	88	89	81	97	96	83	91	62
Responses	300	23	59	155	63	30	121	58	32	58
Salary										
Less then $50,000	34			43						32
$50,000 to $99,999	66			57						68
Mean	$53,290			$51,750						$53,316
Median	$52,500			$50,000						$52,500
Responses	29			14						19
Bonus/Commissions										
Yes	66			50						63
No	34			50						37
Responses	29			14						19
Bonus (among all with salary)										
Zero	34			50						37
$1,000 to $4,999	28									26
$5,000 to $9,999	24			21						21
$10,000 or more	14			29						16
Mean	$5,224			$7,357						$6,000
Median	$3,000			$2,500						$2,500
Responses	29			14						19

Q7. Staff Accountant
(Percent of Respondents)

	2017 Expected Single-Family Starts			Number of Employees			
	1 to 10	11 to 99	100 or more	0 to 2	3 to 4	5 to 9	10 or more
Does Position Exist?							
Yes, full-time	3	9	48			8	23
Yes, part-time	4	5			5	6	3
No	93	86	52	100	95	86	74
Responses	153	108	31	51	63	87	96
Salary							
Less then $50,000		50	27				27
$50,000 to $99,999		50	73				73
Mean		$49,540	$55,000				$53,927
Median		$47,500	$57,000				$53,750
Responses		10	15				22
Bonus/Commissions							
Yes		70	60				64
No		30	40				36
Responses		10	15				22
Bonus (among all with salary)							
Zero		30	40				36
$1,000 to $4,999		20	33				36
$5,000 to $9,999		50	7				14
$10,000 or more			20				14
Mean		$3,400	$6,667				$5,159
Median		$4,000	$2,500				$2,500
Responses		10	15				22

	Total	Region				2017 Expected Dollar Volume				
		Northeast	Midwest	South	West	Less than $1 million	$1 million to $4,999,999	$5 million to $9,999,999	$10 million to $14,999,999	$15 million or over
Bonus (among only those who actually got bonuses)										
$1,000 to $4,999	42									42
$5,000 to $9,999	37									33
$10,000 or more	21									25
Mean	$7,974									$9,500
Median	$5,000									$5,000
Responses	19									12
Benefits										
Health Insurance	93			92						89
Dental Insurance	57			38						63
Vision Program	50			46						53
Prescription Program	46			38						42
Life Insurance	54			46						63
Short Term Disability	29			15						32
Long Term Disability	21			8						26
Flex Spending	32			15						42
401 K	71			62						79
Paid Vacation Leave	86			85						84
Paid Sick Leave	79			62						79
Tuition Reimbursement	25			15						21
Training	43			31						42
Other	4			0						5
Responses	28			13						19

Q7. Staff Accountant
(Percent of Respondents) - continued

	2017 Expected Single-Family Starts			Number of Employees			
	1 to 10	11 to 99	100 or more	0 to 2	3 to 4	5 to 9	10 or more
Bonus (among only those who actually got bonuses)							
$1,000 to $4,999							57
$5,000 to $9,999							21
$10,000 or more							21
Mean							$8,107
Median							$4,000
Responses							14
Benefits							
Health Insurance		90	93				91
Dental Insurance		40	67				59
Vision Program		40	53				50
Prescription Program		50	47				50
Life Insurance		20	73				59
Short Term Disability		0	40				32
Long Term Disability		0	40				27
Flex Spending		10	47				36
401 K		50	80				73
Paid Vacation Leave		80	93				82
Paid Sick Leave		90	67				82
Tuition Reimbursement		10	27				23
Training		20	47				41
Other		0	7				5
Responses		10	15				22

Q7. Bookkeeper
(Percent of Respondents)

	Total	Region				2017 Expected Dollar Volume				
		Northeast	Midwest	South	West	Less than $1 million	$1 million to $4,999,999	$5 million to $9,999,999	$10 million to $14,999,999	$15 million or over
Does Position Exist?										
Yes, full-time	25	33	24	23	29	27	16	28	41	46
Yes, part-time	20	17	12	23	19		27	19	9	5
No	55	50	64	54	52	73	57	53	50	49
Responses	301	24	59	155	63	30	121	58	32	59
Salary										
Less then $50,000	77		79	76	75		76	60	77	88
$50,000 to $99,999	23		21	24	25		24	40	23	12
Mean	$42,478		$42,436	$43,425	$41,382		$40,608	$49,047	$43,028	$39,636
Median	$41,600		$43,550	$42,000	$41,236		$40,000	$48,000	$42,471	$38,000
Responses	71		14	33	16		17	15	13	26
Bonus/Commissions										
Yes	63		64	70	63		41	73	69	69
No	37		36	30	38		59	27	31	31
Responses	71		14	33	16		17	15	13	26
Bonus (among all with salary)										
Zero	37		36	30	38		59	27	31	31
$1 to $999	6			3	19				23	4
$1,000 to $4,999	34		43	36	31		18	33	31	46
$5,000 to $9,999	18		14	27	6		24	20	15	15
$10,000 or more	6		7	3	6			20		4
Mean	$2,879		$2,714	$3,640	$1,706		$1,588	$4,100	$2,090	$3,413
Median	$1,500		$1,750	$2,000	$775		$0	$3,000	$800	$1,500
Responses	71		14	33	16		17	15	13	26

Q7. Bookkeeper
(Percent of Respondents)

	2017 Expected Single-Family Starts			Number of Employees			
	1 to 10	11 to 99	100 or more	0 to 2	3 to 4	5 to 9	10 or more
Does Position Exist?							
Yes, full-time	16	33	48	4	17	22	44
Yes, part-time	27	15		20	27	25	9
No	57	52	52	76	56	53	46
Responses	153	109	31	51	63	87	97
Salary							
Less then $50,000	64	82	87		70	56	88
$50,000 to $99,999	36	18	13		30	44	12
Mean	$44,809	$41,842	$40,500		$41,510	$47,700	$40,411
Median	$45,000	$40,000	$39,500		$43,736	$46,750	$39,750
Responses	22	34	15		10	18	42
Bonus/Commissions							
Yes	59	59	80		70	56	64
No	41	41	20		30	44	36
Responses	22	34	15		10	18	42
Bonus (among all with salary)							
Zero	41	41	20		30	44	36
$1 to $999	9	6			10	6	5
$1,000 to $4,999	23	29	60		20	22	43
$5,000 to $9,999	27	15	13		30	28	10
$10,000 or more		9	7		10		7
Mean	$1,903	$2,546	$5,067		$3,075	$2,239	$3,057
Median	$875	$1,375	$2,000		$2,000	$900	$1,500
Responses	22	34	15		10	18	42

Q7. Bookkeeper
(Percent of Respondents) - continued

	Total	Region				2017 Expected Dollar Volume				
		Northeast	Midwest	South	West	Less than $1 million	$1 million to $4,999,999	$5 million to $9,999,999	$10 million to $14,999,999	$15 million or over
Bonus (among only those who actually got bonuses)										
$1 to $999	9			4	30					6
$1,000 to $4,999	53			52	50			45		67
$5,000 to $9,999	29			39	10			27		22
$10,000 or more	9			4	10			27		6
Mean	$4,543			$5,223	$2,730			$5,591		$4,931
Median	$3,000			$3,000	$1,625			$5,000		$2,000
Responses	45			23	10			11		18
Benefits										
Health Insurance	76		73	72	73		50	64	92	88
Dental Insurance	44		36	41	47		21	29	42	65
Vision Program	26		18	25	20		7	21	25	38
Prescription Program	38		27	41	33		14	14	50	58
Life Insurance	33		36	28	27		14	21	25	54
Short Term Disability	21		27	16	13		14	7	33	27
Long Term Disability	21		18	22	13		0	7	42	31
Flex Spending	17		27	9	20		7	0	17	31
401 K	62		91	50	60		29	43	75	85
Paid Vacation Leave	92		100	91	87		93	93	75	100
Paid Sick Leave	67		36	75	73		43	71	50	85
Tuition Reimbursement	17		18	6	27		0	29	25	15
Training	35		18	28	40		50	36	17	35
Other	6		9	3	0		0	21	0	4
Responses	66		11	32	15		14	14	12	26

Q7. Bookkeeper
(Percent of Respondents) - continued

	2017 Expected Single-Family Starts			Number of Employees			
	1 to 10	11 to 99	100 or more	0 to 2	3 to 4	5 to 9	10 or more
Bonus (among only those who actually got bonuses)							
$1 to $999	15	10				10	7
$1,000 to $4,999	38	50	75			40	67
$5,000 to $9,999	46	25	17			50	15
$10,000 or more		15	8				11
Mean	$3,221	$4,328	$6,333			$4,030	$4,755
Median	$3,000	$3,500	$2,500			$4,500	$2,000
Responses	13	20	12			10	27
Benefits							
Health Insurance	52	83	93		40	57	90
Dental Insurance	33	37	73		10	14	61
Vision Program	14	17	60		0	14	34
Prescription Program	24	30	73		0	14	54
Life Insurance	24	23	67		0	14	49
Short Term Disability	10	27	27		10	7	29
Long Term Disability	5	23	40		0	14	29
Flex Spending	5	10	47		0	0	27
401 K	43	63	87		20	57	76
Paid Vacation Leave	90	90	100		80	86	98
Paid Sick Leave	57	67	80		40	71	71
Tuition Reimbursement	10	17	27		10	21	17
Training	33	33	40		30	29	39
Other	0	10	7		0	0	10
Responses	21	30	15		10	14	41

HUMAN RESOURCES JOBS

Q7. Director of Human Resources
(Percent of Respondents)

	Total	Region				2017 Expected Dollar Volume				
		Northeast	Midwest	South	West	Less than $1 million	$1 million to $4,999,999	$5 million to $9,999,999	$10 million to $14,999,999	$15 million or over
Does Position Exist?										
Yes, full-time	2		5	1	3				3	10
Yes, part-time	*	4								2
No	97	96	95	99	97	100	100	100	97	88
Responses	301	24	59	155	63	30	121	58	32	59

Q7. Recruiter
(Percent of Respondents)

	Total	Region				2017 Expected Dollar Volume				
		Northeast	Midwest	South	West	Less than $1 million	$1 million to $4,999,999	$5 million to $9,999,999	$10 million to $14,999,999	$15 million or over
Does Position Exist?										
Yes, full-time	*		2							2
No	100	100	98	100	100	100	100	100	100	98
Responses	301	24	59	155	63	30	121	58	32	59

Q7. In-house legal counsel
(Percent of Respondents)

	Total	Region				2017 Expected Dollar Volume				
		Northeast	Midwest	South	West	Less than $1 million	$1 million to $4,999,999	$5 million to $9,999,999	$10 million to $14,999,999	$15 million or over
Does Position Exist?										
Yes, full-time	1				3					3
Yes, part-time	*		2							2
No	99	100	98	100	97	100	100	100	100	95
Responses	301	24	59	155	63	30	121	58	32	59

HUMAN RESOURCES JOBS

Q7. Director of Human Resources
(Percent of Respondents)

	2017 Expected Single-Family Starts			Number of Employees			
	1 to 10	11 to 99	100 or more	0 to 2	3 to 4	5 to 9	10 or more
Does Position Exist?							
Yes, full-time		1	16				7
Yes, part-time			3				1
No	100	99	81	100	100	100	92
Responses	153	109	31	51	63	87	97

Q7. Recruiter
(Percent of Respondents)

	2017 Expected Single-Family Starts			Number of Employees			
	1 to 10	11 to 99	100 or more	0 to 2	3 to 4	5 to 9	10 or more
Does Position Exist?							
Yes, full-time							1
No	100	100	100	100	100	100	99
Responses	153	109	31	51	63	87	97

Q7. In-house legal counsel
(Percent of Respondents)

	2017 Expected Single-Family Starts			Number of Employees			
	1 to 10	11 to 99	100 or more	0 to 2	3 to 4	5 to 9	10 or more
Does Position Exist?							
Yes, full-time		1	3				2
Yes, part-time		1					1
No	100	98	97	100	100	100	97
Responses	153	109	31	51	63	87	97

	Total	Region				2017 Expected Dollar Volume				
		Northeast	Midwest	South	West	Less than $1 million	$1 million to $4,999,999	$5 million to $9,999,999	$10 million to $14,999,999	$15 million or over
Does Position Exist?										
Yes, full-time	4	8	5	3	3		1	2	6	15
Yes, part-time	1	4		1						
No	96	88	95	97	97	100	99	98	94	85
Responses	301	24	59	155	63	30	121	58	32	59
Salary										
Less then $50,000	9									
$50,000 to $99,999	73									
$100,000 or more	18									
Mean	$70,491									
Median	$62,000									
Responses	11									
Bonus/Commissions										
Yes	45									
No	55									
Responses	11									
Bonus (among all with salary)										
Zero	55									
$1,000 to $4,999	9									
$5,000 to $9,999	18									
$10,000 or more	18									
Mean	$5,773									
Median	$0									
Responses	11									

	2017 Expected Single-Family Starts			Number of Employees			
	1 to 10	11 to 99	100 or more	0 to 2	3 to 4	5 to 9	10 or more
Does Position Exist?							
Yes, full-time	1	5	19			1	10
Yes, part-time						2	
No	99	95	81	100	100	97	90
Responses	153	109	31	51	63	87	97
Salary							
Less then $50,000							
$50,000 to $99,999							80
$100,000 or more							20
Mean							$74,540
Median							$63,500
Responses							10
Bonus/Commissions							
Yes							50
No							50
Responses							10
Bonus (among all with salary)							
Zero							50
$1,000 to $4,999							10
$5,000 to $9,999							20
$10,000 or more							20
Mean							$6,350
Median							$1,500
Responses							10

Q7. Director of IT
(Percent of Respondents)

		Region				2017 Expected Dollar Volume				
	Total	Northeast	Midwest	South	West	Less than $1 million	$1 million to $4,999,999	$5 million to $9,999,999	$10 million to $14,999,999	$15 million or over
Bonus (among only those who actually got bonuses)										
$1,000 to $4,999										
$5,000 to $9,999										
$10,000 or more										
Mean										
Median										
Responses										
Benefits										
Health Insurance	90									
Dental Insurance	80									
Vision Program	60									
Prescription Program	40									
Life Insurance	70									
Short Term Disability	40									
Long Term Disability	60									
Flex Spending	50									
401 K	90									
Paid Vacation Leave	100									
Paid Sick Leave	90									
Tuition Reimbursement	30									
Training	40									
Other	20									
Responses	10									

Q7. Director of IT
(Percent of Respondents)

	2017 Expected Single-Family Starts			Number of Employees			
	1 to 10	11 to 99	100 or more	0 to 2	3 to 4	5 to 9	10 or more
Bonus (among only those who actually got bonuses)							
$1,000 to $4,999							
$5,000 to $9,999							
$10,000 or more							
Mean							
Median							
Responses							
Benefits							
Health Insurance							90
Dental Insurance							80
Vision Program							60
Prescription Program							40
Life Insurance							70
Short Term Disability							40
Long Term Disability							60
Flex Spending							50
401 K							90
Paid Vacation Leave							100
Paid Sick Leave							90
Tuition Reimbursement							30
Training							40
Other							20
Responses							10

Q7. *Network Engineer*
(Percent of Respondents)

	Total	Region				2017 Expected Dollar Volume				
		Northeast	Midwest	South	West	Less than $1 million	$1 million to $4,999,999	$5 million to $9,999,999	$10 million to $14,999,999	$15 million or over
Does Position Exist?										
Yes, full-time	1	4	2		2					5
Yes, part-time	*			1				2		
No	99	96	98	99	98	100	100	98	100	95
Responses	301	24	59	155	63	30	121	58	32	59

Q7. *Web Design Specialist*
(Percent of Respondents)

	Total	Region				2017 Expected Dollar Volume				
		Northeast	Midwest	South	West	Less than $1 million	$1 million to $4,999,999	$5 million to $9,999,999	$10 million to $14,999,999	$15 million or over
Does Position Exist?										
Yes, full-time	3		5	2	5			3	3	10
Yes, part-time	1	4	2	1	2		2			2
No	96	96	93	97	94	100	98	97	97	88
Responses	301	24	59	155	63	30	121	58	32	59
Salary										
Less then $50,000	44									
$50,000 to $99,999	44									
$100,000 or more	11									
Mean	$56,222									
Median	$50,000									
Responses	9									

Q7. Network Engineer
(Percent of Respondents)

	2017 Expected Single-Family Starts			Number of Employees			
	1 to 10	11 to 99	100 or more	0 to 2	3 to 4	5 to 9	10 or more
Does Position Exist?							
Yes, full-time		1	6			1	3
Yes, part-time	1					1	
No	99	99	94	100	100	99	97
Responses	153	109	31	51	63	87	97

Q7. Web Design Specialist
(Percent of Respondents)

	2017 Expected Single-Family Starts			Number of Employees			
	1 to 10	11 to 99	100 or more	0 to 2	3 to 4	5 to 9	10 or more
Does Position Exist?							
Yes, full-time		5	10			1	8
Yes, part-time	1	2		2	2	1	1
No	99	94	90	98	98	98	91
Responses	153	109	31	51	63	87	97
Salary							
Less then $50,000							
$50,000 to $99,999							
$100,000 or more							
Mean							
Median							
Responses							

Q7. Executive Assistant
(Percent of Respondents)

		Region				2017 Expected Dollar Volume				
	Total	Northeast	Midwest	South	West	Less than $1 million	$1 million to $4,999,999	$5 million to $9,999,999	$10 million to $14,999,999	$15 million or over
Does Position Exist?										
Yes, full-time	11	13	14	10	10	3	4	5	23	29
Yes, part-time	1	4	2	1	1		1	1	3	2
No	88	83	84	89	90	97	95	95	74	69
Responses	300	24	58	155	63	30	121	58	31	59
Salary										
Less then $50,000	70			81						76
$50,000 to $99,999	30			19						24
Mean	$44,732			$43,344						$43,927
Median	$45,000			$41,000						$45,000
Responses	33			16						17
Bonus/Commissions										
Yes	61			63						88
No	39			38						12
Responses	33			16						17
Bonus (among all with salary)										
Zero	39			38						12
$1,000 to $4,999	33			38						47
$5,000 to $9,999	18			13						35
$10,000 or more	9			13						6
Mean	$3,955			$4,938						$5,971
Median	$2,000			$2,000						$3,500
Responses	33			16						17

ADMINISTRATIVE JOBS
Q7. Executive Assistant
(Percent of Respondents)

	2017 Expected Single-Family Starts			Number of Employees			
	1 to 10	11 to 99	100 or more	0 to 2	3 to 4	5 to 9	10 or more
Does Position Exist?							
Yes, full-time	5	12	40		6	7	24
Yes, part-time	1	2				1	2
No	95	86	60	100	94	92	74
Responses	153	109	30	51	63	87	96
Salary							
Less then $50,000		77	75				78
$50,000 to $99,999		23	25				22
Mean		$44,085	$43,333				$43,548
Median		$45,000	$42,250				$45,000
Responses		13	12				23
Bonus/Commissions							
Yes		31	92				74
No		69	8				26
Responses		13	12				23
Bonus (among all with salary)							
Zero		69	8				26
$1,000 to $4,999		31	33				43
$5,000 to $9,999			50				26
$10,000 or more			8				4
Mean		$846	$7,625				$4,587
Median		$0	$5,000				$2,500
Responses		13	12				23

Q7. Executive Assistant
(Percent of Respondents)

| | Total | Region | | | | 2017 Expected Dollar Volume | | | | |
		Northeast	Midwest	South	West	Less than $1 million	$1 million to $4,999,999	$5 million to $9,999,999	$10 million to $14,999,999	$15 million or over
Bonus (among only those who actually got bonuses)										
$1,000 to $4,999	55			60						53
$5,000 to $9,999	30			20						40
$10,000 or more	15			20						7
Mean	$6,525			$7,900						$6,767
Median	$3,750			$3,750						$4,000
Responses	20			10						15
Benefits										
Health Insurance	91			94						100
Dental Insurance	52			50						82
Vision Program	45			50						76
Prescription Program	52			44						65
Life Insurance	52			50						88
Short Term Disability	33			31						47
Long Term Disability	30			31						47
Flex Spending	39			19						59
401 K	70			63						94
Paid Vacation Leave	94			88						100
Paid Sick Leave	76			69						88
Tuition Reimbursement	15			6						29
Training	36			25						53
Other	9			0						12
Responses	33			16						17

Q7. Executive Assistant
(Percent of Respondents)

	2017 Expected Single-Family Starts			Number of Employees				
	1 to 10	11 to 99	100 or more	0 to 2	3 to 4	5 to 9	10 or more
Bonus (among only those who actually got bonuses)								
$1,000 to $4,999			36				59
$5,000 to $9,999			55				35
$10,000 or more			9				6
Mean			$8,318				$6,206
Median			$5,000				$3,500
Responses			11				17
Benefits								
Health Insurance		92	100				96
Dental Insurance		38	92				65
Vision Program		38	75				57
Prescription Program		54	67				57
Life Insurance		38	92				65
Short Term Disability		23	50				43
Long Term Disability		15	58				39
Flex Spending		31	58				43
401 K		54	92				78
Paid Vacation Leave		92	100				96
Paid Sick Leave		77	83				83
Tuition Reimbursement		0	33				22
Training		23	58				43
Other		0	8				9
Responses		13	12				23

A-68

Q7. Office Manager
(Percent of Respondents)

		Region				2017 Expected Dollar Volume				
	Total	Northeast	Midwest	South	West	Less than $1 million	$1 million to $4,999,999	$5 million to $9,999,999	$10 million to $14,999,999	$15 million or over
Does Position Exist?										
Yes, full-time	17	8	19	17	16	3	13	16	22	29
Yes, part-time	3	4	3	1	8	7	2	5	3	
No	80	88	78	82	76	90	84	79	75	71
Responses	301	24	59	155	63	30	121	58	32	59
Salary										
Less then $50,000	56		36	73			75			27
$50,000 to $99,999	40		55	27			25			60
$100,000 or more	4		9							13
Mean	$50,287		$61,971	$42,442			$40,668			$63,773
Median	$46,500		$60,000	$40,000			$40,000			$60,000
Responses	48		11	26			16			15
Bonus/Commissions										
Yes	63		64	54			44			87
No	38		36	46			56			13
Responses	48		11	26			16			15
Bonus (among all with salary)										
Zero	38		36	46			56			13
$1 to $999	2			4			6			
$1,000 to $4,999	15			12			19			13
$5,000 to $9,999	29		27	27			13			40
$10,000 or more	17		36	12			6			33
Mean	$5,430		$11,257	$3,704			$2,456			$9,433
Median	$2,750		$5,000	$1,150			$0			$5,000
Responses	48		11	26			16			15

Q7. Office Manager
(Percent of Respondents)

	2017 Expected Single-Family Starts			Number of Employees			
	1 to 10	11 to 99	100 or more	0 to 2	3 to 4	5 to 9	10 or more
Does Position Exist?							
Yes, full-time	10	23	23		8	21	28
Yes, part-time	3	3	3	2	5	3	2
No	86	74	77	98	87	76	70
Responses	153	109	31	51	63	87	97
Salary							
Less then $50,000	63	65				72	36
$50,000 to $99,999	38	26				28	56
$100,000 or more		9					8
Mean	$42,730	$53,961				$41,250	$58,531
Median	$42,840	$45,000				$39,750	$50,000
Responses	16	23				18	25
Bonus/Commissions							
Yes	50	65				44	80
No	50	35				56	20
Responses	16	23				18	25
Bonus (among all with salary)							
Zero	50	35				56	20
$1 to $999	6						
$1,000 to $4,999	19	13				6	24
$5,000 to $9,999	25	35				22	36
$10,000 or more		17				17	20
Mean	$1,769	$6,623				$4,324	$6,980
Median	$150	$5,000				$0	$5,000
Responses	16	23				18	25

Q7. Office Manager
(Percent of Respondents)

	Total	Region				2017 Expected Dollar Volume				
		Northeast	Midwest	South	West	Less than $1 million	$1 million to $4,999,999	$5 million to $9,999,999	$10 million to $14,999,999	$15 million or over
Bonus (among only those who actually got bonuses)										
$1 to $999	3			7						
$1,000 to $4,999	23			21						15
$5,000 to $9,999	47			50						46
$10,000 or more	27			21						38
Mean	$8,688			$6,879						$10,885
Median	$5,000			$5,000						$5,000
Responses	30			14						13
Benefits										
Health Insurance	70		64	70			46			71
Dental Insurance	36		36	30			15			43
Vision Program	30		36	26			8			36
Prescription Program	36		55	26			8			36
Life Insurance	36		36	35			23			43
Short Term Disability	18		18	17			8			21
Long Term Disability	23		18	22			8			29
Flex Spending	11		27	4			0			14
401 K	64		91	52			31			93
Paid Vacation Leave	98		91	100			92			100
Paid Sick Leave	84		73	83			85			86
Tuition Reimbursement	20		18	22			15			21
Training	36		36	43			31			36
Other	7		9	4			8			7
Responses	44		11	23			13			14

Q7. Office Manager
(Percent of Respondents)

	2017 Expected Single-Family Starts			Number of Employees			
	1 to 10	11 to 99	100 or more	0 to 2	3 to 4	5 to 9	10 or more
Bonus (among only those who actually got bonuses)							
$1 to $999							
$1,000 to $4,999		20					30
$5,000 to $9,999		53					45
$10,000 or more		27					25
Mean		$10,155					$8,725
Median		$6,000					$5,000
Responses		15					20
Benefits							
Health Insurance	60	80				59	79
Dental Insurance	20	45				24	50
Vision Program	13	35				24	38
Prescription Program	20	50				29	46
Life Insurance	40	25				12	54
Short Term Disability	13	15				12	25
Long Term Disability	13	25				18	29
Flex Spending	0	10				6	17
401 K	53	60				47	75
Paid Vacation Leave	100	95				94	100
Paid Sick Leave	80	95				88	79
Tuition Reimbursement	20	15				18	25
Training	40	30				29	33
Other	0	10				6	8
Responses	15	20				17	24

Q7. Administrative Assistant
(Percent of Respondents)

	Total	Region				2017 Expected Dollar Volume				
		Northeast	Midwest	South	West	Less than $1 million	$1 million to $4,999,999	$5 million to $9,999,999	$10 million to $14,999,999	$15 million or over
Does Position Exist?										
Yes, full-time	9	8	7	8	13	3	2	12	3	24
Yes, part-time	6	8	7	3	11	10	7	3	3	5
No	85	83	86	88	76	87	90	84	94	71
Responses	300	24	58	155	63	30	121	58	32	58
Salary										
Less then $50,000	88			83						92
$50,000 to $99,999	12			17						8
Mean	$38,473			$39,292						$38,026
Median	$37,700			$37,000						$37,700
Responses	25			12						13
Bonus/Commissions										
Yes	36			33						54
No	64			67						46
Responses	25			12						13
Bonus (among all with salary)										
Zero	64			67						46
$1 to $999	4									8
$1,000 to $4,999	16			8						31
$5,000 to $9,999	8			8						
$10,000 or more	8			17						15
Mean	$2,278			$3,958						$3,612
Median	$0			$0						$700
Responses	25			12						13

Q7. Administrative Assistant
(Percent of Respondents)

	2017 Expected Single-Family Starts			Number of Employees			
	1 to 10	11 to 99	100 or more	0 to 2	3 to 4	5 to 9	10 or more
Does Position Exist?							
Yes, full-time	2	14	27	2	5	7	19
Yes, part-time	7	7			6	8	6
No	92	79	73	98	89	85	75
Responses	153	109	30	51	63	87	96
Salary							
Less then $50,000		92					94
$50,000 to $99,999		8					6
Mean		$37,856					$37,784
Median		$38,000					$37,700
Responses		13					17
Bonus/Commissions							
Yes		15					41
No		85					59
Responses		13					17
Bonus (among all with salary)							
Zero		85					59
$1 to $999							6
$1,000 to $4,999		8					24
$5,000 to $9,999		8					
$10,000 or more							12
Mean		$500					$2,762
Median		$0					$0
Responses		13					17

Q7. Administrative Assistant
(Percent of Respondents)-continued

	Total	Region				2017 Expected Dollar Volume				
		Northeast	Midwest	South	West	Less than $1 million	$1 million to $4,999,999	$5 million to $9,999,999	$10 million to $14,999,999	$15 million or over
Bonus (among only those who actually got bonuses)										
$1 to $999										
$1,000 to $4,999										
$5,000 to $9,999										
$10,000 or more										
Mean										
Median										
Responses										
Benefits										
Health Insurance	84			75						85
Dental Insurance	52			50						69
Vision Program	40			42						46
Prescription Program	44			25						62
Life Insurance	56			67						77
Short Term Disability	32			33						38
Long Term Disability	20			17						23
Flex Spending	32			25						54
401 K	84			83						92
Paid Vacation Leave	96			92						92
Paid Sick Leave	76			75						85
Tuition Reimbursement	16			8						23
Training	56			42						46
Other	8			0						8
Responses	25			12						13

Q7. Administrative Assistant
(Percent of Respondents)-continued

	2017 Expected Single-Family Starts			Number of Employees			
	1 to 10	11 to 99	100 or more	0 to 2	3 to 4	5 to 9	10 or more
Bonus (among only those who actually got bonuses)							
$1 to $999							
$1,000 to $4,999							
$5,000 to $9,999							
$10,000 or more							
Mean							
Median							
Responses							
Benefits							
Health Insurance		85					82
Dental Insurance		54					59
Vision Program		46					41
Prescription Program		38					59
Life Insurance		38					65
Short Term Disability		38					35
Long Term Disability		15					18
Flex Spending		23					41
401 K		77					82
Paid Vacation Leave		100					94
Paid Sick Leave		85					82
Tuition Reimbursement		8					24
Training		54					41
Other		8					12
Responses		13					17

Q7. Receptionist
(Percent of Respondents)

	Total	Region				2017 Expected Dollar Volume				
		Northeast	Midwest	South	West	Less than $1 million	$1 million to $4,999,999	$5 million to $9,999,999	$10 million to $14,999,999	$15 million or over
Does Position Exist?										
Yes, full-time	8	4	14	6	10	3	1	3	13	29
Yes, part-time	2	8	2	1			1		3	5
No	90	88	85	92	90	97	98	97	84	66
Responses	301	24	59	155	63	30	121	58	32	59
Salary										
Less then $50,000	100									100
Mean	$32,464									$32,444
Median	$30,000									$30,000
Responses	22									16
Bonus/Commissions										
Yes	59									63
No	41									38
Responses	22									16
Bonus (among all with salary)										
Zero	41									38
$1 to $999	5									6
$1,000 to $4,999	45									44
$10,000 or more	9									13
Mean	$2,341									$2,781
Median	$1,000									$1,000
Responses	22									16
Bonus (among only those who actually got bonuses)										
$1 to $999	8									10
$1,000 to $4,999	77									70
$10,000 or more	15									20
Mean	$3,962									$4,450
Median	$2,500									$2,500
Responses	13									10

Q7. Receptionist
(Percent of Respondents)

	2017 Expected Single-Family Starts			Number of Employees			
	1 to 10	11 to 99	100 or more	0 to 2	3 to 4	5 to 9	10 or more
Does Position Exist?							
Yes, full-time	1	10	35	2	2	3	21
Yes, part-time	1	3	3				4
No	98	87	61	98	98	97	75
Responses	153	109	31	51	63	87	97
Salary							
Less then $50,000		100	100				100
Mean		$33,112	$30,735				$31,801
Median		$31,000	$28,200				$30,000
Responses		10	11				19
Bonus/Commissions							
Yes		40	73				58
No		60	27				42
Responses		10	11				19
Bonus (among all with salary)							
Zero		60	27				42
$1 to $999		10					5
$1,000 to $4,999		30	55				42
$10,000 or more			18				11
Mean		$750	$3,773				$2,368
Median		$0	$1,500				$1,000
Responses		10	11				19
Bonus (among only those who actually got bonuses)							
$1 to $999							9
$1,000 to $4,999							73
$10,000 or more							18
Mean							$4,091
Median							$2,000
Responses							11

Q7. Receptionist
(Percent of Respondents)

Benefits	Total	Region				2017 Expected Dollar Volume				
		Northeast	Midwest	South	West	Less than $1 million	$1 million to $4,999,999	$5 million to $9,999,999	$10 million to $14,999,999	$15 million or over
Health Insurance	90									93
Dental Insurance	75									86
Vision Program	60									64
Prescription Program	45									50
Life Insurance	55									57
Short Term Disability	40									43
Long Term Disability	35									29
Flex Spending	35									36
401 K	80									86
Paid Vacation Leave	100									100
Paid Sick Leave	70									71
Tuition Reimbursement	30									29
Training	35									50
Other	0									0
Responses	20									14

Q7. Receptionist
(Percent of Respondents)

	2017 Expected Single-Family Starts			Number of Employees			
	1 to 10	11 to 99	100 or more	0 to 2	3 to 4	5 to 9	10 or more
Benefits							
Health Insurance			90				88
Dental Insurance			80				76
Vision Program			50				59
Prescription Program			40				47
Life Insurance			70				59
Short Term Disability			50				35
Long Term Disability			50				35
Flex Spending			40				35
401 K			80				82
Paid Vacation Leave			100				100
Paid Sick Leave			70				65
Tuition Reimbursement			40				24
Training			40				35
Other			0				0
Responses			10				17

Q7. Settlement Coordinator
(Percent of Respondents)

	Total	Region				2017 Expected Dollar Volume				
		Northeast	Midwest	South	West	Less than $1 million	$1 million to $4,999,999	$5 million to $9,999,999	$10 million to $14,999,999	$15 million or over
Does Position Exist?										
Yes, full-time	8	17	2	10	8		2	3	6	32
No	92	83	98	90	92	100	98	97	94	68
Responses	301	24	59	155	63	30	121	58	32	59
Salary										
Less then $50,000	59			54						56
$50,000 to $99,999	36			38						39
$100,000 or more	5			8						6
Mean	$51,486			$53,400						$53,844
Median	$44,500			$48,000						$46,500
Responses	22			13						18
Bonus/Commissions										
Yes	55			62						56
No	45			38						44
Responses	22			13						18
Bonus (among all with salary)										
Zero	45			38						44
$1,000 to $4,999	18			23						17
$5,000 to $9,999	9			8						11
$10,000 or more	27			31						28
Mean	$7,459			$8,308						$7,506
Median	$2,000			$2,500						$2,000
Responses	22			13						18

Q7. Settlement Coordinator
(Percent of Respondents)

	2017 Expected Single-Family Starts			Number of Employees			
	1 to 10	11 to 99	100 or more	0 to 2	3 to 4	5 to 9	10 or more
Does Position Exist?							
Yes, full-time	1	10	42		3	3	21
No	99	90	58	100	97	97	79
Responses	153	109	31	51	63	87	97
Salary							
Less then $50,000			62				58
$50,000 to $99,999			31				37
$100,000 or more			8				5
Mean			$56,631				$53,116
Median			$45,000				$45,000
Responses			13				19
Bonus/Commissions							
Yes			54				58
No			46				42
Responses			13				19
Bonus (among all with salary)							
Zero			46				42
$1,000 to $4,999			23				16
$5,000 to $9,999							11
$10,000 or more			31				32
Mean			$8,469				$8,426
Median			$1,500				$2,500
Responses			13				19

Q7. Settlement Coordinator
(Percent of Respondents)

| | Total | Region | | | | 2017 Expected Dollar Volume | | | | |
		Northeast	Midwest	South	West	Less than $1 million	$1 million to $4,999,999	$5 million to $9,999,999	$10 million to $14,999,999	$15 million or over
Bonus (among only those who actually got bonuses)										
$1,000 to $4,999	33									30
$5,000 to $9,999	17									20
$10,000 or more	50									50
Mean	$13,675									$13,510
Median	$7,500									$7,500
Responses	12									10
Benefits										
Health Insurance	91			85						94
Dental Insurance	55			38						61
Vision Program	32			23						39
Prescription Program	45			54						44
Life Insurance	45			38						50
Short Term Disability	36			23						33
Long Term Disability	41			23						39
Flex Spending	18			8						22
401 K	68			54						67
Paid Vacation Leave	86			77						89
Paid Sick Leave	77			69						78
Tuition Reimbursement	18			8						11
Training	36			15						33
Other	5			0						6
Responses	22			13						18

Q7. Settlement Coordinator
(Percent of Respondents)

	2017 Expected Single-Family Starts			Number of Employees			
	1 to 10	11 to 99	100 or more	0 to 2	3 to 4	5 to 9	10 or more
Bonus (among only those who actually got bonuses)							
$1,000 to $4,999							27
$5,000 to $9,999							18
$10,000 or more							55
Mean							$14,555
Median							$10,000
Responses							11
Benefits							
Health Insurance			92				95
Dental Insurance			54				63
Vision Program			31				37
Prescription Program			38				47
Life Insurance			54				47
Short Term Disability			38				37
Long Term Disability			38				42
Flex Spending			31				21
401 K			69				68
Paid Vacation Leave			85				84
Paid Sick Leave			77				74
Tuition Reimbursement			15				11
Training			38				32
Other			8				5
Responses			13				19

PRODUCTION JOBS
Q7. Production Manager
(Percent of Respondents)

		Region				2017 Expected Dollar Volume				
	Total	Northeast	Midwest	South	West	Less than $1 million	$1 million to $4,999,999	$5 million to $9,999,999	$10 million to $14,999,999	$15 million or over
Does Position Exist?										
Yes, full-time	15	17	20	10	19		10	22	16	22
Yes, part-time	*	4					1			
No	85	79	80	90	81	100	89	78	84	78
Responses	301	24	59	155	63	30	121	58	32	59
Is it filled by person(s) with experience in construction trades?										
Always	78									
Sometimes	22									
Responses	23									
Salary										
Less then $50,000	16		9	31			25	33		
$50,000 to $99,999	74		82	69	75		75	67		69
$100,000 or more	9		9		25					31
Mean	$69,520		$74,468	$65,766	$72,457		$58,458	$58,083		$91,202
Median	$65,000		$75,000	$73,250	$61,250		$60,000	$53,929		$82,500
Responses	43		11	16	12		12	12		13
Bonus/Commissions										
Yes	79		100	69	83		58	83		85
No	21			31	17		42	17		15
Responses	43		11	16	12		12	12		13
Bonus (among all with salary)										
Zero	21			31	17		42	17		15
$1,000 to $4,999	14		9		42		17	8		8
$5,000 to $9,999	28		45	31	8		25	33		15
$10,000 or more	37		45	38	33		17	42		62
Mean	$11,137		$13,277	$13,938	$6,821		$3,708	$14,920		$17,181
Median	$6,000		$7,000	$6,000	$2,500		$2,250	$5,200		$15,000
Responses	43		11	16	12		12	12		13

PRODUCTION JOBS
Q7. Production Manager
(Percent of Respondents)

	2017 Expected Single-Family Starts			Number of Employees			
	1 to 10	11 to 99	100 or more	0 to 2	3 to 4	5 to 9	10 or more
Does Position Exist?							
Yes, full-time	8	17	29	2	8	17	24
Yes, part-time	1					1	
No	92	83	71	98	92	82	76
Responses	153	109	31	51	63	87	97
Is it filled by person(s) with experience in construction trades?							
Always							86
Sometimes							14
Responses							14
Salary							
Less then $50,000	18	21				27	
$50,000 to $99,999	82	74				73	82
$100,000 or more		5					18
Mean	$62,859	$63,875				$56,453	$82,117
Median	$60,200	$60,000				$54,000	$80,000
Responses	11	19				15	22
Bonus/Commissions							
Yes	73	79				60	91
No	27	21				40	9
Responses	11	19				15	22
Bonus (among all with salary)							
Zero	27	21				40	9
$1,000 to $4,999	27	16				13	18
$5,000 to $9,999	27	26				20	32
$10,000 or more	18	37				27	41
Mean	$4,400	$11,929				$5,976	$12,284
Median	$2,500	$6,000				$1,500	$7,000
Responses	11	19				15	22

Q7. Production Manager
(Percent of Respondents) - continued

	Total	Region				2017 Expected Dollar Volume				
		Northeast	Midwest	South	West	Less than $1 million	$1 million to $4,999,999	$5 million to $9,999,999	$10 million to $14,999,999	$15 million or over
Bonus (among only those who actually got bonuses)										
$1,000 to $4,999	18		9		50			10		9
$5,000 to $9,999	35		45	45	10			40		18
$10,000 or more	47		45	55	40			50		73
Mean	$14,085		$13,277	$20,273	$8,185			$17,904		$20,305
Median	$7,750		$7,000	$10,000	$5,000			$12,700		$15,000
Responses	34		11	11	10			10		11
Benefits										
Health Insurance	72		82	64	70			67		100
Dental Insurance	44		64	29	50			42		77
Vision Program	33		55	21	30			33		62
Prescription Program	36		55	29	30			25		69
Life Insurance	44		55	29	40			25		77
Short Term Disability	33		55	21	20			17		54
Long Term Disability	26		36	14	20			8		54
Flex Spending	28		45	14	30			17		62
401 K	64		91	36	70			58		85
Paid Vacation Leave	100		100	100	100			100		100
Paid Sick Leave	77		73	71	80			50		92
Tuition Reimbursement	18		27	7	10			17		38
Training	46		45	36	40			25		62
Other	10		9	7	10			0		23
Responses	39		11	14	10			12		13

Q7. Production Manager
(Percent of Respondents) - continued

	2017 Expected Single-Family Starts			Number of Employees			
	1 to 10	11 to 99	100 or more	0 to 2	3 to 4	5 to 9	10 or more
Bonus (among only those who actually got bonuses)							
$1,000 to $4,999		20					20
$5,000 to $9,999		33					35
$10,000 or more		47					45
Mean		$15,110					$13,513
Median		$8,000					$7,250
Responses		15					20
Benefits							
Health Insurance	45	75				54	82
Dental Insurance	27	38				31	55
Vision Program	9	31				23	45
Prescription Program	18	31				15	55
Life Insurance	27	31				23	59
Short Term Disability	18	19				15	45
Long Term Disability	0	13				8	36
Flex Spending	0	13				15	41
401 K	55	56				54	77
Paid Vacation Leave	100	100				100	100
Paid Sick Leave	73	75				69	82
Tuition Reimbursement	0	19				15	23
Training	27	44				46	41
Other	9	6				0	14
Responses	11	16				13	22

Q7. Land Manager
(Percent of Respondents)

	Total	Region				2017 Expected Dollar Volume				
		Northeast	Midwest	South	West	Less than $1 million	$1 million to $4,999,999	$5 million to $9,999,999	$10 million to $14,999,999	$15 million or over
Does Position Exist?										
Yes, full-time	2		2	1	5					10
No	98	100	98	99	95	100	100	100	100	90
Responses	301	24	59	155	63	30	121	58	32	59
Is it filled by person(s) with experience in construction trades?										
Always										
Sometimes										
Responses										
Salary										
$50,000 to $99,999	67									
$100,000 or more	33									
Mean	$87,500									
Median	$92,500									
Responses	6									

Q7. Land Manager
(Percent of Respondents)

	2017 Expected Single-Family Starts			Number of Employees			
	1 to 10	11 to 99	100 or more	0 to 2	3 to 4	5 to 9	10 or more
Does Position Exist?							
Yes, full-time		1	13				6
No	100	99	87	100	100	100	94
Responses	153	109	31	51	63	87	97
Is it filled by person(s) with experience in construction trades?							
Always							
Sometimes							
Responses							
Salary							
$50,000 to $99,999							
$100,000 or more							
Mean							
Median							
Responses							

A-90

Q7. Purchasing Manager
(Percent of Respondents)

	Total	Region				2017 Expected Dollar Volume				
		Northeast	Midwest	South	West	Less than $1 million	$1 million to $4,999,999	$5 million to $9,999,999	$10 million to $14,999,999	$15 million or over
Does Position Exist?										
Yes, full-time	5	4	5	5	6				6	24
No	95	96	95	95	94	100	100	100	94	76
Responses	301	24	59	155	63	30	121	58	32	59
Is it filled by person(s) with experience in construction trades?										
Always	70									
Sometimes	20									
Never/Almost never	10									
Responses	10									
Salary										
Less then $50,000	6									7
$50,000 to $99,999	81									79
$100,000 or more	13									14
Mean	$69,875									$70,929
Median	$65,000									$65,000
Responses	16									14
Bonus/Commissions										
Yes	81									79
No	19									21
Responses	16									14
Bonus (among all with salary)										
Zero	19									21
$1,000 to $4,999	13									7
$5,000 to $9,999	25									21
$10,000 or more	44									50
Mean	$12,031									$13,179
Median	$5,500									$8,000
Responses	16									14

Q7. Purchasing Manager
(Percent of Respondents)

	2017 Expected Single-Family Starts			Number of Employees			
	1 to 10	11 to 99	100 or more	0 to 2	3 to 4	5 to 9	10 or more
Does Position Exist?							
Yes, full-time		5	32				16
No	100	95	68	100	100	100	84
Responses	153	109	31	51	63	87	97
Is it filled by person(s) with experience in construction trades?							
Always							70
Sometimes							20
Never/Almost never							10
Responses							10
Salary							
Less then $50,000			10				6
$50,000 to $99,999			80				81
$100,000 or more			10				13
Mean			$67,100				$69,875
Median			$62,500				$65,000
Responses			10				16
Bonus/Commissions							
Yes			70				81
No			30				19
Responses			10				16
Bonus (among all with salary)							
Zero			30				19
$1,000 to $4,999			10				13
$5,000 to $9,999			20				25
$10,000 or more			40				44
Mean			$8,400				$12,031
Median			$5,500				$5,500
Responses			10				16

Q7. Purchasing Manager
(Percent of Respondents) - continued

	Total	Region				2017 Expected Dollar Volume				
		Northeast	Midwest	South	West	Less than $1 million	$1 million to $4,999,999	$5 million to $9,999,999	$10 million to $14,999,999	$15 million or over
Bonus (among only those who actually got bonuses)										
$1,000 to $4,999	15									9
$5,000 to $9,999	31									27
$10,000 or more	54									64
Mean	$14,808									$16,773
Median	$10,000									$12,000
Responses	13									11
Benefits										
Health Insurance	93									92
Dental Insurance	73									69
Vision Program	53									54
Prescription Program	47									54
Life Insurance	53									54
Short Term Disability	47									46
Long Term Disability	47									46
Flex Spending	47									38
401 K	80									77
Paid Vacation Leave	100									100
Paid Sick Leave	87									92
Tuition Reimbursement	40									38
Training	40									46
Other	13									15
Responses	15									13

Q7. Purchasing Manager
(Percent of Respondents) - continued

	2017 Expected Single-Family Starts			Number of Employees			
	1 to 10	11 to 99	100 or more	0 to 2	3 to 4	5 to 9	10 or more
Bonus (among only those who actually got bonuses)							
$1,000 to $4,999							15
$5,000 to $9,999							31
$10,000 or more							54
Mean							$14,808
Median							$10,000
Responses							13
Benefits							
Health Insurance							93
Dental Insurance							73
Vision Program							53
Prescription Program							47
Life Insurance							53
Short Term Disability							47
Long Term Disability							47
Flex Spending							47
401 K							80
Paid Vacation Leave							100
Paid Sick Leave							87
Tuition Reimbursement							40
Training							40
Other							13
Responses							15

Q7. Home Services/Warranty Manager
(Percent of Respondents)

	Total	Region				2017 Expected Dollar Volume				
		Northeast	Midwest	South	West	Less than $1 million	$1 million to $4,999,999	$5 million to $9,999,999	$10 million to $14,999,999	$15 million or over
Does Position Exist?										
Yes, full-time	16	13	17	14	19	7	2		10	22	51
Yes, part-time	2	8		1	5				9	5
No	82	79	83	85	76	93	98		90	69	44
Responses	301	24	59	155	63	30	121		58	32	59
Is it filled by person(s) with experience in construction trades?										
Always	70			70						71
Sometimes	30			30						29
Responses	23			10						17
Salary										
Less then $50,000	31			29	33					27
$50,000 to $99,999	69			71	67					73
Mean	$53,373			$51,662	$56,167					$54,753
Median	$50,000			$50,000	$55,000					$53,950
Responses	45			21	12					30
Bonus/Commissions										
Yes	76			67	100					70
No	24			33						30
Responses	45			21	12					30
Bonus (among all with salary)										
Zero	24			33						30
$1,000 to $4,999	33			24						30
$5,000 to $9,999	22			19						17
$10,000 or more	20			24						23
Mean	$6,938			$8,238	$4,808					$7,933
Median	$3,000			$3,000	$4,000					$3,500
Responses	45			21	12					30

Q7. Home Services/Warranty Manager
(Percent of Respondents)

	2017 Expected Single-Family Starts			Number of Employees			
	1 to 10	11 to 99	100 or more	0 to 2	3 to 4	5 to 9	10 or more
Does Position Exist?							
Yes, full-time	5	18	58	2	2	6	41
Yes, part-time	1	4	3			1	5
No	94	78	39	98	98	93	54
Responses	153	109	31	51	63	87	97
Is it filled by person(s) with experience in construction trades?							
Always		100	50				71
Sometimes			50				29
Responses		10	10				21
Salary							
Less then $50,000		40	22				26
$50,000 to $99,999		60	78				74
Mean		$51,380	$55,456				$55,226
Median		$50,000	$58,600				$53,000
Responses		20	18				39
Bonus/Commissions							
Yes		75	78				74
No		25	22				26
Responses		20	18				39
Bonus (among all with salary)							
Zero		25	22				26
$1,000 to $4,999		20	39				33
$5,000 to $9,999		35	17				23
$10,000 or more		20	22				18
Mean		$5,300	$9,139				$6,949
Median		$5,000	$3,000				$3,000
Responses		20	18				39

Q7. Home Services/Warranty Manager
(Percent of Respondents) - continued

	Total	Region				2017 Expected Dollar Volume				
		Northeast	Midwest	South	West	Less than $1 million	$1 million to $4,999,999	$5 million to $9,999,999	$10 million to $14,999,999	$15 million or over
Bonus (among only those who actually got bonuses)										
$1,000 to $4,999	44			36	67					43
$5,000 to $9,999	29			29	17					24
$10,000 or more	26			36	17					33
Mean	$9,182			$12,357	$4,808					$11,333
Median	$5,000			$5,000	$4,000					$5,000
Responses	34			14	12					21
Benefits										
Health Insurance	89			95	83					90
Dental Insurance	66			60	75					69
Vision Program	41			35	50					45
Prescription Program	45			45	42					55
Life Insurance	48			45	33					59
Short Term Disability	32			30	17					31
Long Term Disability	27			20	17					24
Flex Spending	30			20	33					34
401 K	80			65	92					79
Paid Vacation Leave	98			95	100					100
Paid Sick Leave	84			80	92					86
Tuition Reimbursement	18			10	17					17
Training	30			15	42					38
Other	9			10	0					7
Responses	44			20	12					29

Q7. Home Services/Warranty Manager
(Percent of Respondents) - continued

	2017 Expected Single-Family Starts			Number of Employees			
	1 to 10	11 to 99	100 or more	0 to 2	3 to 4	5 to 9	10 or more
Bonus (among only those who actually got bonuses)							
$1,000 to $4,999		27	50				45
$5,000 to $9,999		47	21				31
$10,000 or more		27	29				24
Mean		$7,067	$11,750				$9,345
Median		$5,000	$4,500				$5,000
Responses		15	14				29
Benefits							
Health Insurance		85	94				92
Dental Insurance		75	65				71
Vision Program		35	47				42
Prescription Program		35	59				50
Life Insurance		40	65				53
Short Term Disability		25	35				34
Long Term Disability		20	35				29
Flex Spending		25	41				32
401 K		85	71				82
Paid Vacation Leave		95	100				97
Paid Sick Leave		90	76				82
Tuition Reimbursement		0	29				18
Training		20	41				32
Other		10	6				8
Responses		20	17				38

Q7. Contract Manager
(Percent of Respondents)

	Total	Region				2017 Expected Dollar Volume				
		Northeast	Midwest	South	West	Less than $1 million	$1 million to $4,999,999	$5 million to $9,999,999	$10 million to $14,999,999	$15 million or over
Does Position Exist?										
Yes, full-time	3	4	5	3	2	3				14
No	97	96	95	97	98	97	100	100	100	86
Responses	301	24	59	155	63	30	121	58	32	59
Salary										
Less then $50,000	44									
$50,000 to $99,999	33									
$100,000 or more	22									
Mean	$62,222									
Median	$50,000									
Responses	9									

Q7. Contract Manager
(Percent of Respondents)

	2017 Expected Single-Family Starts			Number of Employees			
	1 to 10	11 to 99	100 or more	0 to 2	3 to 4	5 to 9	10 or more
Does Position Exist?							
Yes, full-time	1	1	19			1	8
No	99	99	81	100	100	99	92
Responses	153	109	31	51	63	87	97
Salary							
Less then $50,000							
$50,000 to $99,999							
$100,000 or more							
Mean							
Median							
Responses							

A-100

Q7. Project Manager
(Percent of Respondents)

	Total	Region				2017 Expected Dollar Volume				
		Northeast	Midwest	South	West	Less than $1 million	$1 million to $4,999,999	$5 million to $9,999,999	$10 million to $14,999,999	$15 million or over
Does Position Exist?										
Yes, full-time	30	30	36	29	27	7	20	41	34	47
Yes, part-time	*				2		1			
No	70	70	64	71	71	93	79	59	66	53
Responses	297	23	59	153	62	30	118	58	32	58
Salary										
Less then $50,000	16		19	19	6		46	9	10	
$50,000 to $99,999	77		76	70	94		50	87	70	93
$100,000 or more	7		5	12			4	4	20	7
Mean	$67,247		$65,643	$70,331	$62,666		$54,586	$66,281	$77,370	$76,011
Median	$65,000		$60,000	$68,000	$62,500		$52,000	$65,000	$60,000	$70,000
Responses	87		21	43	16		24	23	10	27
Bonus/Commissions										
Yes	74		81	70	81		58	74	70	89
No	26		19	30	19		42	26	30	11
Responses	87		21	43	16		24	23	10	27
Bonus (among all with salary)										
Zero	26		19	30	19		42	26	30	11
$1 to $999	1		2	2			17			
$1,000 to $4,999	10		14	9	13		21	4	20	4
$5,000 to $9,999	20		19	21	25		21	17	20	22
$10,000 or more	43		48	37	44			52	30	63
Mean	$11,670		$13,202	$10,733	$12,283		$7,625	$13,022	$7,400	$16,918
Median	$5,000		$8,000	$5,000	$5,000		$2,500	$15,000	$3,750	$10,000
Responses	87		21	43	16		24	23	10	27

Q7. Project Manager
(Percent of Respondents)

	2017 Expected Single-Family Starts			Number of Employees			
	1 to 10	11 to 99	100 or more	0 to 2	3 to 4	5 to 9	10 or more
Does Position Exist?							
Yes, full-time	25	36	35	6	16	34	49
Yes, part-time		1			2		
No	75	63	65	94	82	66	51
Responses	150	108	31	51	62	85	96
Salary							
Less then $50,000	25	11	9		50	21	7
$50,000 to $99,999	64	89	73		50	72	84
$100,000 or more	11		18			7	9
Mean	$65,788	$64,367	$79,927		$50,044	$65,816	$71,832
Median	$56,060	$65,000	$80,000		$49,000	$60,000	$70,000
Responses	36	38	11		10	29	45
Bonus/Commissions							
Yes	56	82	100		60	55	87
No	44	18			40	45	13
Responses	36	38	11		10	29	45
Bonus (among all with salary)							
Zero	44	18			40	45	13
$1 to $999	17	3				7	2
$1,000 to $4,999	17	5	9		10	7	13
$5,000 to $9,999	22	18	27		20	17	18
$10,000 or more		55	64		30	31	53
Mean	$6,250	$13,954	$20,094		$11,900	$7,690	$14,384
Median	$2,250	$12,500	$12,500		$4,000	$3,000	$10,000
Responses	36	38	11		10	29	45

Q7. Project Manager
(Percent of Respondents) – continued

	Total	Region				2017 Expected Dollar Volume				
		Northeast	Midwest	South	West	Less than $1 million	$1 million to $4,999,999	$5 million to $9,999,999	$10 million to $14,999,999	$15 million or over
Bonus (among only those who actually got bonuses)										
$1 to $999	2			3						
$1,000 to $4,999	14		18	13	15		29	6		4
$5,000 to $9,999	27		24	30	31		36	24		25
$10,000 or more	58		59	53	54		36	71		71
Mean	$15,864		$16,309	$15,383	$15,118		$13,071	$17,618		$19,033
Median	$10,000		$12,500	$10,000	$10,000		$5,500	$15,000		$11,250
Responses	64		17	30	13		14	17		24
Benefits										
Health Insurance	73		65	73	75		60	65	90	89
Dental Insurance	39		35	40	38		15	26	40	70
Vision Program	27		25	28	25		5	26	30	44
Prescription Program	29		35	28	19		5	13	50	56
Life Insurance	27		30	33	6		10	17	30	48
Short Term Disability	23		25	28	13		5	13	40	41
Long Term Disability	17		20	20	13		0	4	40	33
Flex Spending	12		20	10	6		0	9	10	26
401 K	69		90	60	69		35	74	80	89
Paid Vacation Leave	92		95	93	100		95	100	80	89
Paid Sick Leave	70		60	78	75		60	65	70	81
Tuition Reimbursement	17		15	20	6		15	13	30	19
Training	35		20	43	31		30	35	30	41
Other	7		15	3	6		10	13	0	4
Responses	83		20	40	16		20	23	10	27

A-103

Q7. Project Manager
(Percent of Respondents) - continued

	2017 Expected Single-Family Starts			Number of Employees			
	1 to 10	11 to 99	100 or more	0 to 2	3 to 4	5 to 9	10 or more
Bonus (among only those who actually got bonuses)							
$1 to $999		3					3
$1,000 to $4,999	30	6	9			13	15
$5,000 to $9,999	30	23	27			31	21
$10,000 or more	40	68	64			56	62
Mean	$11,250	$17,105	$20,094			$13,938	$16,597
Median	$5,500	$15,000	$12,500			$12,500	$10,000
Responses	20	31	11			16	39
Benefits							
Health Insurance	65	72	100			59	87
Dental Insurance	18	42	91			19	58
Vision Program	9	31	64			22	36
Prescription Program	15	33	55			4	51
Life Insurance	15	19	82			15	40
Short Term Disability	9	19	73			11	36
Long Term Disability	3	11	73			7	27
Flex Spending	0	8	55			4	20
401 K	59	69	91			63	80
Paid Vacation Leave	91	92	91			93	91
Paid Sick Leave	59	78	73			74	69
Tuition Reimbursement	15	8	45			19	18
Training	29	31	64			30	38
Other	6	8	0			7	7
Responses	34	36	11			27	45

Q7. Architect
(Percent of Respondents)

		Region				2017 Expected Dollar Volume				
	Total	Northeast	Midwest	South	West	Less than $1 million	$1 million to $4,999,999	$5 million to $9,999,999	$10 million to $14,999,999	$15 million or over
Does Position Exist?										
Yes, full-time	10	4	15	7	13	3	2	5	19	27
Yes, part-time	1	4		1			1	3		
No	89	92	85	92	87	97	97	91	81	73
Responses	301	24	59	155	63	30	121	58	32	59
Salary										
Less then $50,000	21			18						25
$50,000 to $99,999	68			82						63
$100,000 or more	11									13
Mean	$80,858			$62,136						$66,219
Median	$64,500			$65,000						$62,000
Responses	28			11						16
Bonus/Commissions										
Yes	68			82						88
No	32			18						13
Responses	28			11						16
Bonus (among all with salary)										
Zero	32			18						13
$1,000 to $4,999	18			9						19
$5,000 to $9,999	18			18						25
$10,000 or more	32			55						44
Mean	$10,461			$17,864						$12,969
Median	$4,500			$10,000						$5,000
Responses	28			11						16

Q7. Architect
(Percent of Respondents)

	2017 Expected Single-Family Starts			Number of Employees			
	1 to 10	11 to 99	100 or more	0 to 2	3 to 4	5 to 9	10 or more
Does Position Exist?							
Yes, full-time	4	13	29		2	7	23
Yes, part-time		3				3	
No	96	84	71	100	98	90	77
Responses	153	109	31	51	63	87	97
Salary							
Less then $50,000		23					24
$50,000 to $99,999		69					62
$100,000 or more		8					14
Mean		$65,374					$87,032
Median		$64,000					$64,000
Responses		13					21
Bonus/Commissions							
Yes		77					86
No		23					14
Responses		13					21
Bonus (among all with salary)							
Zero		23					14
$1,000 to $4,999		23					24
$5,000 to $9,999		15					24
$10,000 or more		38					38
Mean		$10,577					$11,567
Median		$5,000					$5,000
Responses		13					21

Q7. Architect
(Percent of Respondents)

	Total	Region				2017 Expected Dollar Volume				
		Northeast	Midwest	South	West	Less than $1 million	$1 million to $4,999,999	$5 million to $9,999,999	$10 million to $14,999,999	$15 million or over
Bonus (among only those who actually got bonuses)										
$1,000 to $4,999	26									21
$5,000 to $9,999	26									29
$10,000 or more	47									50
Mean	$15,416									$14,821
Median	$5,400									$7,500
Responses	19									14
Benefits										
Health Insurance	88									100
Dental Insurance	62									80
Vision Program	35									40
Prescription Program	38									60
Life Insurance	38									47
Short Term Disability	27									33
Long Term Disability	23									33
Flex Spending	23									33
401 K	81									93
Paid Vacation Leave	85									100
Paid Sick Leave	58									87
Tuition Reimbursement	19									20
Training	35									47
Other	0									0
Responses	26									15

Q7. Architect
(Percent of Respondents)

	2017 Expected Single-Family Starts			Number of Employees			
	1 to 10	11 to 99	100 or more	0 to 2	3 to 4	5 to 9	10 or more
Bonus (among only those who actually got bonuses)							
$1,000 to $4,999		30					28
$5,000 to $9,999		20					28
$10,000 or more		50					44
Mean		$13,750					$13,494
Median		$7,500					$5,200
Responses		10					18
Benefits							
Health Insurance		100					100
Dental Insurance		73					74
Vision Program		27					42
Prescription Program		36					53
Life Insurance		27					47
Short Term Disability		18					37
Long Term Disability		9					32
Flex Spending		18					32
401 K		91					89
Paid Vacation Leave		73					95
Paid Sick Leave		55					74
Tuition Reimbursement		9					26
Training		18					47
Other		0					0
Responses		11					19

Q7. Estimator
(Percent of Respondents)

		Region				2017 Expected Dollar Volume				
	Total	Northeast	Midwest	South	West	Less than $1 million	$1 million to $4,999,999	$5 million to $9,999,999	$10 million to $14,999,999	$15 million or over
Does Position Exist?										
Yes, full-time	15	17	24	14	8	3	6	16	19	38
Yes, part-time	2	4	2	3			4	2	3	3
No	83	79	75	82	92	97	90	83	78	62
Responses	299	24	59	154	62	29	121	58	32	58
Salary										
Less then $50,000	21		38	10						18
$50,000 to $99,999	79		62	90						82
Mean	$55,306		$50,462	$57,823						$55,568
Median	$55,000		$50,000	$58,000						$56,500
Responses	43		13	21						22
Bonus/Commissions										
Yes	70		77	67						86
No	30		23	33						14
Responses	43		13	21						22
Bonus (among all with salary)										
Zero	30		23	33						14
$1,000 to $4,999	26		38	19						32
$5,000 to $9,999	26		23	33						23
$10,000 or more	19		15	14						32
Mean	$5,466		$4,000	$6,286						$8,411
Median	$3,000		$2,500	$4,000						$5,000
Responses	43		13	21						22

Q7. Estimator
(Percent of Respondents)

	2017 Expected Single-Family Starts			Number of Employees			
	1 to 10	11 to 99	100 or more	0 to 2	3 to 4	5 to 9	10 or more
Does Position Exist?							
Yes, full-time	10	12	45		2	7	39
Yes, part-time	4	1				7	1
No	86	87	55	100	98	86	60
Responses	153	107	31	51	63	87	95
Salary							
Less then $50,000	14	23	21				22
$50,000 to $99,999	86	77	79				78
Mean	$57,446	$53,462	$55,564				$55,479
Median	$57,443	$55,000	$56,500				$55,000
Responses	14	13	14				36
Bonus/Commissions							
Yes	50	69	86				81
No	50	31	14				19
Responses	14	13	14				36
Bonus (among all with salary)							
Zero	50	31	14				19
$1,000 to $4,999	21	31	21				31
$5,000 to $9,999	29	23	29				31
$10,000 or more		15	36				19
Mean	$1,929	$3,923	$10,396				$6,251
Median	$500	$4,000	$5,000				$4,500
Responses	14	13	14				36

Q7. Estimator
(Percent of Respondents) - continued

| | Total | Region | | | | 2017 Expected Dollar Volume | | | | |
		Northeast	Midwest	South	West	Less than $1 million	$1 million to $4,999,999	$5 million to $9,999,999	$10 million to $14,999,999	$15 million or over
Bonus (among only those who actually got bonuses)										
$1,000 to $4,999	37		50	29						37
$5,000 to $9,999	37		30	50						26
$10,000 or more	27		20	21						37
Mean	$7,835		$5,200	$9,429						$9,739
Median	$5,000		$4,000	$5,000						$5,000
Responses	30		10	14						19
Benefits										
Health Insurance	81		69	90						91
Dental Insurance	49		46	57						68
Vision Program	40		38	43						59
Prescription Program	40		31	48						59
Life Insurance	49		46	57						64
Short Term Disability	35		38	33						45
Long Term Disability	30		31	33						45
Flex Spending	26		31	19						45
401 K	79		92	71						91
Paid Vacation Leave	88		92	86						95
Paid Sick Leave	70		54	76						77
Tuition Reimbursement	26		23	24						27
Training	51		38	52						50
Other	7		15	0						9
Responses	43		13	21						22

	2017 Expected Single-Family Starts			Number of Employees			
	1 to 10	11 to 99	100 or more	0 to 2	3 to 4	5 to 9	10 or more
Bonus (among only those who actually got bonuses)							
$1,000 to $4,999			25				38
$5,000 to $9,999			33				38
$10,000 or more			42				24
Mean			$12,129				$7,760
Median			$5,500				$5,000
Responses			12				29
Benefits							
Health Insurance	71	77	93				89
Dental Insurance	29	31	79				53
Vision Program	21	15	71				42
Prescription Program	21	31	64				47
Life Insurance	36	31	79				53
Short Term Disability	29	8	57				36
Long Term Disability	14	8	64				33
Flex Spending	0	15	50				28
401 K	64	85	86				81
Paid Vacation Leave	71	92	100				94
Paid Sick Leave	64	69	71				72
Tuition Reimbursement	21	8	36				22
Training	57	38	50				50
Other	0	8	7				8
Responses	14	13	14				36

Q7. Superintendent
(Percent of Respondents)

		Region				2017 Expected Dollar Volume				
	Total	Northeast	Midwest	South	West	Less than $1 million	$1 million to $4,999,999	$5 million to $9,999,999	$10 million to $14,999,999	$15 million or over
Does Position Exist?										
Yes, full-time	44	38	41	40	59	20	31	47	50	76
Yes, part-time	1	4	1	1	2		1	4	3	3
No	55	58	59	59	40	80	68	49	47	24
Responses	299	24	59	153	63	30	120	57	32	59
Salary										
Less then $50,000	20		17	28	14		26	24	7	13
$50,000 to $99,999	78		83	71	83		71	72	87	87
$100,000 or more	2			2	3		3	4	7	
Mean	$59,888		$57,346	$56,288	$64,925		$54,997	$59,978	$65,473	$63,365
Median	$60,000		$55,000	$55,000	$65,000		$52,000	$55,000	$65,000	$65,000
Responses	126		23	58	36		35	25	15	45
Bonus/Commissions										
Yes	67		52	71	81		49	76	67	80
No	33		48	29	19		51	24	33	20
Responses	126		23	58	36		35	25	25	45
Bonus (among all with salary)										
Zero	33		48	29	19		51	24	24	20
$1 to $999	2		3	3	3		3	4	4	
$1,000 to $4,999	10		9	9	14		11	8	20	4
$5,000 to $9,999	21		22	19	28		14	32	20	24
$10,000 or more	33		22	40	36		20	32	27	51
Mean	$7,818		$3,951	$9,941	$8,293		$3,403	$7,360	$4,567	$13,520
Median	$5,000		$1,500	$5,000	$5,000		$0	$5,000	$2,500	$10,000
Responses	126		23	58	36		35	25	15	45

Q7. Superintendent
(Percent of Respondents)

	2017 Expected Single-Family Starts			Number of Employees			
	1 to 10	11 to 99	100 or more	0 to 2	3 to 4	5 to 9	10 or more
Does Position Exist?							
Yes, full-time	35	45	84	16	29	42	70
Yes, part-time	1	2		2	3	1	
No	64	53	16	82	68	56	30
Responses	152	108	31	51	63	85	97
Salary							
Less then $50,000	20	21	15		22	21	17
$50,000 to $99,999	74	79	85		78	74	82
$100,000 or more	6					6	2
Mean	$59,734	$57,961	$64,385		$51,278	$62,356	$61,675
Median	$55,500	$55,000	$65,000		$51,000	$61,000	$60,000
Responses	50	47	26		18	34	66
Bonus/Commissions							
Yes	56	68	88		50	59	77
No	44	32	12		50	41	23
Responses	50	47	26		18	34	66
Bonus (among all with salary)							
Zero	44	32	12		50	41	23
$1 to $999	4	2			6	6	2
$1,000 to $4,999	16	9	23		6	12	11
$5,000 to $9,999	16	26	23		22	18	24
$10,000 or more	20	32	65		22	24	41
Mean	$4,090	$6,712	$17,636		$4,061	$4,309	$10,703
Median	$1,250	$5,000	$14,500		$750	$1,750	$5,000
Responses	50	47	26		18	34	66

Q7. Superintendent
(Percent of Respondents) - continued

	Total	Region				2017 Expected Dollar Volume				
		Northeast	Midwest	South	West	Less than $1 million	$1 million to $4,999,999	$5 million to $9,999,999	$10 million to $14,999,999	$15 million or over
Bonus (among only those who actually got bonuses)										
$1 to $999	4			5	3		6	5		
$1,000 to $4,999	15		17	12	17		24	11	30	6
$5,000 to $9,999	32		42	27	34		29	42	30	31
$10,000 or more	49		42	56	45		41	42	40	64
Mean	$11,588		$7,573	$14,063	$10,294		$7,006	$9,684	$6,850	$16,900
Median	$8,000		$6,500	$10,000	$6,000		$5,000	$7,000	$6,500	$11,938
Responses	85		12	41	29		17	19	10	36
Benefits										
Health Insurance	73		75	67	79		55	63	79	91
Dental Insurance	42		45	31	52		10	29	43	71
Vision Program	25		20	20	33		3	13	29	47
Prescription Program	32		35	30	33		3	25	29	56
Life Insurance	31		30	33	27		14	13	36	53
Short Term Disability	22		30	17	21		7	21	21	33
Long Term Disability	17		20	13	21		3	4	21	33
Flex Spending	18		25	11	24		3	13	14	33
401 K	63		85	48	76		34	58	71	80
Paid Vacation Leave	94		85	94	97		90	96	93	98
Paid Sick Leave	73		45	78	82		72	58	64	84
Tuition Reimbursement	15		15	11	15		10	17	7	20
Training	37		30	31	42		34	38	21	42
Other	6		10	4	3		3	13	0	7
Responses	115		20	54	33		29	24	14	45

Q7. Superintendent
(Percent of Respondents) - continued

	2017 Expected Single-Family Starts			Number of Employees			
	1 to 10	11 to 99	100 or more	0 to 2	3 to 4	5 to 9	10 or more
Bonus (among only those who actually got bonuses)							
$1 to $999	7	3				10	2
$1,000 to $4,999	29	13				20	14
$5,000 to $9,999	29	38	26			30	31
$10,000 or more	36	47	74			40	53
Mean	$7,304	$9,859	$19,936			$7,325	$13,851
Median	$5,000	$8,000	$15,000			$6,000	$10,000
Responses	28	32	23			20	51
Benefits							
Health Insurance	60	71	96		33	65	88
Dental Insurance	16	50	69		8	29	57
Vision Program	7	26	50		0	16	35
Prescription Program	16	33	58		0	16	49
Life Insurance	13	29	65		0	19	45
Short Term Disability	11	19	38		8	19	26
Long Term Disability	4	14	42		0	10	26
Flex Spending	2	17	42		17	6	25
401 K	56	62	73		42	58	71
Paid Vacation Leave	91	95	96		92	84	98
Paid Sick Leave	69	74	77		75	61	77
Tuition Reimbursement	9	12	23		8	16	15
Training	38	26	46		25	42	37
Other	2	10	4		8	0	9
Responses	45	42	26		12	31	65

SALES & MARKETING JOBS
Q7. Sales Manager
(Percent of Respondents)

	Total	Region				2017 Expected Dollar Volume				
		Northeast	Midwest	South	West	Less than $1 million	$1 million to $4,999,999	$5 million to $9,999,999	$10 million to $14,999,999	$15 million or over
Does Position Exist?										
Yes, full-time	7	4	12	5	10	3	2	3	9	22
Yes, part-time	1	1		1						3
No	92	96	88	94	90	97	98	97	91	75
Responses	301	24	59	155	63	30	121	58	32	59
Salary										
Less then $50,000	33									31
$50,000 to $99,999	50									54
$100,000 or more	17									15
Mean	$65,142									$65,120
Median	$62,500									$65,000
Responses	18									13
Bonus/Commissions										
Yes	83									85
No	17									15
Responses	18									13
Bonus (among all with salary)										
Zero	17									15
$1,000 to $4,999	6									8
$10,000 or more	78									77
Mean	$48,444									$43,385
Median	$17,500									$15,000
Responses	18									13
Bonus (among only those who actually got bonuses)										
$1,000 to $4,999	7									9
$10,000 or more	93									91
Mean	$58,133									$51,273
Median	$22,500									$22,500
Responses	15									11

	2017 Expected Single-Family Starts			Number of Employees			
	1 to 10	11 to 99	100 or more	0 to 2	3 to 4	5 to 9	10 or more
Does Position Exist?							
Yes, full-time	3	6	26		3	3	16
Yes, part-time		1	3			1	1
No	97	93	71	100	97	95	82
Responses	153	109	31	51	63	87	97
Salary							
Less then $50,000							27
$50,000 to $99,999							53
$100,000 or more							20
Mean							$72,038
Median							$75,000
Responses							15
Bonus/Commissions							
Yes							87
No							13
Responses							15
Bonus (among all with salary)							
Zero							13
$1,000 to $4,999							7
$10,000 or more							80
Mean							$39,800
Median							$15,000
Responses							15
Bonus (among only those who actually got bonuses)							
$1,000 to $4,999							8
$10,000 or more							92
Mean							$45,923
Median							$20,000
Responses							13

Q7. Sales Manager
(Percent of Respondents)

	Total	Region				2017 Expected Dollar Volume				
		Northeast	Midwest	South	West	Less than $1 million	$1 million to $4,999,999	$5 million to $9,999,999	$10 million to $14,999,999	$15 million or over
Benefits										
Health Insurance	86									100
Dental Insurance	62									79
Vision Program	48									57
Prescription Program	43									64
Life Insurance	52									57
Short Term Disability	52									57
Long Term Disability	43									50
Flex Spending	33									43
401 K	86									93
Paid Vacation Leave	95									100
Paid Sick Leave	81									93
Tuition Reimbursement	38									50
Training	48									57
Other	10									14
Responses	21									14

Q7. Model Home Host
(Percent of Respondents)

	Total	Region				2017 Expected Dollar Volume				
		Northeast	Midwest	South	West	Less than $1 million	$1 million to $4,999,999	$5 million to $9,999,999	$10 million to $14,999,999	$15 million or over
Does Position Exist?										
Yes, full-time	3	3	5	3	2				3	14
Yes, part-time	5	4	7	5	5		1	3	13	14
No	92	96	88	92	94	100	99	97	84	73
Responses	301	24	59	155	63	30	121	58	32	59
Salary										
Less then $50,000	100									
Mean	$33,938									
Median	$32,250									
Responses	8									

Q7. Sales Manager
(Percent of Respondents)

Benefits	2017 Expected Single-Family Starts			Number of Employees			
	1 to 10	11 to 99	100 or more	0 to 2	3 to 4	5 to 9	10 or more
Benefits							
Health Insurance							100
Dental Insurance							76
Vision Program							53
Prescription Program							53
Life Insurance							53
Short Term Disability							59
Long Term Disability							47
Flex Spending							41
401 K							88
Paid Vacation Leave							100
Paid Sick Leave							88
Tuition Reimbursement							47
Training							53
Other							12
Responses							17

Q7. Model Home Host
(Percent of Respondents)

	2017 Expected Single-Family Starts			Number of Employees			
	1 to 10	11 to 99	100 or more	0 to 2	3 to 4	5 to 9	10 or more
Does Position Exist?							
Yes, full-time		3	19				9
Yes, part-time	1	7	13	2	2	5	9
No	99	90	68	98	98	95	81
Responses	153	109	31	51	63	87	97
Salary							
Less then $50,000							
Mean							
Median							
Responses							

Q7. Salesperson
(Percent of Respondents)

	Total	Region				2017 Expected Dollar Volume				
		Northeast	Midwest	South	West	Less than $1 million	$1 million to $4,999,999	$5 million to $9,999,999	$10 million to $14,999,999	$15 million or over
Does Position Exist?										
Yes, full-time	16	8	22	15	15	3	4	10	19	52
No	84	92	78	85	85	97	96	90	81	48
Responses	299	24	59	155	61	30	121	58	31	58
Salary										
Less then $50,000	72		45	82	82					76
$50,000 to $99,999	22		45	14	18					14
$100,000 or more	7		9	5						10
Mean	$34,050		$43,500	$25,318	$34,073					$34,855
Median	$30,000		$50,000	$24,000	$32,000					$30,000
Responses	46		11	22	11					29
Bonus/Commissions										
Yes	76		64	86	82					83
No	24		36	14	18					17
Responses	46		11	22	11					29
Bonus (among all with salary)										
Zero	24		36	14	18					17
$5,000 to $9,999	2				9					3
$10,000 or more	74		64	86	73					79
Mean	$64,365		$49,000	$75,945	$68,273					$67,648
Median	$55,000		$44,000	$75,000	$50,000					$60,000
Responses	46		11	22	11					29
Bonus (among only those who actually got bonuses)										
$5,000 to $9,999	3									4
$10,000 or more	97			100						96
Mean	$84,594			$87,937						$81,742
Median	$70,000			$90,000						$65,000
Responses	35			19						24

Q7. Salesperson
(Percent of Respondents)

	2017 Expected Single-Family Starts			Number of Employees			
	1 to 10	11 to 99	100 or more	0 to 2	3 to 4	5 to 9	10 or more
Does Position Exist?							
Yes, full-time	1	23	68		5	8	40
No	99	77	32	100	95	92	60
Responses	153	107	31	51	63	87	95
Salary							
Less then $50,000		68	84				76
$50,000 to $99,999		24	11				16
$100,000 or more		8	5				8
Mean		$37,252	$27,842				$34,166
Median		$30,000	$25,000				$30,000
Responses		25	19				38
Bonus/Commissions							
Yes		72	89				79
No		28	11				21
Responses		25	19				38
Bonus (among all with salary)							
Zero		28	11				21
$5,000 to $9,999		4					3
$10,000 or more		68	89				76
Mean		$57,432	$80,263				$66,758
Median		$50,000	$65,000				$57,500
Responses		25	19				38
Bonus (among only those who actually got bonuses)							
$5,000 to $9,999		6					3
$10,000 or more		94	100				97
Mean		$79,767	$89,706				$84,560
Median		$75,000	$65,000				$72,500
Responses		18	17				30

Q7. Salesperson
(Percent of Respondents) - continued

Benefits	Total	Region				2017 Expected Dollar Volume				
		Northeast	Midwest	South	West	Less than $1 million	$1 million to $4,999,999	$5 million to $9,999,999	$10 million to $14,999,999	$15 million or over
Benefits										
Health Insurance	83		73	85	90					96
Dental Insurance	52		45	40	80					64
Vision Program	38		27	25	70					46
Prescription Program	43		36	40	50					50
Life Insurance	45		36	45	50					57
Short Term Disability	31		27	30	30					39
Long Term Disability	29		27	25	30					32
Flex Spending	29		45	10	40					32
401 K	71		82	55	90					82
Paid Vacation Leave	86		91	80	90					86
Paid Sick Leave	76		64	75	90					82
Tuition Reimbursement	19		27	10	20					21
Training	26		18	15	50					39
Other	5		0	5	0					4
Responses	42		11	20	10					28

Q7. Salesperson
(Percent of Respondents) - continued

	2017 Expected Single-Family Starts			Number of Employees			
	1 to 10	11 to 99	100 or more	0 to 2	3 to 4	5 to 9	10 or more
Benefits							
Health Insurance		80	95				86
Dental Insurance		45	65				58
Vision Program		30	50				42
Prescription Program		40	50				44
Life Insurance		30	65				50
Short Term Disability		20	45				36
Long Term Disability		15	45				33
Flex Spending		20	40				28
401 K		70	75				75
Paid Vacation Leave		90	85				86
Paid Sick Leave		80	75				78
Tuition Reimbursement		5	35				19
Training		10	45				31
Other		5	5				3
Responses		20	20				36

Q7. Design Center Manager
(Percent of Respondents)

	Total	Region				2017 Expected Dollar Volume				
		Northeast	Midwest	South	West	Less than $1 million	$1 million to $4,999,999	$5 million to $9,999,999	$10 million to $14,999,999	$15 million or over
Does Position Exist?										
Yes, full-time	7	4	8	9	3		2	3	6	25
Yes, part-time	1	4		1			1			2
No	92	92	92	90	97	100	97	97	94	73
Responses	301	24	59	155	63	30	121	58	32	59
Salary										
Less then $50,000	32			36						27
$50,000 to $99,999	68			64						73
Mean	$57,701			$58,429						$60,162
Median	$53,000			$55,000						$55,000
Responses	22			14						15
Bonus/Commissions										
Yes	59			57						67
No	41			43						33
Responses	22			14						15
Bonus (among all with salary)										
Zero	41			43						33
$1,000 to $4,999	27			29						27
$5,000 to $9,999	5									7
$10,000 or more	27			29						33
Mean	$7,852			$6,143						$10,183
Median	$2,000			$2,000						$3,000
Responses	22			14						15
Bonus (among only those who actually got bonuses)										
$1,000 to $4,999	46									40
$5,000 to $9,999	8									10
$10,000 or more	46									50
Mean	$13,288									$15,275
Median	$7,500									$8,750
Responses	13									10

Q7. *Design Center Manager*
(Percent of Respondents)

	2017 Expected Single-Family Starts			Number of Employees			
	1 to 10	11 to 99	100 or more	0 to 2	3 to 4	5 to 9	10 or more
Does Position Exist?							
Yes, full-time	2	6	35		2	2	20
Yes, part-time	1	1				1	1
No	97	93	65	100	98	97	79
Responses	153	109	31	51	63	87	97
Salary							
Less then $50,000			36				32
$50,000 to $99,999			64				68
Mean			$57,727				$59,444
Median			$55,000				$55,000
Responses			11				19
Bonus/Commissions							
Yes			73				63
No			27				37
Responses			11				19
Bonus (among all with salary)							
Zero			27				37
$1,000 to $4,999			27				26
$5,000 to $9,999			9				5
$10,000 or more			36				32
Mean			$12,955				$8,987
Median			$4,000				$2,000
Responses			11				19
Bonus (among only those who actually got bonuses)							
$1,000 to $4,999							42
$5,000 to $9,999							8
$10,000 or more							50
Mean							$14,229
Median							$8,750
Responses							12

Q7. Design Center Manager
(Percent of Respondents) - continued

	Total	Region				2017 Expected Dollar Volume				
		Northeast	Midwest	South	West	Less than $1 million	$1 million to $4,999,999	$5 million to $9,999,999	$10 million to $14,999,999	$15 million or over
Benefits										
Health Insurance	82			79						100
Dental Insurance	59			43						67
Vision Program	32			14						40
Prescription Program	50			43						67
Life Insurance	59			50						73
Short Term Disability	50			36						60
Long Term Disability	36			21						40
Flex Spending	45			21						60
401 K	77			64						87
Paid Vacation Leave	86			79						93
Paid Sick Leave	73			71						93
Tuition Reimbursement	27			14						33
Training	45			29						53
Other	9			0						13
Responses	22			14						15

Q7. Design Center Manager
(Percent of Respondents) - continued

Benefits	2017 Expected Single-Family Starts			Number of Employees			
	1 to 10	11 to 99	100 or more	0 to 2	3 to 4	5 to 9	10 or more
Health Insurance			100				95
Dental Insurance			64				68
Vision Program			45				37
Prescription Program			64				58
Life Insurance			73				68
Short Term Disability			55				58
Long Term Disability			55				42
Flex Spending			55				53
401 K			82				79
Paid Vacation Leave			91				89
Paid Sick Leave			82				79
Tuition Reimbursement			36				32
Training			45				47
Other			9				11
Responses			11				19

A-128

Q7. Selections Coordinator
(Percent of Respondents)

	Total	Region				2017 Expected Dollar Volume				
		Northeast	Midwest	South	West	Less than $1 million	$1 million to $4,999,999	$5 million to $9,999,999	$10 million to $14,999,999	$15 million or over
Does Position Exist?										
Yes, full-time	10	8	14	10	5		2	10	16	27
Yes, part-time	3	4		4	5	3	3	3	9	9
No	87	88	86	86	90	97	95	86	75	73
Responses	301	24	59	155	63	30	121	58	32	59
Salary										
Less then $50,000	63			43						56
$50,000 to $99,999	37			57						44
Mean	$47,285			$49,829						$48,563
Median	$45,000			$50,000						$45,500
Responses	27			14						16
Bonus/Commissions										
Yes	63			50						63
No	37			50						38
Responses	27			14						16
Bonus (among all with salary)										
Zero	37			50						38
$1,000 to $4,999	19			14						19
$5,000 to $9,999	22			21						19
$10,000 or more	22			14						25
Mean	$6,393			$5,179						$6,694
Median	$3,000			$1,500						$3,000
Responses	27			14						16
Bonus (among only those who actually got bonuses)										
$1,000 to $4,999	29									30
$5,000 to $9,999	35									30
$10,000 or more	35									40
Mean	$10,153									$10,710
Median	$6,500									$7,050
Responses	17									10

Q7. Selections Coordinator
(Percent of Respondents)

	2017 Expected Single-Family Starts			Number of Employees			
	1 to 10	11 to 99	100 or more	0 to 2	3 to 4	5 to 9	10 or more
Does Position Exist?							
Yes, full-time	2	15	29	2	3	5	23
Yes, part-time	3	5			2	7	3
No	95	81	71	98	95	89	74
Responses	153	109	31	51	63	87	97
Salary							
Less then $50,000		67					59
$50,000 to $99,999		33					41
Mean		$44,492					$48,932
Median		$45,000					$45,000
Responses		15					22
Bonus/Commissions							
Yes		60					68
No		40					32
Responses		15					22
Bonus (among all with salary)							
Zero		40					32
$1,000 to $4,999		20					14
$5,000 to $9,999		20					27
$10,000 or more		20					27
Mean		$5,433					$7,595
Median		$3,000					$5,000
Responses		15					22
Bonus (among only those who actually got bonuses)							
$1,000 to $4,999							20
$5,000 to $9,999							40
$10,000 or more							40
Mean							$11,140
Median							$7,600
Responses							15

Benefits	Total	Region				2017 Expected Dollar Volume				
		Northeast	Midwest	South	West	Less than $1 million	$1 million to $4,999,999	$5 million to $9,999,999	$10 million to $14,999,999	$15 million or over
Health Insurance	93			100						94
Dental Insurance	67			64						81
Vision Program	41			43						50
Prescription Program	48			50						63
Life Insurance	63			64						81
Short Term Disability	48			43						63
Long Term Disability	52			36						69
Flex Spending	37			29						56
401 K	85			79						94
Paid Vacation Leave	89			86						100
Paid Sick Leave	74			79						94
Tuition Reimbursement	33			29						31
Training	48			43						63
Other	7			0						13
Responses	27			14						16

Q7. *Customer service Manager*
(Percent of Respondents)

	Total	Region				2017 Expected Dollar Volume				
		Northeast	Midwest	South	West	Less than $1 million	$1 million to $4,999,999	$5 million to $9,999,999	$10 million to $14,999,999	$15 million or over
Does Position Exist?										
Yes, full-time	3	4	2	2	5			3	2	10
Yes, part-time	1		2	1			1			2
No	97	96	97	97	95	100	99	98	97	88
Responses	301	24	59	155	63	30	121	58	32	59
Salary										
Less then $50,000	25									
$50,000 to $99,999	75									
Mean	$53,913									
Median	$54,550									
Responses	8									

Q7. Selections Coordinator
(Percent of Respondents)

	2017 Expected Single-Family Starts			Number of Employees			
	1 to 10	11 to 99	100 or more	0 to 2	3 to 4	5 to 9	10 or more
Benefits							
Health Insurance		87					91
Dental Insurance		53					73
Vision Program		20					45
Prescription Program		33					50
Life Insurance		40					68
Short Term Disability		27					55
Long Term Disability		27					59
Flex Spending		13					45
401 K		80					91
Paid Vacation Leave		87					91
Paid Sick Leave		60					86
Tuition Reimbursement		7					36
Training		27					55
Other		0					9
Responses		15					22

Q7. Customer service Manager
(Percent of Respondents)

	2017 Expected Single-Family Starts			Number of Employees			
	1 to 10	11 to 99	100 or more	0 to 2	3 to 4	5 to 9	10 or more
Does Position Exist?							
Yes, full-time		5	10				8
Yes, part-time	1	1			2		1
No	99	94	90	100	98	100	91
Responses	153	109	31	51	63	87	97
Salary							
Less then $50,000							
$50,000 to $99,999							
Mean							
Median							
Responses							

Appendix B. Positions & Compensation

	Percent Who Have Full-Time Position	Average Salary	Average Bonus (among all with salary)	Average Total Compensation	Average Bonus (among only those who acutally got bonuses)
	A	B	C	D	E
EXECUTIVE JOBS					
President/CEO	95	$113,222	$44,179	$157,401	$90,007
CFO/Head of Finance	26	$107,758	$40,825	$148,583	$58,788
CIO/Head of IT	3	$79,600	$19,250	$98,850	
VP of Construction	36	$94,293	$37,625	$131,918	$49,532
OPERATIONS JOBS					
Head/Director of Purchasing	17	$80,884	$20,014	$100,898	$27,242
Head /Director of Land Acquisition	8	$124,114	$49,352	$173,466	$63,868
Head /Director of Production	14	$74,496	$26,337	$100,833	$40,518
Head /Director of Development and Training	*				
Head /Director of Sales & Marketing	19	$88,027	$47,863	$135,890	$65,973
FINANCE JOBS					
Controller	18	$72,002	$11,697	$83,699	$16,570
Payroll Manager	5	$54,571	$4,107	$58,678	
Staff Accountant	10	$53,290	$5,224	$58,514	$7,974
Bookkeeper	25	$42,478	$2,879	$45,357	$4,543
HUMAN RESOURCES					
Director of Human Resources	2				
Recruiter	*				
In-house legal counsel	1				
IT JOBS					
Director of IT	4	$70,491	$5,773	$76,264	
Network Engineer	1				
Web Design Specialist	3	$56,222			
ADMINISTRATIVE JOBS					
Executive Assistant	11	$44,732	$3,955	$48,687	$6,525
Office Manager	17	$50,287	$5,430	$55,717	$8,688
Administrative Assistant	9	$38,473	$2,278	$40,751	
Receptionist	8	$32,464	$2,341	$34,805	$3,962
Settlement Coordinator	8	$51,486	$7,459	$58,945	$13,675
PRODUCTION JOBS					
Production Manager	15	$69,520	$11,137	$80,657	$14,085
Land Manager	2	$87,500			
Purchasing Manager	5	$69,875	$12,031	$81,906	$14,808
Home Services/Warranty Manager	16	$53,373	$6,938	$60,311	$9,182
Contract Manager	3	$62,222			
Project Manager	30	$67,247	$11,670	$78,917	$15,864
Architect	10	$80,858	$10,461	$91,319	$15,416
Estimator	15	$55,306	$5,466	$60,772	$7,835
Superintendent	44	$59,888	$7,818	$67,706	$11,588
SALES & MARKETING JOBS					
Sales Manager	7	$65,142	$48,444	$113,586	$58,133
Model Home Host	3	$33,938			
Salesperson	16	$34,050	$64,365	$98,415	$84,594
Design Center Manager	7	$57,701	$7,852	$65,553	$13,288
Selections Coordinator	10	$47,285	$6,393	$53,678	$10,153
Customer Service Manager	3	$53,913			

* Less than 0.5%.

Appendix C. Compensation and Benefits by Job Category

Executive Jobs

(Percent of Respondents)

	President/CEO	CFO/Head of Finance	CIO/Head of IT	VP of Construction
Does this Position Exist?				
Yes, full-time	95	26	3	36
Yes, part-time	3	4	1	1
No	2	70	95	63
Responses	*301*	*300*	*301*	*300*
Is it filled by person(s) with experience in construction trades?				
Always	89			96
Sometimes	4			2
Never/Almost never	7			1
Responses	*269*			*81*
Salary				
Less then $50,000	11	4	20	7
$50,000 to $99,999	42	47	50	51
$100,000 or more	47	49	30	42
Mean	$113,222	$107,758	$79,600	$94,293
Responses	*273*	*72*	*10*	*104*
Bonus/Commissions				
Yes	49	69	40	76
No	51	31	60	24
Responses	*273*	*72*	*10*	*104*
Bonus (among all with salary)				
Zero	51	31	60	24
$1,000 to $4,999	1	6	40	3
$5,000 to $9,999	1	8		3
$10,000 or more	47	56		70
Mean	$44,179	$40,825	$19,250	$37,625
Responses	*273*	*72*	*10*	*104*
Bonus (among only those who actually got bonuses)				
$1,000 to $4,999	3	8		4
$5,000 to $9,999	1	12		4
$10,000 or more	96	80		92
Mean	$90,007	$58,788		$49,532
Responses	*134*	*50*		*79*
Benefits				
Health Insurance	72	90		88
Dental Insurance	33	53		46
Vision Program	20	40		29
Prescription Program	27	40		36
Life Insurance	36	53		42
Short Term Disability	16	31		27
Long Term Disability	17	34		26
Flex Spending	13	29		25
401 K	53	66		63
Paid Vacation Leave	83	87		90
Paid Sick Leave	62	69		73
Tuition Reimbursement	13	18		17
Training	31	35		34
Other	8	10		11
Responses	*259*	*68*		*99*

Operations Jobs
(Percent of Respondents)

	Head/Director of Purchasing	Head /Director of Land Acquisition	Head /Director of Production	Head /Director of Development and Training	Head /Director of Sales & Marketing
Does this Position Exist?					
Yes, full-time	17	8	14	*	1
Yes, part-time	1			*	
No	82	92	86	99	7
Responses	*301*	*301*	*301*	*301*	*30*
Is it filled by person(s) with experience in construction trades?					
Always	67	87	81		5
Sometimes	26		15		3
Never/Almost never	8	13	4		
Responses	*39*	*15*	*26*		*26*
Salary					
Less then $50,000	8				1
$50,000 to $99,999	67	32	88		4
$100,000 or more	24	68	13		4
Mean	$80,884	$124,114	$74,496		$88,027
Responses	*49*	*22*	*40*		*51*
Bonus/Commissions					
Yes	73	77	65		73
No	27	23	35		27
Responses	*49*	*22*	*40*		*51*
Bonus (among all with salary)					
Zero	27	23	35		27
$1,000 to $4,999	4	5	3		6
$5,000 to $9,999	12	5	15		4
$10,000 or more	57	68	48		63
Mean	$20,014	$49,352	$26,337		$47,863
Responses	*49*	*22*	*40*		*51*
Bonus (among only those who actually got bonuses)					
$1,000 to $4,999	6	6	4		8
$5,000 to $9,999	17	6	23		5
$10,000 or more	78	88	73		86
Mean	$27,242	$63,868	$40,518		$65,973
Responses	*36*	*17*	*26*		*37*
Benefits					
Health Insurance	90	91	76		88
Dental Insurance	63	82	47		56
Vision Program	49	50	29		42
Prescription Program	49	59	32		42
Life Insurance	51	59	34		52
Short Term Disability	33	32	24		34
Long Term Disability	39	50	34		30
Flex Spending	33	41	16		24
401 K	73	82	66		82
Paid Vacation Leave	96	95	97		90
Paid Sick Leave	80	77	71		72
Tuition Reimbursement	22	23	16		16
Training	29	41	26		28
Other	8		5		6
Responses	*49*	*22*	*38*		*50*

* Less than 0.5%.

Finance Jobs
(Percent of Respondents)

	Controller	Payroll Manager	Staff Accountant	Bookkeeper
Does this Position Exist?				
Yes, full-time	18	5	10	25
Yes, part-time	5	2	4	20
No	77	92	86	55
Responses	*301*	*301*	*300*	*301*
Salary				
Less then $50,000	14	36	34	77
$50,000 to $99,999	75	64	66	23
$100,000 or more	12			
Mean	$72,002	$54,571	$53,290	$42,478
Responses	*51*	*14*	*29*	*71*
Bonus/Commissions				
Yes	71	50	66	63
No	29	50	34	37
Responses	*51*	*14*	*29*	*71*
Bonus (among all with salary)				
Zero	29	50	34	37
$1 to $999				6
$1,000 to $4,999	6		28	34
$5,000 to $9,999	25	36	24	18
$10,000 or more	39	14	14	6
Mean	$11,697	$4,107	$5,224	$2,879
Responses	*51*	*14*	*29*	*71*
Bonus (among only those who actually got bonuses)				
$1 to $999				9
$1,000 to $4,999	8		42	53
$5,000 to $9,999	36		37	29
$10,000 or more	56		21	9
Mean	$16,570.22		$7,974	$4,543
Responses	*36*		*19*	*45*
Benefits				
Health Insurance	88	79	93	76
Dental Insurance	63	50	57	44
Vision Program	43	36	50	26
Prescription Program	45	29	46	38
Life Insurance	53	64	54	33
Short Term Disability	31	43	29	21
Long Term Disability	37	21	21	21
Flex Spending	37	36	32	17
401 K	80	57	71	62
Paid Vacation Leave	98	79	86	92
Paid Sick Leave	86	64	79	67
Tuition Reimbursement	20	14	25	17
Training	33	36	43	35
Other	10	7	4	6
Responses	*49*	*14*	*28*	*66*

Human Resources Jobs

(Percent of Respondents)

	Director of Human Resources	Recruiter	In-house legal counsel
Does this Position Exist?			
Yes, full-time	2	*	1
Yes, part-time	*		*
No	97	100	99
Responses	*301*	*301*	*301*
Salary			
Less then $50,000			
$50,000 to $99,999			
$100,000 or more			
Mean			
Responses			
Bonus/Commissions			
Yes			
No			
Responses			
Bonus (among all with salary)			
Zero			
$1,000 to $4,999			
$5,000 to $9,999			
$10,000 or more			
Mean			
Responses			
Bonus (among only those who actually got bonuses)			
$1,000 to $4,999			
$5,000 to $9,999			
$10,000 or more			
Mean			
Responses			
Benefits			
Health Insurance			
Dental Insurance			
Vision Program			
Prescription Program			
Life Insurance			
Short Term Disability			
Long Term Disability			
Flex Spending			
401 K			
Paid Vacation Leave			
Paid Sick Leave			
Tuition Reimbursement			
Training			
Other			
Responses			

* Less than 0.5%.

IT Jobs
(Percent of Respondents)

	Director of IT	Network Engineer	Web Design Specialist
Does this Position Exist?			
Yes, full-time	4	1	3
Yes, part-time	1	*	1
No	96	99	96
Responses	*301*	*301*	*301*
Salary			
Less then $50,000	9		44
$50,000 to $99,999	73		44
$100,000 or more	18		11
Mean	$70,491		$56,222
Responses	*11*		*9*
Bonus/Commissions			
Yes	45		
No	55		
Responses	*11*		
Bonus (among all with salary)			
Zero	55		
$1,000 to $4,999	9		
$5,000 to $9,999	18		
$10,000 or more	18		
Mean	$5,773		
Responses	*11*		
Bonus (among only those who actually got bonuses)			
$1,000 to $4,999			
$5,000 to $9,999			
$10,000 or more			
Mean			
Responses			
Benefits			
Health Insurance	90		
Dental Insurance	80		
Vision Program	60		
Prescription Program	40		
Life Insurance	70		
Short Term Disability	40		
Long Term Disability	60		
Flex Spending	50		
401 K	90		
Paid Vacation Leave	100		
Paid Sick Leave	90		
Tuition Reimbursement	30		
Training	40		
Other	20		
Responses	*10*		

* Less than 0.5%.

Administrative Jobs

(Percent of Respondents)

	Executive Assistant	Office Manager	Administrative Assistant	Receptionist	Settlement Coordinator
Does this Position Exist?					
Yes, full-time	11	17	9	8	8
Yes, part-time	1	3	6	2	
No	88	80	85	90	92
Responses	*300*	*301*	*300*	*301*	*301*
Salary					
Less then $50,000	70	56	88	100	59
$50,000 to $99,999	30	40	12		36
$100,000 or more		4			5
Mean	$44,732	$50,287	$38,473	$32,464	$51,486
Responses	*33*	*48*	*25*	*22*	*22*
Bonus/Commissions					
Yes	61	63	36	59	55
No	39	38	64	41	45
Responses	*33*	*48*	*25*	*22*	*22*
Bonus (among all with salary)					
Zero	39	38	64	41	45
$1 to $999		2	4	5	
$1,000 to $4,999	33	15	16	45	18
$5,000 to $9,999	18	29	8		9
$10,000 or more	9	17	8	9	27
Mean	$3,955	$5,430	$2,278	$2,341	$7,459
Responses	*33*	*48*	*25*	*22*	*22*
Bonus (among only those who actually got bonuses)					
$1 to $999		3		8	
$1,000 to $4,999	55	23		77	33
$5,000 to $9,999	30	47			17
$10,000 or more	15	27		15	50
Mean	$6,525	$8,688		$3,962	$13,675
Responses	*20*	*30*		*13*	*12*
Benefits					
Health Insurance	91	70	84	90	91
Dental Insurance	52	36	52	75	55
Vision Program	45	30	40	60	32
Prescription Program	52	36	44	45	45
Life Insurance	52	36	56	55	45
Short Term Disability	33	18	32	40	36
Long Term Disability	30	23	20	35	41
Flex Spending	39	11	32	35	18
401 K	70	64	84	80	68
Paid Vacation Leave	94	98	96	100	86
Paid Sick Leave	76	84	76	70	77
Tuition Reimbursement	15	20	16	30	18
Training	36	36	56	35	36
Other	9	7	8	0	5
Responses	*33*	*44*	*25*	*20*	*22*

Production Jobs
(Percent of Respondents)

	Production Manager	Land Manager	Purchasing Manager	Home Services/ Warranty Manager	Contract Manager	Project Manager	Architect	Estimator	Superintendent
Does this Position Exist?									
Yes, full-time	15	2	5	16	3	30	10	15	44
Yes, part-time	*			2		*	1	2	1
No	85	98	95	82	97	70	89	83	55
Responses	*301*	*301*	*301*	*301*	*301*	*297*	*301*	*299*	*299*
Is it filled by person(s) with experience in construction trades?									
Always	78		70	70					
Sometimes	22		20	30					
Never/Almost never			10						
Responses	*23*		*10*	*23*					
Salary									
Less then $50,000	16		6	31	44	16	21	21	20
$50,000 to $99,999	74	67	81	69	33	77	68	79	78
$100,000 or more	9	33	13		22	7	11		2
Mean	$69,520	$87,500	$69,875	$53,373	$62,222	$67,247	$80,858	$55,306	$59,888
Responses	*43*	*6*	*16*	*45*	*9*	*87*	*28*	*43*	*126*
Bonus/Commissions									
Yes	79		81	76		74	68	70	67
No	21		19	24		26	32	30	33
Responses	*43*		*16*	*45*		*87*	*28*	*43*	*126*
Bonus(among all with salary)									
Zero	21		19	24		26	32	30	33
$1 to $999						1			2
$1,000 to $4,999	14		13	33		10	18	26	10
$5,000 to $9,999	28		25	22		20	18	26	21
$10,000 or more	37		44	20		43	32	19	33
Mean	$11,137		$12,031	$6,938		$11,670	$10,461	$5,466	$7,818
Responses	*43*		*16*	*45*		*87*	*28*	*43*	*126*
Bonus (among only those who actually got bonuses)									
$1 to $999						2			4
$1,000 to $4,999	18		15	44		14	26	37	15
$5,000 to $9,999	35		31	29		27	26	37	32
$10,000 or more	47		54	26		58	47	27	49
Mean	$14,085		$14,808	$9,182		$15,864	$15,416	$7,835	$11,588
Responses	*34*		*13*	*34*		*64*	*19*	*30*	*85*
Benefits									
Health Insurance	72		93	89		73	88	81	73
Dental Insurance	44		73	66		39	62	49	42
Vision Program	33		53	41		27	35	40	25
Prescription Program	36		47	45		29	38	40	32
Life Insurance	44		53	48		27	38	49	31
Short Term Disability	33		47	32		23	27	35	22
Long Term Disability	26		47	27		17	23	30	17
Flex Spending	28		47	30		12	23	26	18
401 K	64		80	80		69	81	79	63
Paid Vacation Leave	100		100	98		92	85	88	94
Paid Sick Leave	77		87	84		70	58	70	73
Tuition Reimbursement	18		40	18		17	19	26	15
Training	46		40	30		35	35	51	37
Other	10		13	9		7	0	7	6
Responses	*39*		*15*	*44*		*83*	*26*	*43*	*115*

* Less than 0.5%.

Sales & Marketing Jobs

(Percent of Respondents)

	Sales Manager	Model Home Host	Salesperson	Design Center Manager	Selections Coordinator	Customer Service Manager
Does this Position Exist?						
Yes, full-time	7	3	16	7	10	
Yes, part-time	1	5		1	3	
No	92	92	84	92	87	9
Responses	*301*	*301*	*299*	*301*	*301*	*30*
Salary						
Less then $50,000	33	100	72	32	63	2
$50,000 to $99,999	50		22	68	37	7
$100,000 or more	17		7			
Mean	$65,142	$33,938	$34,050	$57,701	$47,285	$53,913
Responses	*18*	*8*	*46*	*22*	*27*	*8*
Bonus/Commissions						
Yes	83		76	59	63	
No	17		24	41	37	
Responses	*18*		*46*	*22*	*27*	
Bonus(among all with salary)						
Zero	17		24	41	37	
$1 to $999						
$1,000 to $4,999	6			27	19	
$5,000 to $9,999	78		2	5	22	
$10,000 or more			74	27	22	
Mean	$48,444		$64,365	$7,852	$6,393	
Responses	*18*		*46*	*22*	*27*	
Bonus (among only those who actually got bonuses)						
$1 to $999						
$1,000 to $4,999	7			46	29	
$5,000 to $9,999	93		3	8	35	
$10,000 or more			97	46	35	
Mean	$58,133		$84,594	$13,288	$10,153	
Responses	*15*		*35*	*13*	*17*	
Benefits						
Health Insurance	86		83	82	93	
Dental Insurance	62		52	59	67	
Vision Program	48		38	32	41	
Prescription Program	43		43	50	48	
Life Insurance	52		45	59	63	
Short Term Disability	52		31	50	48	
Long Term Disability	43		29	36	52	
Flex Spending	33		29	45	37	
401 K	86		71	77	85	
Paid Vacation Leave	95		86	86	89	
Paid Sick Leave	81		76	73	74	
Tuition Reimbursement	38		19	27	33	
Training	48		26	45	48	
Other	10		5	9	7	
Responses	*21*		*42*	*22*	*27*	

Appendix D. Positions and Compensation by Single-Family Starts in 2017

	1-10 Starts		11-99 Starts		100 + Starts	
	Percent Who Have Full-time Position	Average Total Compensation	Percent Who Have Full-time Position	Average Total Compensation	Percent Who Have Full-time Position	Average Total Compensation
EXECUTIVE JOBS						
President/CEO	96	$113,658	93	$165,823	97	$294,121
CFO/Head of Finance	11	$86,333	33	$112,744	71	$211,032
CIO/Head of IT	1		3		6	
VP of Construction	24	$88,076	40	$128,782	81	$179,940
OPERATIONS JOBS						
Head/Director of Purchasing	3		22	$75,135	68	$117,014
Head /Director of Land Acquisition	1		9		35	$161,682
Head /Director of Production	7		20	$78,266	26	
Head /Director of Development&Training	0		0		3	
Head /Director of Sales & Marketing	5		26	$119,494	61	$178,438
FINANCE JOBS						
Controller	5		26	$74,420	55	$98,220
Payroll Manager	2		6		13	
Staff Accountant	3		9	$52,940	48	$61,667
Bookkeeper	16	$46,712	33	$44,388	48	$45,567
HUMAN RESOURCES						
Director of Human Resources	0		1		16	
Recruiter	0		0		0	
In-house legal counsel	0		1		3	
IT JOBS						
Director of IT	0		5		19	
Network Engineer	0		1		6	
Web Design Specialist	0		5		10	
ADMINISTRATIVE JOBS						
Executive Assistant	5		12	$44,931	40	$50,958
Office Manager	10	$44,499	23	$60,584	23	
Administrative Assistant	2		14	$38,356	27	
Receptionist	1		10	$33,862	35	$34,508
Settlement Coordinator	1		10		42	$65,100
PRODUCTION JOBS						
Production Manager	8	$67,259	17	$75,804	29	
Land Manager	0		1		13	
Purchasing Manager	0		5		32	$75,500
Home Services/Warranty Manager	5		18	$56,680	58	$64,595
Contract Manager	1		1		19	
Project Manager	25	$72,038	36	$78,321	35	$100,021
Architect	4		13	$75,951	29	
Estimator	10	$59,375	12	$57,385	45	$65,960
Superintendent	35	$63,824	45	$64,673	84	$82,021
SALES & MARKETING JOBS						
Sales Manager	3		6		26	
Model Home Host	0		3		19	
Salesperson	1		23	$94,684	68	$108,105
Design Center Manager	2		6		35	$70,682
Selections Coordinator	2		15	$49,925	29	
Customer service Manager	0		5		10	

APPENDIX E. Other Fringe Benefits by Job Category

Q7. EXECUTIVE JOBS

President/CEO

* 9 paid holidays
* Aflac insurances
* All auto costs paid including truck purchase
* All vehicle expenses paid
* Auto (2)
* Auto Allowance $9,000/year
* Auto, Cell Phone
* Bonus based on profit, family insurance fully paid by company
* Bonuses Vary: depending on profit that year
* Car
* Car, phone
* Company auto
* Company Car
* Company vehicle (3)
* Critical Illness, Accident Insurance, 529 College Savings Plan
* Equity/Stock in Company
* Half of S corp profit, Simple IRA
* IRA
* No regular salary taken, Just bonus at year end
* Owner
* Owner Receives no bonus because all profits are the owner's.
* Ownership shares
* Paid Bereavement Leave
* Paid Holidays (2)
* Profit sharing (2)
* SIMPLE IRA
* This is the founder and gets profits, so low salary
* Travel stipend of $6,000 annually
* Travel to NAHB, etc., if not picked up by local association
* Truck
* Truck&gas
* Vehicle (6)
* Vehicle allowance
* Vehicle allowance 1,000, phone and club 300 monthly
* Vehicle and gas expense
* Vehicle/fuel

CFO/Head of Finance

* $300/month Health reimbursement
* Auto allowance, long term care insurance
* Bonus based on profit, family insurance fully paid by company
* Company Car
* Company Equity/Stock
* Company Truck
* Free vacation beach house
* Half of S corp profit, Simple IRA
* Matching 401k
* Ownership shares
* Paid Bereavement Leave
* Paid Holidays (2)
* PROFIT SHARING
* Critical Illness, Accident Insurance, 529 College Savings Plan
* Spouse of owner
* Subcontracted, part-time
* Vehicle allowance 300, phone and club 300 monthly
* Works three days per week

CIO **Head of IT**

* Company vehicle
* Matching 401k
* Critical Illness, Accident Insurance, 529 College Savings Plan

VP **of Construction**

* Aflac
* Auto Allowance $9,000/yr.
* Company Equity/Stock
* Company Truck
* Company truck, 20% OF Net profit (est. 100k), Simple Ira
* Company vehicle
* Critical Illness, Accident Insurance, 529 College Savings Plan
* Fuel card for vehicle
* IRA
* Matching 401k
* Ownership shares
* Paid Bereavement Leave
* Paid holidays
* Reimbursement for mileage
* Travel stipend of $6,000 annually
* Truck, Cell Phone
* Vehicle (2)
* Vehicle - Truck & gas & insurance
* Vehicle allowance

Q7. OPERATIONS JOBS

Head/Director of Purchasing

* Cell Phone
* Company Equity/Stock
* Critical Illness, Accident Insurance, 529 College Savings Plan
* Ownership Shares
* Paid Bereavement Leave
* Vehicle allowance

Head/Director of Land Acquisition

* Auto allowance
* Critical Illness, Accident Insurance, 529 College Savings Plan
* Paid Bereavement Leave
* Travel stipend of $6,000 annually

Head/Director of Production

* 10% ownership
* Auto Allowance
* Car, phone
* Cell Phone
* Company car
* Company Equity/Stock
* Critical Illness, Accident Insurance, 529 College Savings Plan
* Paid Holidays
* Vehicle and fuel supplied

Head/Director of Development and Training

* Critical Illness, Accident Insurance, 529 College Savings Plan
* Ownership Shares

Head/Director of Sales and Marketing

* Auto allowance
* Auto Allowance $9,000/year
* Company Vehicle
* Critical Illness, Accident Insurance, 529 College Savings Plan
* Matching 401k
* Ownership Shares
* Paid Bereavement Leave
* Subcontracted
* Vehicle allowance
* Vehicle and gas expense

Q7. FINANCE JOBS

Controller

* Auto
* Bonus based on profit, family insurance fully paid by company
* Bonuses vary depending on year end profit
* Critical Illness, Accident Insurance, 529 College Savings Plan
* Paid Bereavement Leave
* Paid Holidays
* Profit sharing
* Subcontracted part-time
* Vehicle

Payroll Manager

*   Critical Illness, Accident Insurance, 529 College Savings Plan
*   Subcontracted part-time
*   This person also does AP, bookkeeper, warranty

Staff Accountant

*   Paid Bereavement Leave
*   Paid holidays
*   Subcontracted part-time

Bookkeeper

*   9 paid holidays
*   Bonuses vary depending on year end profit
*   Gas reimbursement
*   IRA
*   Paid as retirement
*   Paid Bereavement Leave
*   Paid Holidays
*   Same person that does Payroll
*   SIMPLE IRA
*   Subcontracted part-time
*   Subcontracted, not an employee

Q7. HUMAN RESOURCES JOBS

Director of Human Resources

*   Critical Illness, Accident Insurance, 529 College Savings Plan
*   Paid holidays
*   These positions are shared with one person who does payroll.

Recruiter

*   Critical Illness, Accident Insurance, 529 College Savings Plan

In-house Legal Counsel

* Works three days per week
* Paid holidays

Q7. IT JOBS

Director of IT

* Ownership Shares
* Paid Bereavement Leave
* Paid holidays
* Subcontracted part-time

Network Engineer

* Paid Bereavement Leave
* Subcontracted as needed

Web Design Specialist

* Critical Illness, Accident Insurance, 529 College Savings Plan
* Paid holidays
* Subcontracted

Q7. ADMINISTRATIVE JOBS

Executive Assistant

* Auto allowance
* Critical Illness, Accident Insurance, 529 College Savings Plan
* Paid Bereavement Leave

Office Manager

*   Bonus based on profit, family insurance fully paid by company
*   Matching 401k
*   Critical Illness, Accident Insurance, 529 College Savings Plan
*   Same position as payroll
*   Simple IRA
*   Subcontracted part-time
*   Very flexible hours

Administrative Assistant

*   Critical Illness, Accident Insurance, 529 College Savings Plan
*   Paid holidays

Receptionist

*   Profit sharing
*   Same position as marketing coordinator/web designer

Settlement Coordinator

*   Office manager does
*   Paid Bereavement Leave
*   Paid Holidays
*   This position is with Office manager
*   Very flexible hours

Q7. PRODUCTION JOBS

Production Manager

* All vehicle expenses paid
* Bonus based on profit, family insurance fully paid by company
* Company Vehicle
* Critical Illness, Accident Insurance, 529 College Savings Plan
* Paid Bereavement Leave
* Paid holidays
* Truck provided
* Vehicle

Land Manager

* Critical Illness, Accident Insurance, 529 College Savings Plan
* Paid holidays

Purchasing Manager

* Critical Illness, Accident Insurance, 529 College Savings Plan
* Paid Bereavement Leave

Home Services/Warranty Manager

* Auto allowance
* Auto allowance $9000/year
* Company truck, Simple IRA
* Company Vehicle
* Contract labor
* Critical Illness, Accident Insurance, 529 College Savings Plan
* IRA
* Matching 401k
* Paid Bereavement Leave
* Vehicle allowance

Contract Manager

* Critical Illness, Accident Insurance, 529 College Savings Plan
* Paid Bereavement Leave

Q7. PRODUCTION JOBS - *continued*

Project Manager
* Bonuses and profit sharing
* Company Car
* Company truck, Simple IRA
* Company vehicle (2)
* Contract labor
* Paid holidays
* Phone, mileage reimbursement
* Critical Illness, Accident Insurance, 529 College Savings Plan
* SIMPLE IRA
* Take home vehicle
* Truck
* Vehicle

Architect
* Contract labor
* SIMPLE IRA
* Subcontracted as needed

Estimator
* Critical Illness, Accident Insurance, 529 College Savings Plan
* Paid Bereavement Leave
* Paid holidays
* SIMPLE IRA

Superintendent
* 9 Paid Holidays
* Auto allowance (2)
* Company Car
* Company Vehicle (3)
* Contract labor
* Critical Illness, Accident Insurance, 529 College Savings Plan
* IRA
* Matching 401k
* Paid Bereavement Leave
* Paid Holidays (2)
* Profit sharing
* SIMPLE IRA
* Travel stipend of $6,000 annually
* Truck & gas
* Truck provided
* Vehicle
* Vehicle allowance
* Vehicle and fuel
* Vehicle Reimbursement $300/month
* Vehicle-Truck & Gas & insurance

Q7. SALES AND MARKETING JOBS

Sales Manager

* Critical Illness, Accident Insurance, 529 College Savings Plan
* Paid Bereavement Leave
* This is same person Head of Sales and Marketing

Model Home Host
**** *None – No "other" comments indicated for this position*

Salesperson

* Bonus based on profitability, single insurance fully paid by company
* Licensing reimbursement
* Matching 401k
* Paid Bereavement Leave
* Profit sharing
* Simple Ira

Design Center Manager

* Auto allowance
* Critical Illness, Accident Insurance, 529 College Savings Plan
* Paid Bereavement Leave

Selections Coordinator

* Critical Illness, Accident Insurance, 529 College Savings Plan
* Paid Bereavement Leave
* Paid Holidays
* Vehicle mileage

Customer Service Manager

* Paid holidays (2)
* Profit sharing

Appendix F. 2017 Single-Family Builder Compensation Survey

1. What is your company's principal operation?

☐ Single-Family Spec/Tract Builder

☐ Single-Family Custom Builder

☐ Single-Family General Contractor

☐ Other

[If not a single-family builder, end survey].

2. How many <u>single-family units</u> did your company start in 2016? How many do you expect to start in 2017?

2016: _____   2017:_____

3. Approximately, what will be the company's total <u>dollar volume</u> of business in <u>2017</u>?

☐ Under $500,000   ☐ $10 million - $14,999,999

☐ $500,000 - $999,999   ☐ $15 million or over

☐ $1 million - $4,999,999   ☐ No business activity

☐ $5 million - $9,999,999

4. How many years has your company been in the home building business? _____ Years

5. How many employees were on your payroll as of June 30, 2017? (Include Owner/President/CEO). _____

6. What was your total payroll as of June 30, 2017? (Include Owner/President/CEO). $_____

7. Please indicate whether each of the following positions exists in your company, its current annual salary, bonus/commission, and any fringe benefits currently offered.
   - For positions with only one employee, report the actual salary/bonus/commission.
   - For positions with multiple employees, report the average of all salaries in that position. If a person does more than one job, report job that takes most of his/her time.
   - If job titles do not exactly match those in your company, please respond by matching job descriptions.
   - For some positions, report if job is filled by a person(s) with hands-on experience in construction trades.

EXECUTIVE JOBS				
	President/CEO *(Owner, leader, senior manager of the company)*	**CFO/Head of Finance** *(Lead decision maker about company's finances. Provides financial analysis, budgets, and forecasts)*	**CIO/Head of IT** *(Lead decision maker about company's information technology needs)*	**VP of Construction** *(Lead decision maker about company's construction practices and policies)*
Does position exist?	☐ Yes, full-time ☐ Yes, part-time ☐ No	☐ Yes, full-time ☐ Yes, part-time ☐ No	☐ Yes, full-time ☐ Yes, part-time ☐ No	☐ Yes, full-time ☐ Yes, part-time ☐ No
Is it filled by person(s) with experience in construction trades?	☐ Always ☐ Sometimes ☐ Never/Almost never		☐ Always ☐ Sometimes ☐ Never/Almost never	☐ Always ☐ Sometimes ☐ Never/Almost never
Annual salary	$_____	$_____	$_____	$_____
Bonus/ Commissions	☐ None $_____	☐ None $_____	☐ None $_____	☐ None $_____
Fringe Benefits	☐ Health Insurance ☐ Dental Insurance ☐ Vision Program ☐ Prescription Program ☐ Life Insurance ☐ Short Term Disability ☐ Long Term Disability ☐ Flex Spending ☐ 401 K ☐ Paid vacation ☐ Paid sick leave ☐ Tuition Reimbursement ☐ Training ☐ Other (specify):__	☐ Health Insurance ☐ Dental Insurance ☐ Vision Program ☐ Prescription Program ☐ Life Insurance ☐ Short Term Disability ☐ Long Term Disability ☐ Flex Spending ☐ 401 K ☐ Paid vacation leave ☐ Paid sick leave ☐ Tuition Reimbursement ☐ Training ☐ Other (specify):____	☐ Health Insurance ☐ Dental Insurance ☐ Vision Program ☐ Prescription Program ☐ Life Insurance ☐ Short Term Disability ☐ Long Term Disability ☐ Flex Spending ☐ 401 K ☐ Paid vacation leave ☐ Paid sick leave ☐ Tuition Reimbursement ☐ Training ☐ Other (specify):__	☐ Health Insurance ☐ Dental Insurance ☐ Vision Program ☐ Prescription Program ☐ Life Insurance ☐ Short Term Disability ☐ Long Term Disability ☐ Flex Spending ☐ 401 K ☐ Paid vacation leave ☐ Paid sick leave ☐ Tuition Reimbursement ☐ Training ☐ Other (specify):____

	OPERATIONS JOBS			
	Head /Director of Purchasing *(in charge of ordering and negotiating building materials)*	**Head /Director of Land Acquisition** *(in charge of land acquisition, development, and zoning issues)*	**Head /Director of Production** *(manages engineers, production managers and implements company's production policies)*	**Head /Director of Development and Training** *(in charge of developing all in-house or external training)*
Does position exist?	☐Yes, full-time ☐Yes, part-time ☐No	☐Yes, full-time ☐Yes, part-time ☐No	☐Yes, full-time ☐Yes, part-time ☐No	☐Yes, full-time ☐Yes, part-time ☐No
Is it filled by person(s) with experience in construction trades?	☐Always ☐Sometimes ☐Never/Almost never	☐Always ☐Sometimes ☐Never/Almost never	☐Always ☐Sometimes ☐Never/Almost never	☐Always ☐Sometimes ☐Never/Almost never
Annual salary	$_____	$_____	$_____	$_____
Bonus/ Commissions	☐None $_____	☐None $_____	☐None $_____	☐None $_____
Fringe Benefits	☐ Health Insurance ☐ Dental Insurance ☐ Vision Program ☐ Prescription Program ☐ Life Insurance ☐ Short Term Disability ☐ Long Term Disability ☐ Flex Spending ☐401 K ☐Paid vacation ☐Paid sick leave ☐Tuition Reimbursement ☐Training ☐Other (specify):__	☐ Health Insurance ☐ Dental Insurance ☐ Vision Program ☐ Prescription Program ☐ Life Insurance ☐ Short Term Disability ☐ Long Term Disability ☐ Flex Spending ☐401 K ☐Paid vacation ☐Paid sick leave ☐Tuition Reimbursement ☐Training ☐Other (specify):__	☐ Health Insurance ☐ Dental Insurance ☐ Vision Program ☐ Prescription Program ☐ Life Insurance ☐ Short Term Disability ☐ Long Term Disability ☐ Flex Spending ☐401 K ☐Paid vacation leave ☐Paid sick leave ☐Tuition Reimbursement ☐Training ☐Other (specify):___	☐ Health Insurance ☐ Dental Insurance ☐ Vision Program ☐ Prescription Program ☐ Life Insurance ☐ Short Term Disability ☐ Long Term Disability ☐ Flex Spending ☐401 K ☐Paid vacation leave ☐Paid sick leave ☐Tuition Reimbursement ☐Training ☐Other (specify):___

	OPERATIONS JOBS	FINANCE JOBS		
	Head /Director of Sales & Marketing *(in charge of marketing strategy to promote the company and product)*	**Controller** *(plans, organizes, and controls accounting system)*	**Payroll Manager** *(manages payroll process)*	**Staff Accountant** *(Assembles and analyzes accounting data to prepare financial statements)*
Does position exist?	☐ Yes, full-time ☐ Yes, part-time ☐ No	☐ Yes, full-time ☐ Yes, part-time ☐ No	☐ Yes, full-time ☐ Yes, part-time ☐ No	☐ Yes, full-time ☐ Yes, part-time ☐ No
Is it filled by person(s) with experience in construction trades?	☐ Always ☐ Sometimes ☐ Never/Almost never			
Annual salary	$_____	$_____	$_____	$_____
Bonus/ Commissions	☐ None $_____	☐ None $_____	☐ None $_____	☐ None $_____
Fringe Benefits	☐ Health Insurance ☐ Dental Insurance ☐ Vision Program ☐ Prescription Program ☐ Life Insurance ☐ Short Term Disability ☐ Long Term Disability ☐ Flex Spending ☐ 401 K ☐ Paid vacation ☐ Paid sick leave ☐ Tuition Reimbursement ☐ Training ☐ Other (specify):__	☐ Health Insurance ☐ Dental Insurance ☐ Vision Program ☐ Prescription Program ☐ Life Insurance ☐ Short Term Disability ☐ Long Term Disability ☐ Flex Spending ☐ 401 K ☐ Paid vacation ☐ Paid sick leave ☐ Tuition Reimbursement ☐ Training ☐ Other (specify):__	☐ Health Insurance ☐ Dental Insurance ☐ Vision Program ☐ Prescription Program ☐ Life Insurance ☐ Short Term Disability ☐ Long Term Disability ☐ Flex Spending ☐ 401 K ☐ Paid vacation leave ☐ Paid sick leave ☐ Tuition Reimbursement ☐ Training ☐ Other (specify):___	☐ Health Insurance ☐ Dental Insurance ☐ Vision Program ☐ Prescription Program ☐ Life Insurance ☐ Short Term Disability ☐ Long Term Disability ☐ Flex Spending ☐ 401 K ☐ Paid vacation leave ☐ Paid sick leave ☐ Tuition Reimbursement ☐ Training ☐ Other (specify):___

	FINANCE JOBS	HUMAN RESOURCES JOBS		
	Bookkeeper *(processes accounts payable and enters accounting data)*	**Director of Human Resources** *(manages all functions related to recruiting and retaining employees)*	**Recruiter** *(handles all functions related to recruiting employees)*	**In-house Legal Counsel** *(lead internal attorney for company)*
Does position exist?	☐ Yes, full-time ☐ Yes, part-time ☐ No	☐ Yes, full-time ☐ Yes, part-time ☐ No	☐ Yes, full-time ☐ Yes, part-time ☐ No	☐ Yes, full-time ☐ Yes, part-time ☐ No
Annual salary	$_____	$_____	$_____	$_____
Bonus/ Commissions	☐ None $_____	☐ None $_____	☐ None $_____	☐ None $_____
Fringe	☐ Health Insurance ☐ Dental Insurance ☐ Vision Program ☐ Prescription Program ☐ Life Insurance ☐ Short Term Disability ☐ Long Term Disability ☐ Flex Spending ☐ 401 K ☐ Paid vacation ☐ Paid sick leave ☐ Tuition Reimbursement ☐ Training ☐ Other (specify):__	☐ Health Insurance ☐ Dental Insurance ☐ Vision Program ☐ Prescription Program ☐ Life Insurance ☐ Short Term Disability ☐ Long Term Disability ☐ Flex Spending ☐ 401 K ☐ Paid vacation ☐ Paid sick leave ☐ Tuition Reimbursement ☐ Training ☐ Other (specify):__	☐ Health Insurance ☐ Dental Insurance ☐ Vision Program ☐ Prescription Program ☐ Life Insurance ☐ Short Term Disability ☐ Long Term Disability ☐ Flex Spending ☐ 401 K ☐ Paid vacation leave ☐ Paid sick leave ☐ Tuition Reimbursement ☐ Training ☐ Other (specify):___	☐ Health Insurance ☐ Dental Insurance ☐ Vision Program ☐ Prescription Program ☐ Life Insurance ☐ Short Term Disability ☐ Long Term Disability ☐ Flex Spending ☐ 401 K ☐ Paid vacation leave ☐ Paid sick leave ☐ Tuition Reimbursement ☐ Training ☐ Other (specify):___

	IT JOBS			ADMINISTRATIVE JOBS
	Director of IT *(directly manages company's networks, computer resources, and website)*	**Network Engineer** *(installs software, maintains network and computer inventory)*	**Web Design Specialist** *(designs, monitors, and updates company's website)*	**Executive Assistant** *(provides administrative and clerical support to company's executives)*
Does position exist?	☐ Yes, full-time ☐ Yes, part-time ☐ No	☐ Yes, full-time ☐ Yes, part-time ☐ No	☐ Yes, full-time ☐ Yes, part-time ☐ No	☐ Yes, full-time ☐ Yes, part-time ☐ No
Annual salary	$_____	$_____	$_____	$_____
Bonus/ Commissions	☐ None $_____	☐ None $_____	☐ None $_____	☐ None $_____
Fringe benefits	☐ Health Insurance ☐ Dental Insurance ☐ Vision Program ☐ Prescription Program ☐ Life Insurance ☐ Short Term Disability ☐ Long Term Disability ☐ Flex Spending ☐ 401 K ☐ Paid vacation ☐ Paid sick leave ☐ Tuition Reimbursement ☐ Training ☐ Other (specify):__	☐ Health Insurance ☐ Dental Insurance ☐ Vision Program ☐ Prescription Program ☐ Life Insurance ☐ Short Term Disability ☐ Long Term Disability ☐ Flex Spending ☐ 401 K ☐ Paid vacation leave ☐ Paid sick leave ☐ Tuition Reimbursement ☐ Training ☐ Other (specify):__	☐ Health Insurance ☐ Dental Insurance ☐ Vision Program ☐ Prescription Program ☐ Life Insurance ☐ Short Term Disability ☐ Long Term Disability ☐ Flex Spending ☐ 401 K ☐ Paid vacation leave ☐ Paid sick leave ☐ Tuition Reimbursement ☐ Training ☐ Other (specify):	☐ Health Insurance ☐ Dental Insurance ☐ Vision Program ☐ Prescription Program ☐ Life Insurance ☐ Short Term Disability ☐ Long Term Disability ☐ Flex Spending ☐ 401 K ☐ Paid vacation leave ☐ Paid sick leave ☐ Tuition Reimbursement ☐ Training ☐ Other (specify):___

ADMINISTRATIVE JOBS

	Office Manager *(manages administrative office staff)*	**Administrative Assistant** *(handles office administrative duties, typing, filing)*	**Receptionist** *(receives and routes incoming calls and visitors, performs clerical duties)*	**Settlement Coordinator** *(serves as liaison between customers and the rest of the company)*
Does position exist?	☐ Yes, full-time ☐ Yes, part-time ☐ No	☐ Yes, full-time ☐ Yes, part-time ☐ No	☐ Yes, full-time ☐ Yes, part-time ☐ No	☐ Yes, full-time ☐ Yes, part-time ☐ No
Annual salary	$_____	$_____	$_____	$_____
Bonus/ Commissions	☐ None $_____	☐ None $_____	☐ None $_____	☐ None $_____
Fringe benefits	☐ Health Insurance ☐ Dental Insurance ☐ Vision Program ☐ Prescription Program ☐ Life Insurance ☐ Short Term Disability ☐ Long Term Disability ☐ Flex Spending ☐ 401 K ☐ Paid vacation ☐ Paid sick leave ☐ Tuition Reimbursement ☐ Training ☐ Other (specify):__	☐ Health Insurance ☐ Dental Insurance ☐ Vision Program ☐ Prescription Program ☐ Life Insurance ☐ Short Term Disability ☐ Long Term Disability ☐ Flex Spending ☐ 401 K ☐ Paid vacation ☐ Paid sick leave ☐ Tuition Reimbursement ☐ Training ☐ Other (specify):__	☐ Health Insurance ☐ Dental Insurance ☐ Vision Program ☐ Prescription Program ☐ Life Insurance ☐ Short Term Disability ☐ Long Term Disability ☐ Flex Spending ☐ 401 K ☐ Paid vacation leave ☐ Paid sick leave ☐ Tuition Reimbursement ☐ Training ☐ Other (specify):___	☐ Health Insurance ☐ Dental Insurance ☐ Vision Program ☐ Prescription Program ☐ Life Insurance ☐ Short Term Disability ☐ Long Term Disability ☐ Flex Spending ☐ 401 K ☐ Paid vacation leave ☐ Paid sick leave ☐ Tuition Reimbursement ☐ Training ☐ Other (specify):___

PRODUCTION JOBS

	Production Manager *(responsible for field operations, including budgeting and cost controls at the divisional level or for smaller company)*	Land Manager *(responsible for land acquisition/development at the divisional level or for smaller company)*	Purchasing Manager *(orders and negotiates for building products at the divisional level or for smaller company)*	Home Services/ Warranty Manager *(maintains quality assurance and provides warranty service to homeowners after closing)*
Does position exist?	☐ Yes, full-time ☐ Yes, part-time ☐ No	☐ Yes, full-time ☐ Yes, part-time ☐ No	☐ Yes, full-time ☐ Yes, part-time ☐ No	☐ Yes, full-time ☐ Yes, part-time ☐ No
Is it filled by person(s) with experience in construction trades?	☐ Always ☐ Sometimes ☐ Never/Almost never	☐ Always ☐ Sometimes ☐ Never/Almost never	☐ Always ☐ Sometimes ☐ Never/Almost never	☐ Always ☐ Sometimes ☐ Never/Almost never
Annual salary	$_____	$_____	$_____	$_____
Bonus/ Commissions	☐ None $_____	☐ None $_____	☐ None $_____	☐ None $_____
Fringe benefits	☐ Health Insurance ☐ Dental Insurance ☐ Vision Program ☐ Prescription Program ☐ Life Insurance ☐ Short Term Disability ☐ Long Term Disability ☐ Flex Spending ☐ 401 K ☐ Paid vacation leave ☐ Paid sick leave ☐ Tuition Reimbursement ☐ Training ☐ Other (specify):__	☐ Health Insurance ☐ Dental Insurance ☐ Vision Program ☐ Prescription Program ☐ Life Insurance ☐ Short Term Disability ☐ Long Term Disability ☐ Flex Spending ☐ 401 K ☐ Paid vacation leave ☐ Paid sick leave ☐ Tuition Reimbursement ☐ Training ☐ Other (specify):___	☐ Health Insurance ☐ Dental Insurance ☐ Vision Program ☐ Prescription Program ☐ Life Insurance ☐ Short Term Disability ☐ Long Term Disability ☐ Flex Spending ☐ 401 K ☐ Paid vacation leave ☐ Paid sick leave ☐ Tuition Reimbursement ☐ Training ☐ Other (specify):___	☐ Health Insurance ☐ Dental Insurance ☐ Vision Program ☐ Prescription Program ☐ Life Insurance ☐ Short Term Disability ☐ Long Term Disability ☐ Flex Spending ☐ 401 K ☐ Paid vacation leave ☐ Paid sick leave ☐ Tuition Reimbursement ☐ Training ☐ Other (specify):___

PRODUCTION JOBS

	Contract Manager *(responsible for producing and monitoring sales contracts)*	**Project Manager** *(monitors production schedules and ensures that homes are completed on time and meet quality and profit levels as well as client needs)*	**Architect** *(responsible for architectural and structural design aspects of the home building process)*	**Estimator** *(ensures accuracy of house take-offs)*
Does position exist?	☐ Yes, full-time ☐ Yes, part-time ☐ No	☐ Yes, full-time ☐ Yes, part-time ☐ No	☐ Yes, full-time ☐ Yes, part-time ☐ No	☐ Yes, full-time ☐ Yes, part-time ☐ No
Annual salary	$_____	$_____	$_____	$_____
Bonus/ Commissions	☐ None $_____	☐ None $_____	☐ None $_____	☐ None $_____
Fringe benefits	☐ Health Insurance ☐ Dental Insurance ☐ Vision Program ☐ Prescription Program ☐ Life Insurance ☐ Short Term Disability ☐ Long Term Disability ☐ Flex Spending ☐ 401 K ☐ Paid vacation ☐ Paid sick leave ☐ Tuition Reimbursement ☐ Training ☐ Other (specify):_	☐ Health Insurance ☐ Dental Insurance ☐ Vision Program ☐ Prescription Program ☐ Life Insurance ☐ Short Term Disability ☐ Long Term Disability ☐ Flex Spending ☐ 401 K ☐ Paid vacation leave ☐ Paid sick leave ☐ Tuition Reimbursement ☐ Training ☐ Other (specify):__	☐ Health Insurance ☐ Dental Insurance ☐ Vision Program ☐ Prescription Program ☐ Life Insurance ☐ Short Term Disability ☐ Long Term Disability ☐ Flex Spending ☐ 401 K ☐ Paid vacation ☐ Paid sick leave ☐ Tuition Reimbursement ☐ Training ☐ Other (specify):__	☐ Health Insurance ☐ Dental Insurance ☐ Vision Program ☐ Prescription Program ☐ Life Insurance ☐ Short Term Disability ☐ Long Term Disability ☐ Flex Spending ☐ 401 K ☐ Paid vacation ☐ Paid sick leave ☐ Tuition Reimbursement ☐ Training ☐ Other (specify):__

	PRODUCTION JOBS	SALES & MARKETING JOBS		
	Superintendent *(manages daily construction activities)*	**Sales Manager** *(manages sales functions and personnel, establishes procedures for doing sales presentations and qualifying prospects)*	**Model Home Host** *(meets and greets public, collects customer registration cards)*	**Salesperson** *(conducts sales presentation for prospective customers, prepares home purchase agreements, follow up with clients about construction, design, financing)*
Does position exist?	☐ Yes, full-time ☐ Yes, part-time ☐ No	☐ Yes, full-time ☐ Yes, part-time ☐ No	☐ Yes, full-time ☐ Yes, part-time ☐ No	☐ Yes, full-time ☐ Yes, part-time ☐ No
Annual salary	$_____	$_____	$_____	$_____
Bonus/ Commissions	☐ None $_____	☐ None $_____	☐ None $_____	☐ None $_____
Fringe benefits	☐ Health Insurance ☐ Dental Insurance ☐ Vision Program ☐ Prescription Program ☐ Life Insurance ☐ Short Term Disability ☐ Long Term Disability ☐ Flex Spending ☐ 401 K ☐ Paid vacation ☐ Paid sick leave ☐ Tuition Reimbursement ☐ Training ☐ Other (specify):_	☐ Health Insurance ☐ Dental Insurance ☐ Vision Program ☐ Prescription Program ☐ Life Insurance ☐ Short Term Disability ☐ Long Term Disability ☐ Flex Spending ☐ 401 K ☐ Paid vacation leave ☐ Paid sick leave ☐ Tuition Reimbursement ☐ Training ☐ Other (specify):__	☐ Health Insurance ☐ Dental Insurance ☐ Vision Program ☐ Prescription Program ☐ Life Insurance ☐ Short Term Disability ☐ Long Term Disability ☐ Flex Spending ☐ 401 K ☐ Paid vacation ☐ Paid sick leave ☐ Tuition Reimbursement ☐ Training ☐ Other (specify):__	☐ Health Insurance ☐ Dental Insurance ☐ Vision Program ☐ Prescription Program ☐ Life Insurance ☐ Short Term Disability ☐ Long Term Disability ☐ Flex Spending ☐ 401 K ☐ Paid vacation leave ☐ Paid sick leave ☐ Tuition Reimbursement ☐ Training ☐ Other (specify):__

SALES & MARKETING JOBS

	Design Center Manager (manages company's design center)	Selections Coordinator (helps customers make finish selections in company's design center)	Customer Service Manager (manages customer service at the divisional level or for a smaller company)
Does position exist?	☐ Yes, full-time ☐ Yes, part-time ☐ No	☐ Yes, full-time ☐ Yes, part-time ☐ No	☐ Yes, full-time ☐ Yes, part-time ☐ No
Annual salary	$_____	$_____	$_____
Bonus/ Commissions	☐ None $_____	☐ None $_____	☐ None $_____
Fringe benefits	☐ Health Insurance ☐ Dental Insurance ☐ Vision Program ☐ Prescription Program ☐ Life Insurance ☐ Short Term Disability ☐ Long Term Disability ☐ Flex Spending ☐ 401 K ☐ Paid vacation leave ☐ Paid sick leave ☐ Tuition Reimbursement ☐ Training ☐ Other (specify):__	☐ Health Insurance ☐ Dental Insurance ☐ Vision Program ☐ Prescription Program ☐ Life Insurance ☐ Short Term Disability ☐ Long Term Disability ☐ Flex Spending ☐ 401 K ☐ Paid vacation leave ☐ Paid sick leave ☐ Tuition Reimbursement ☐ Training ☐ Other (specify):__	☐ Health Insurance ☐ Dental Insurance ☐ Vision Program ☐ Prescription Program ☐ Life Insurance ☐ Short Term Disability ☐ Long Term Disability ☐ Flex Spending ☐ 401 K ☐ Paid vacation leave ☐ Paid sick leave ☐ Tuition Reimbursement ☐ Training ☐ Other (specify):__

8. If there are other position(s) in your company not listed above, please provide title and a description of duties.

_____

_____

_____

THANK YOU!